# Teens, TV and Tunes

# Teens, TV and Tunes

## The Manufacturing of American Adolescent Culture

DOYLE GREENE

McFarland & Company, Inc., Publishers
*Jefferson, North Carolina, and London*

LIBRARY OF CONGRESS CATALOGUING-IN-PUBLICATION DATA

Greene, Doyle, 1962–
    Teens, TV and tunes : the manufacturing of American
adolescent culture / Doyle Greene.
        p.    cm.
    Includes bibliographical references and index.

    ISBN 978-0-7864-6642-9
    softcover : acid free paper ∞

    1. Television and politics—United States.    2. Young
consumers—United States.    3. Music and youth—Social
aspects.    4. Mass media and culture—United States.
5. Branding (Marketing)—Social aspects.    6. United States—
Social life and customs—20th century.    7. United States—
Social life and customs—21st century.    8. Nickelodeon (Firm)
9. Walt Disney Company.    I. Title.
PN1992.6.G735  2012
305.230973—dc23                                    2012002936

BRITISH LIBRARY CATALOGUING DATA ARE AVAILABLE

On the cover: Miranda Cosgrove, *iCarly* (Nickelodeon/Photofest)

Manufactured in the United States of America

*McFarland & Company, Inc., Publishers*
    *Box 611, Jefferson, North Carolina 28640*
    *www.mcfarlandpub.com*

To Joe and Julie:
For hanging out and time well spent.

# Acknowledgments

My thanks to the Lynch family (Rodney, Jeni, and Jack), Ann Klee, Matt Potts, Steve Fier and Phanomvanh Daoheuang ("Nacho and Nikki"), Jay Beck, Laurie Ouellette, and in particular Joe Tompkins and Julie Wilson for the various and varied perspectives they brought to this study. Earl A. Greene, John "Ray" Link, and Sophia Green provided valuable support over the course of this project. Special thanks are owed to Gary C. Thomas, Keya Ganguly, and especially Richard Leppert, for their critical readings and comments. Thanks also to Photofest (www.photofestnyc.com) for their services in providing the illustrations.

# Table of Contents

Acknowledgments   vi

Preface   1

Introduction: Reading Teen Culture   3

### Part One: Don't Trust Anyone Over Thirty

1: Teen Culture Industry (or, You Pays Your Money
and You Takes Your Choice)   15

2. On the Importance of Being Hip   23

### Part Two: The Society of the Teen Sitcom

3. The Form and Function of the Sitcom   39

4. Free, White, and Teenage Male (or, How to Con Friends
and Manipulate People): *Saved by the Bell*   48

5. Nickelodeon Nation Building:
From *Clarissa Explains It All* to *Zoey 101*   55

6. The Political Dilemmas of *iCarly*   72

7. I Have a Dream Job: *True Jackson, VP*   90

### Part Three: Pop Goes Teen Culture

8. The Birth of the Pop-Music Sitcom: The Monkees,
the Archies, and the Partridge Family   101

9. Teen Pop in Opposition: Britney Spears versus Madonna   119

10. My Generation: *School of Rock* and the Revival of Rock Ideology   133

11. Keeping It Real and Imaginary: The Ideological
Contradictions of *Hannah Montana*   146

12.  The Boy Brands Are Back in Town
       (or, Triumph of the Hip): *Big Time Rush*                            162

*Conclusion: The Youth of Today Are the Leaders of Tomorrow*               173

*Appendix: Cast Listings*                                                  177

*Chapter Notes*                                                            181

*Bibliography*                                                             209

*Index*                                                                    213

# Preface

To a certain degree, this project dates back to critical work analyzing the relationship between culture, history, and ideology that eventually resulted in *Politics and the American Television Comedy* (2008). The emphasis of that book was prior to 1980, the year I turned 18, and especially TV that greatly impacted me during my tween/teen years in the 1970s. Except for *South Park*, and perhaps a few other shows that occasionally had their moments, I decided that little if anything worthwhile on TV was produced since.

Indeed, my view at the time was that American popular culture rolled over and died. Most Hollywood films and TV shows now make me ill — and I mean that literally. The blitz of CGI effects, constant camera movement, varying speed images, color processing, and rapid-fire editing all combine to generate motion sickness, not any sense of visual enjoyment. My albums, singles, cassettes, and 8-tracks were all sold, given away, discarded, or simply lost over the years. For various reasons, in 2005 I sold off much of my music library, which probably numbered around two thousand CDs. What I kept was a highly select batch that included some modern classical and free jazz; otherwise, it was all 1970s art rock, hard rock, and punk/post-punk. After 30-plus years, I whittled it down to mostly the music I originally bought as a teenager. In effect, I'd become the cultural dinosaur I swore I'd never become: the middle-aged adult who was incapable of making a statement unless it was prefaced by "Back in my day...." In fact, I was rather proud of it.

Watching TV for research as much as entertainment ca. 2007–8, I became intrigued by Nickelodeon's teen sitcom line at the time: *Drake and Josh*, *Zoey 101*, *H₂O ... Just Add Water*, and especially *iCarly*. A friend of mine who has since become a fan of *iCarly* put it best: "It's not a great show, but it's as good as the rest of the shit on TV." One attraction was still TV nostalgia. However, it wasn't *That 70's Show* nostalgia and vicariously reliving the halcyon days of smoking marijuana and listening to classic rock (I'm speaking as someone who *was* a Midwestern teenager in the 1970s). Rather, I was struck by how much *Drake and Josh* and *iCarly* reminded me of older sitcoms; *iCarly* may have well been *The Lucy Show* with a teenage cast. Moreover, teen sitcoms offered as much in terms of textual analysis as the primetime sitcoms I was wading through at the time, and becoming increasingly disgusted with in the process. *Zoey 101* and *iCarly* seemed a lot more "mature" than *According to Jim* or *Two and a Half Men*.

A steady diet of Nickelodeon had another "advantage," for lack of a better word. The onslaught of commercials and the saturation programming of the same shows made me a lot more informed about teen culture, whether I really wanted to be or not. Names and faces started to become familiar, and I noticed it was the *same* names and faces as far as the teen advertising, the teen sitcoms, and teen pop — and the teen pop I was now hearing was *not* what I recalled from the late 1990s. Of that era, all I remembered was being mortified by Britney Spears' "Baby One More Time" music video, for months I thought Christina Aguilera's "Genie in a Bottle" was a Britney Spears song, and I despised boy bands. The first time I saw Miley Cyrus's "Start All Over" music video I had a Proust moment, as if I was suddenly flung back in time to my parents' family room watching MTV in the early 1980s. When I first saw Britney Spears's "Womanizer" video, I was stunned how much the musical setting compared to early 1980s industrial music as much as late 1990s teen pop.

An old saying goes, "There are two kinds of fools: one says 'This is old and, therefore, good' and the other says, 'This is new and, therefore, better.'" My view is that adult thinking, especially as far as the contempt for current teen culture, often falls prey to the former. As far as expressing any interest in cultural history, teen thinking frequently becomes victim of the latter. My goal is to provide a critical assessment that avoids both these modes of thinking. Whether it amounts to its own foolishness readers can decide.

# Introduction:
# Reading Teen Culture

## Teen Culture: "Ideology Marketing" and "Imagined Audience"

Recounting the teenage experience in the 1970s seems like describing a cultural Dark Age. Radio was a limited selection of local AM and FM radio stations; network TV was a choice between the CBS, NBC, ABC, and PBS (always the last resort). Satellite radio, cable TV, and DBS TV — along with a multitude of TV networks — had yet to proliferate across America. While VHS radically changed home entertainment in the 1980s, it now borders on obsolescence against DVD, TIVO, and "view on demand." As for music, CDs and MP3 files have largely, if not entirely, replaced albums and cassettes while home stereo systems that often took up as much space as the furniture can be jettisoned in favor of Discmans, iPods, and PC media players. Above all, personal computers and the Internet revolutionized daily life at all levels of economics, education, and entertainment.

As much as the technology of culture, American politics considerably changed. Ronald Reagan and the "Reagan Revolution" of the 1980s rigidly branded American conservatism around Calvin Coolidge's maxim that "the business of America is business," hard-line national security domestic and foreign policies, fundamentalist morality politics, and the mantra, "Government is the problem, not the solution." Since the 1990s, a younger generation has grown up amid "postindustrial" global capitalism driven by the computer and consumption rather than the factory and production. In response, American liberalism was rebranded into the centrist, middle-class neoliberalism of "New Democrats" like Bill Clinton and Barack Obama at the expense of labor-liberalism and welfare-state liberalism (the New Deal of the 1930s or the Great Society of the 1960s). Teens in the 21st century now have the two-party option effectively defined by the Clintonism of the Democratic Party and the Reaganism of the Republican Party: a choice between moderate-left or right- to far-right neoliberalism.[1]

In this context, my project politically analyzes "teen culture," emphasizing teen sitcoms, teen pop, and their points of convergence. It examines the historical and ideological development of American youth culture, the economic and ideological relationship between television and popular music, and the industry and ideological rivalry between Nickelodeon and Disney. Nonetheless, teen culture cannot be reduced to the maxim: "When you have them by their pocketbooks their hearts and minds will follow." The primary concern is how these texts engage in the complicated and ongoing process of *ideology marketing*.

Here it is necessary to define what is meant by "ideology marketing" and how it compares and contrasts to "lifestyle marketing." Ideology marketing and lifestyle marketing both entail a complex interaction of consumer, cultural, individual, political, and social identities. As a lifestyle network, Nickelodeon brands itself as the Hip "kids only network" alternative to the Square "family network" Disney Channel. Along with a deluge of tween/teen-targeted advertising, Nickelodeon teen sitcoms represent adolescents as the central agents within their social milieus, *Nick News* specials address controversial political issues, and Nickelodeon's Big Help public service campaigns actively promote local, national, and global community involvement. As Sarah Banet-Wesier argued in *Kids Rule!: Nickelodeon and Consumer Citizenship* (2007), "The network addresses its child audience as empowered citizens who are able to make decisions about politics, culture, and relevant social issues, by virtue of membership in the [Nickelodeon] brand identity."[2] This brand identity functions as a means by which participation in consumer culture becomes a form of "citizenship" not only in the nation-state of America but as part of the "Nickelodeon Nation." *Hannah Montana* had a reported worldwide audience of *200 million* people, ca. 2008. In the global marketplace, this "Hannah Montana nation" was not only one of the larger populations in the world, but a "nation" of citizens constructed around media and consumer culture.[3]

There is also a distinction that needs to be drawn between lifestyle marketing and ideology marketing. "Lifestyle marketing" is often used to describe how TV networks adopt certain strategies to solicit particular viewing demographics and resonate with a particular *target audience*: Nickelodeon and Disney Channel for adolescents, MTV for teens and young adults, Spike for young adult males, We and Lifetime for women, BET for African Americans, Univision for Latin Americans, PBS for liberals, FOX News for conservatives, etc. More correctly, this target audience is an *assumed audience* and even an *imagined audience*. John Hartley contended, "Audiences may be imagined empirically, theoretically, or politically, but in all cases the product is a fiction that serves the needs of an imagining institution [entertainment industries, the State, academia, journalism].... There is no 'actual' audience that lies beyond its production as a category ... as *representations*."[4] To this extent, audiences as "categorical representations" are fabricated around various agendas, assumptions, perceptions, presumptions, and stereotypes; in the case of teen culture, the imagined audience of "teenyboppers" and "tweens." In short, audiences are a manufactured cultural product as much as the movies, music, or TV shows they consume. Teen culture cannot be divorced from how the audience-consumer is imagined, represented, and manufactured by Nickelodeon and Disney Channel, as well as *Rolling Stone* or *Tiger Beat.*

The potential pitfall with "lifestyle marketing" as applied to an analysis of teen culture is how the term is often interpreted and implemented, specifically the almost standardized critical line that its sole function is conning impressionable adolescent consumers to waste money on its bogus insipidness. In effect, teen culture is often assessed around simplistic applications of Theodor W. Adorno's denunciations of the Culture Industry, and this is not at all denying the pervasive Culture Industry standards and practices in teen culture that merit investigation and criticism. The problem is that many of the same criticisms can be applied to adult culture, even as much as adult culture strives to exempt itself from the grip of the Culture Industry.

"Ideology marketing" is intended to stress the extent that teen culture is also a set of *competing* cultural discourses that debate current political issues, conflicting world-views, and the tenets of American society where the messages are part and parcel of the cultural product. Edward R. Murrow proclaimed television has the ability to act as "the world's largest classroom." To press the metaphor, teen culture and the various "lesson plans" offered by movies, songs, and TV shows have the potential to serve as the world's largest school. Whether defined as target audience, assumed audience, or imagined audience, teen culture is primarily consumed by adolescents who are in diverse stages of cultural, political, and social "puberty." It engages in various forms of political *instruction* encompassing rebellion as well as conformity, and the convenient simplicity of an "either-or" binary between oppositional culture and mass culture works far better in cultural theory than everyday cultural practice. Britney Spears is just as political as the Dead Kennedys and *iCarly* is just as political as *TV Nation.* The difference is *how* the political positions are manifest in the texts, *what kinds* of political readings are applied to the texts, and the various political pressures *outside* the specific texts. Pierre Bourdieu suggested, "Aesthetic conflicts about the legitimate vision of the world — in the last resort, *about what deserves to be represented and the right way to represent it*— are political conflicts ... emphasizing the power to impose the dominant definition of reality, and social reality in particular."[5] In this respect, the politics of teen culture as "representation" are very much debates about the "*right way* to represent" social reality as much as they are about "*what deserves* to be represented." Bruce Springsteen and Hannah Montana both offer ambivalent critiques of American society. The separation lies in *whose* critique is critically validated as artistically authentic and politically oppositional.

To be sure, the views expressed in this project are highly "opinionated." However, my concern is *not* which TV shows, movies, or songs are "good" or "bad." As Lester Bangs put it, "I'll take my bad taste and you're welcome to yours, and maybe someday something will actually happen again that makes us both happy."[6] The intent is offering textual interpretations and contextual considerations as a means to debate the stakes of teen culture historically and politically, not become mired in time-consuming and tedious arguments over "quality" or lack thereof. I am much more inclined to consider culture around terms like "brand," "commodity," "discourse," "product," and "text"—and far less around questions of "art." Capitalism, culture, and ideology cannot be separated into autonomous forces but are inherently related. Nevertheless, I am increasingly reluctant to consider culture a means by which ideology is uniformly instilled and enforced in the body-politic. If capitalism and its ideology are inherently contradictory, it follows that its cultural products are also contradictory. In this sense, the business of teen culture is also the *marketing of ideological contradiction*.

## The Terrain of Teen Culture

This project is comparative and far from comprehensive, and numerous forms of tween and teen culture are not addressed or fully addressed: John Hughes's films, the CW line of teen dramas, ABC Family Channel shows, the plethora of teen "reality shows," *Glee*, the *Bratz* franchise, the *Harry Potter* and *Twilight* phenomena, Nickelodeon's stable of animated shows (*SpongeBob SquarePants*) and comedy-action shows (*The Troop, Supah Ninjas*), or Disney products like the *Camp Rock, Cheetah Girls*, and *High School Musical* films. Moreover, the sheer amount of teen sitcoms and teen pop that could have been considered, or analyzed in much more detail, far exceeded the parameters. It became necessary to exclude, limit, or condense discussion of pertinent teen sitcoms like *Ned's Declassified School Survival Guide, Wizards of Waverly Place, The Naked Brothers Band, Sonny with a Chance*, and *Victorious*. The same was done with teen pop, such as the boy band genre, the Spice Girls, the Jonas Brothers, Justin Bieber, Taylor Swift, or Ke$ha. Readers are invited to use the arguments presented to draw their own comparisons, conclusions, and contrasts, particularly in areas not included in this project. The goal is not to iron out the problematics, but examine and exacerbate the contradictions of teen culture historically as well in as the present.

The theoretical and contextual terrain of this project is outlined in Part One. Chapter 1 posits a core contradiction of "teen culture" is that it is *produced by adults and consumed by adolescents*. Teen culture defines itself as the "voice" of an adolescent audience-market; in turn, adolescents decide which brands of teen culture best "speak" for them. In this context, the production-versus-consumption mass culture debates, along with traditional liberal-conservative political arguments, provide useful methodologies but also prove limited. The issue is the "generation gap" manifest in teen culture. Adults as producers of teen culture often *mythologize* their own cultural experience and social visions of the past, be it the "good old days" of traditional American values or the "good old days" of youth rebellion (hippies, punks, slackers, etc.). Adolescents as consumers of teen culture struggle with the *contradictions* of 21st century American life around issues of adult authority, the computer age, consumerism, education systems, family structures, identity politics, mass culture, neoliberalism, and postindustrial capitalism. In this way, teen culture is *both* product and producer of the ideological tensions between generational schisms.

Chapter 2 provides an analysis of teen culture ideology historically constructed and sustained around "Hip versus Square." In Norman Mailer's famous and highly flawed essay "The White Negro" (1957), Hip was romantically, even stereotypically, defined around the African-American urban experience, male libidinal liberation, and social rebellion while Square was defined around white, middle-class repression and conformity. American popular culture exhibits an ongoing conflict as the politics of Hipness are continually reconfigured in specific cultural texts and historical contexts. More specifically, the struggle in popular culture is over *whom and what* is represented as Hip through a complicated and shifting interplay of identity politics revolving around age, class, ethnicity, gender, geography, nationality, race, and sexuality. Teen culture does not so much offer a uniform representation of an idealized Hip teenage lifestyle but *competing representations of normative teenage life around idealized Hipness.* While race is still a pivotal factor, increasingly and equally important demarcation points are *gender* and *age.* Through the construction of "the teenybopper" and "the tween," adolescent girls as cultural producers, and especially as cultural consumers, become the perennial scapegoats for the alleged scourge of mass culture.

Part Two focuses on readings of select teen sitcoms from 1989 to 2011. In Chapter 3, the formal characteristics and distinction between the "classical sitcom" and "contemporary sitcom" is outlined; as a brief example, the classical sitcom style is typified by *Everybody Loves Raymond* and the contemporary sitcom style by *Everybody Hates Chris.* Whether a sitcom falls within classical or contemporary conventions (or somewhere in between), the structure of the sitcom is "*ethical form*" converting disordered into ordered situations through transformative action.[7] The ethical form also becomes the means by which the sitcom engages in civic education, if not outright ideological indoctrination. Moreover, while gender politics have been a primary concern of the sitcoms since the 1950s, the championing of masculinity became increasingly integral to sitcoms since the 1990s with the advent of the men's movement.

In this context, Chapter 4 focuses on a defining teen sitcom, *Saved by the Bell* (NBC, 1989–93) as an early example of how a teen sitcom "imagines" a certain normative lifestyle that teenagers are presumed to inhabit; in turn, *Saved by the Bell* proscribed what constituted the normative yet "imaginary" teenage life. Emerging in the wake of Reaganism and the dawn of the men's movement, *Saved by the Bell* served as a highly conservative cultural discourse affirming dominant ideology while representing rebel Hipness around white, middle-class masculinity and an unabashed pursuit of self-interest speciously framed as ethical awareness.

Chapter 5 assesses Nickelodeon's status as a "kids only" network and Nickelodeon's relationship to New Democrat neoliberalism since the 1990s. Nickelodeon's prototype "girl power" teen sitcom *Clarissa Explains It All* (1991–4) emerged as a progressive neoliberal, postfeminist competing discourse to the conservatism of *Family Ties* and *Saved by the Bell* as the decade of Reaganism gave way to the decade of Clintonism. This chapter also discusses two subsequent Nickelodeon teen sitcoms, *Drake and Josh* (2004–7) and *Zoey 101* (2005–8). Both were pivotal texts as far representations of gender, Hipness, and especially the status of the tween/teen girl as a crucial determining agent capable of both jeopardizing and establishing community order.

While "girl power ideology" needs to be considered around feminist and postfeminist politics, it must also be assessed in its relationship to neoliberal ideology. In this respect, two Nickelodeon teen sitcoms are the focus of Chapters 6 and 7: *iCarly* (2007– ) and *True Jackson, VP* (2008–11). Centered on a teenage girl who attains celebrity with a self-produced comedy webshow, analysis of *iCarly* reveals a series of highly problematic and interrelated political negotiations around gender roles, adult authority within the family and educational apparatus, DYI culture versus mass culture, and, ultimately, the friction between community, work, and liberal-conservative politics in an era of computers, postindustrial capitalism, and neoliberalism. The central problematic of *iCarly* is the tension between the "old" constructs of 20th century American society versus the "new" conditions of 21st century American life, and the extent to which *both* are satirized as well as valorized.

*True Jackson, VP* revolved around an African-American teenage girl who lands a job as an executive designer with an international fashion corporation; it was not coincidental that the show premiered the weekend after Barack Obama was elected president. In this context, *True Jackson, VP* problematically negotiated liberal indenity politics in terms of gender, race and even sexuality alongside conservative messages of adult authority, social mobility, and especially the importance of a work ethic in the schema of ethical capitalism. As a New Democrat brand of teen culture for a post–Obama era of American politics, *True Jackson, VP* not only functioned as the antithesis to the conservatism of *Saved by the Bell*, but served a competing discourse to the more ambivalent critique of neoliberalism offered by *iCarly*.

Part Three examines teen culture around popular music and its relationship to TV. Chapter 8 considers "bubblegum" as a musical style and genre, a critical and marketing category, and its implementation by pop-music sitcoms ca. 1966–74. The bands, or *brands*, respectively offered by NBC (the Monkees),

CBS (the Archies), and ABC (the Partridge Family) were not only manufactured cultural commodities but ideological representations of American teens and young adults amid counterculture and post-counterculture turbulence. As important, these shows perpetuated a critical position "authentic" rock music was inevitably commodified, co-opted, and corrupted into banal pop music the moment it came into contact with television, a view exacerbated by the advent of MTV in 1981.

From the cancellation of *The Partridge Family* in 1974 to the debut of *Hannah Montana* in 2006, the pop-music sitcom genre was all but extinct. To be sure, rock and popular music underwent numerous historical changes and permutations during the pop-music sitcom's lengthy hibernation. Chapters 9 and 10 discuss two cultural discourses that were significant in the emergence of *Hannah Montana*: the teen pop of Britney Spears and the film *School of Rock*. Britney Spears personified what I have termed "First Wave Teen Pop" in American pop culture consciousness. This brand of slickly produced and shamelessly marketed pop music merged black dance music genres, white bubblegum pop, and an emphasis on image as much as music; Madonna, British "New Pop" bands, and New Kids on the Block served as the formative figures during the 1980s. From approximately 1995–2003 First Wave Teen Pop dominated the charts while it was critically reviled as the nadir of manufactured pop music and a feminized mass culture in its cadre of boy bands (Backstreet Boys, *N Sync, 98 Degrees), the Spice Girls, and teenage pop singers like Spears and Christina Aguilera.[8] Through a comparative study of Madonna and Spears's controversial career paths, as well as analysis of Madonna's song "Music" (2000) versus Spears's songs "Piece of Me" (2007) and "Circus" (2008), Madonna's role as pop-culture provocateur extraordinaire affirms progressive neoliberal ideology whereas Britney Spears, the poster girl for mass culture *par excellance*, provides an unnerving if unintended radical critique of capitalism, class and the contradictions of American society.[9]

The 2003 film *School of Rock* served as a clarion call for rock traditionalism in response to the rise and fall of First Wave Teen Pop. In addition to sustaining the sexism and other elements of conservatism in rock ideology, *School of Rock*'s generational politics are crucial. *School of Rock* seeks to inhibit the contradiction of "anti–Establishment" teens of decades past from becoming the middle-aged Establishment adults of today. To do so, *School of Rock* converts rock history and rock ideology into a rock mythology of timeless rebellion at two levels. One is through film's canonization of classic rock, hard rock, heavy metal, punk, grunge, and Alternative into a unified body of eternally authentic and inherently subversive popular music. Second is through the cultural stereotype of the "eternal teenager" and defining Hipness as the domain of the white, male adult who retains his adolescent passions—namely his undying love for "real" rock and roll—while refusing to conform to Square society. Conversely, the 2003 film *What a Girl Wants* can be read as the girl power competing discourse to *School of Rock*. In both films, similar if not identical ideological positions concerning individualism, self-determination, and social mobility are manifest; they are represented far differently in terms of the gender, generational, and Hip-Square politics.

Chapter 11 addresses the Hannah Montana phenomenon. Launched by Disney as a pop-music teen sitcom in 2006 and running until 2011, *Hannah Montana* revolved around Miley Stewart (Miley Cyrus), an unsophisticated, teenage girl from the South, who lived a double life as a teen pop superstar through her brassy alter-ego "Hannah Montana" with the inevitable comparison being Britney Spears. In terms of popular music, Hannah Montana/Miley Cyrus heralded the emergence of a "Second Wave Teen Pop." Like First Wave Teen Pop, Second Wave Teen Pop utilizes bubblegum pop and black music like disco, funk, rap, and techno. However, and in the wake of *School of Rock*, Second Wave Teen Pop draws much more extensively from a white pop/rock lineage ranging from 1970s hard rock and punk to 1990s Alternative and grunge, and especially 1980s New Wave and "stadium rock."[10] As important, and also like *School of Rock*, Second Wave Teen Pop frames the individualism of rock ideology around productive self-determination rather than destructive social rebellion. Nonetheless, through analysis of the Hannah Montana musical product, the *Hannah Montana* sitcom, and especially *Hannah Montana: The Movie* (2009), Hannah Montana can be read beyond the standard interpretation as a syrupy symbol of the American Dream. Like Britney Spears, Hannah Montana functions as an overdetermined cultural figure that reveals as much as conceals the ideological contradictions of American society.

Nickelodeon's chief response to *Hannah Montana* was the pop-music sitcom *Big Time Rush* (2009- ), the focus of Chapter 12. While the formal and marketing model of *Big Time Rush* is clearly *The Monkees*, the ideology owes much to *Saved by the Bell* and *School of Rock*. Centered on a boy band's pursuit of stardom, *Big Time Rush* becomes highly disingenuous in its frequent satire of the Culture Industry while the show simultaneously and brazenly cross-markets Big Time Rush as a boy band into pop music through the very same strategies and tactics the show cynically and speciously criticizes. Quite consciously presenting itself as anti–Establishment, *Big Time Rush* also seeks to defuse the popular and pejorative view of boy bands as feminine and inauthentic by constructing a "rebel" image of the boy band around the "authentic masculine" ingrained in rock ideology. Indeed, *Big Time Rush* champions Hipness as white, middle-class, Middle American male adolescence that thoroughly dominates all things female in relentless pursuit of the American Dream.

By way of conclusion, teen culture is both product and producer of ideological contradictions, and serves as a critical point to assess the larger crisis of American popular culture. Raymond Williams formulated the maintenance of "dominant culture" as a complex and continuous process of reincorporating "residual culture" along with the incorporation of "emergent culture." Entering the 21st century, emergent culture entails the possibilities afforded (pun intended) by the proliferation of cable and satellite TV, satellite radio, and especially the personal computer and the internet. At the same time, this emergent culture is increasingly constrained by the drive to not only sustain but instill residual culture on younger generations, namely the cultural canon developed around TV and rock music in the latter half of the 20th century. In other words, as much as teen culture proclaims, "Out with the old, in with the new," it also insists, "Out with the new, in with the old."

My goal is not to predict the future. If that were my intent, I'd be writing in vague quatrains. However, I am adamant in my view that what is occurring in teen culture now is not only significant as cultural and political discourse, but has a crucial bearing as teens become adults and the dominant generation in the impending decades. If the Nickelodeon ethos is that "kids matter," my contention is that "teen culture matters" as well.

# PART ONE

---

# DON'T TRUST ANYONE OVER THIRTY

The crisis consists precisely of the fact that the old is dying and the new cannot be born; in this interregnum a great variety of morbid symptoms appear.—*Antonio Gramsci, "State and Civil Society" (1930)*

In the new millennium there is much less of a generation gap.—*Bret Michaels,* People *magazine (12/29/2009)*

# 1

# Teen Culture Industry
# (or, You Pays Your Money
# and You Takes Your Choice)

## Adult Production and Teen Consumption

In the scope of this project, "teen culture" is defined as cultural production primarily marketed towards an audience of cultural consumers ages 17 and under; in this respect, it could be said the focus is as much on *tween culture* as it is increasingly differentiated from *teen culture* as far as critical and marketing discourses. Another way to define it is that "teen culture" is the stuff of the annual Kid's Choice and Teen Choice Awards, and here the word "Choice" becomes crucial. The core contradiction of teen culture is that it is, and always has been, primarily *produced by adults in entertainment industries for adolescent consumers* save for its occasional teenage stars like Michael Jackson and Donny Osmond in the early 1970s, Britney Spears and Christina Aguilera in the late 1990s, or, most recently, Miranda Cosgrove and Miley Cyrus. Conversely, David Cassidy was 20 when *The Partridge Family* debuted in 1970 and the Spice Girls were all in their early 20s when their breakthrough hit "Wannabe" was released in 1996. In this way, the term "teen idols" not only (pejoratively) refers to the adult performers but the adolescent fan base who, as far as the teen culture industry goes, might have rancid taste but not filthy lucre. Nevertheless, as much as teen culture is determined by a teen culture industry, teen culture is also determined by teens as far as what brands of teen culture they consume and for how long they consume them. To this extent, teen culture manifests the problematics of mass culture, and the extent the focus cannot be strictly placed on cultural production or cultural consumption.

At several levels the production of teen culture epitomizes Theodor W. Adorno's analysis of the Culture Industry. Adorno decried the standardization of culture in modern capitalism into mass produced, easily consumed, and ideologically affirmative "mass culture" that negates "true culture" as a challenge and critique of social conditions.[1] For Adorno, so-called "true culture" in the twentieth century was a highly select body of avant-garde modernism (e.g., the music of Arnold Schoenberg or the literature of Samuel Beckett) whereas "mass culture" is "popular culture" as a *whole*: popular music, Hollywood films, television, mainstream novels, etc.[2] Rather than resistance, mass culture manufactures pseudo-individuality at both the level of production and consumption; as Adorno defined it, "By pseudo-individualization we mean endowing cultural mass production with the halo of free choice or open market on the basis of standardization itself."[3]

In *Why TV Is Not Our Fault* (2005), Eileen R. Meehan noted ownership and control of broadcast TV is dominated by the "Big Five" of Disney, General Electric, News Corporation, Time Warner, and Viacom. As well as Disney Channel, Disney owns ABC and ABC Family channels; Viacom is the parent company of Nickelodeon as well as CBS, Comedy Central, MTV, Spike, and VH-1. Defining the TV industry as an "oligopoly," Meehan suggested:

> Each company in an oligopoly strives to be number one without destabilizing the oligopoly from which they all benefit, whether as the first or last firm.... True competition would destabilize the oligopoly, putting some of the oligopolists out of business and create a more fluid market structure. Eliminating competition and maintaining the oligopoly is in the interest of each oligopolist. Rivalry exists only to the degree that each oligopolist tries to be the first among equals.[4]

As far as teen sitcoms and Second Wave Teen Pop, this largely boils down to the "Big Two" of Disney Channel and Nickelodeon.[5] The *rivalry* rather than competition between Disney Channel and Nickelodeon in the teen culture industry has become one of producing almost identical products. The success of Nickelodeon's *Drake and Josh*, a teen sitcom about two highly dissimilar stepbrothers (one carefree Hip and one uptight Square) was followed by Disney Channel's *The Suite Life of Zack and Cody*, a teen sitcom about two highly dissimilar twin brothers (one impetuous Hip and the other reserved Square, if not quite as pronounced as the Hip-Square binary of *Drake and Josh*). With the immense success of Disney's *Hannah Montana* and the Jonas Brothers, Nickelodeon responded with teen sitcoms about a teenage rock band (*The Naked Brothers Band*), a boy band (*Big Time Rush*), and a teenage girl at a performing arts high school with the career goal of becoming a pop star (*Victorious*). The popularity of Disney's *High School Musical* films spawned the almost identical Nickelodeon made-for-TV film *Spectacular!* (The more "mature" brand of *High School Musical* is offered by FOX with *Glee*.) The success of Nickelodeon's *iCarly*, about a teenage girl who produces her own comedy webshow and allows for show-within-a-show skits, was followed by Disney Channel's *Sonny with a Chance*, a self-described "TV comedy about a TV comedy" wherein a teenage girl lands a role on a popular teen comedy-variety show which allows for show-within-a-show skits.[6]

Beyond the almost parasitic TV product and production, cross-marketing between teen sitcoms and teen pop is now standard operating procedure.[7] Most overtly, this entails the manufacture of teen pop performers out of pop music sitcoms including *Hannah Montana*, *The Naked Brothers Band*, and *Big Time Rush*. Moreover, a *partial* listing of current and former Disney Channel and Nickelodeon teen sitcom cast members who entered the pop music market includes Hilary Duff (*Lizzie McGuire*), Drake Bell (*Drake and Josh*), Emma Roberts (*Unfabulous*), Miley Cyrus (*Hannah Montana*), Emily Osment (*Hannah Montana*), Mitchel Musso (*Hannah Montana*), Miranda Cosgrove (*iCarly*), Jennette McCurdy (*iCarly*), Selena Gomez (*Wizards of Waverly Place*), Keke Palmer (*True Jackson, VP*), Demi Lovato (*Sonny with a Chance*), Victoria Justice (*Victorious*), and Leon Thomas III (*Victorious*).[8] Each popular teen sitcom is accompanied by a plethora of merchandise ranging from DVDs, CDs, books, video games, sundry fan collectables, toys, and fashion. *True Jackson, VP* cross-marketed a "Mad Style by True Jackson" line of clothing in partnership with Wal-Mart; one commercial featured a multicultural group of tween girls dancing to the *True Jackson, VP* theme song. Miley Cyrus also markets clothing through Wal-Mart, and Selena Gomez markets a "Dream Out Loud" fashion line through K-Mart.

Here two points need to be stressed. One is that the Culture Industry aspects of teen culture are hardly some recent and diabolical invention of Disney and Nickelodeon. Since *Howdy Doody* premiered in 1947, the close relationship between "kiddie TV" and advertising has been the ongoing subject of concerns and complaints; hence, the appeal of PBS as a site of educational TV is that the network is "commercial free" as well as politically liberal-to-moderate in message. While a more "mature" brand of teen culture — meaning an adult isn't embarrassed to admit being a fan of the show — *Glee* similarly cross-markets between TV, pop music, and a plethora of related merchandise.[9] Elvis Presley, the Beatles, the Grateful Dead and Led Zeppelin were business enterprises as well as rock performers. The Rolling Stones are as much a corporation as a rock band, with cross-marketed products in 2010 including "Rolling Stones Special Editions" of the Trivia Pursuit and Monopoly board games. The most glaring contradiction becomes U2 as the saviors of rock progressive populism and global humanitarianism while U2 singer Bono shakes hands with George W. Bush, hugs Vladimir Putin, and promotes the ethical capitalism of his Product Red line in conjunction with multinationals like Apple, Gap, and Starbucks.[10] As Norma Coates noted, such practices are "conveniently ignored or denied by rock critics in their attempt to somehow blame teenybopper fans, artists, and television for such abominations."[11]

Indeed, the Monkees were reviled for their manufactured TV origins, their lack of "authenticity," extensive and excessive marketing, and predominantly "teenybopper" assumed audience in the 1960s. Nonetheless, the Monkees underwent a critical redemption as producers of well-crafted pop music and the inventors of music video in the 1980s (discussed further in Chapter 8). In the 1970s, Kiss was unmercifully flayed by rock critics not only for their hard rock/heavy metal music and monster movie/superhero imagery, but the accompanying flood of merchandise that ranged from a special edition Kiss comic book, Kiss make-up kits, and a horrendous made-for TV movie, *Kiss Meets the Phantom of the Park* (NBC, 1978). Kiss is now considered an eminent 1970s classic rock band. To this extent, the revisionism is not only historical but political, and owes to the fact that the Monkees and Kiss are now part of the *middle-age adult* pop culture canon, and therefore elevated to a status of new respectability and superiority in comparison to current teen culture.[12]

The other issue is the extent that popular culture allows any spaces for individual and collective resistance. Simon Frith suggested:

> Production and consumption were ... the focus of the mass culture debate.... Out of Adorno have come analysis of the economics of entertainment in which the ideological effects ... the transformation of a creative people into a passive massare taken for granted.... From [Walter] Benjamin have come subcultural theories ... youth subcultures are said to make their own meanings, to create cultures in the act of consumption.[13]

Again, "choice" becomes pivotal as far as teen culture consumption. At worst, teen culture criticism denies tweens and teens have any capacity to make informed consumer decisions and instead mindlessly race to the store to buy any and all products remotely connected to their favorite and unvaryingly "bad" assortment of TV shows, music, movies, etc. In effect, this argument takes an Adorno-Culture Industry view of teen culture as mass production and market deception. At best, teen culture criticism grants tweens and teens make consumer choices although much of their taste is still deemed awful until they become more mature cultural consumers and appreciate the same cultural products as adults. This argument is a backhanded application of the Benjamin-subculture argument in which teen consumption manufactures a counterfeit cultural identity until they "grow up." Both of these positions ultimately "devalue" teen culture and teen consumers and instead reflect an elitism that permeates adult attitudes around contemporary teen culture.

## Teen Culture and the New Generation Gap

> If the modern mass audience no longer understands *Oedipus Rex*, I would go so far as to say this is the fault of *Oedipus Rex* and not the fault of the audience.[14]— *Antonin Artaud*

While it appears to be stating the obvious, generational conflict permeates teen culture at the levels of text and context. Historically, primetime domestic sitcoms focus on precocious toddlers and pernicious teenagers being molded by effective parenting. This can be represented by content families (*Leave It to*

*Beaver, The Partridge Family, The Brady Bunch,* or *The Cosby Show*), fathers besieged by insolent wives and children (*Married ... With Children, Home Improvement, George Lopez, My Wife and Kids, According to Jim,* or *The War at Home*), or beleaguered single moms coping with uncooperative ex-husbands and kids (*One Day at a Time, Reba,* or *The New Adventures of Old Christine*). Even teen-centered primetime sitcoms—the more notable recent examples being *That 70's Show, Malcolm in the Middle,* and *Everybody Hates Chris*—gave equal time to the problems of the teenagers (school, romance, parental control) and the adults (work, marriage, troublesome kids).[15]

Dan Schneider's teen programming for Nickelodeon did not develop around gauging current teen consumer taste and trends, but TV *he* watched as a kid—the classical sitcoms and comedy-variety shows. As important, Schneider was cognizant that teens and tweens demand shows that offer a sense of empowerment, a view quite compatible with Nickelodeon's programming agenda as a "kids only" TV network. As Schneider put it,

> When you're a kid, most of the time you're being told to shut up by adults. In school: be quiet. Your dad's watching a show: be quiet. Even the kids who seem to have a lot of freedom, their lives are pretty controlled. So what I try to do on my shows is have the kids come out on top. They're the smartest ones in the room. They're the ones in charge.[16]

As discussed in Chapters 5 and 6, this also becomes the ideological tension in Schneider's teen sitcoms. *Zoey 101* and *iCarly* can read as neoliberal updates of the hippie battle cry "Don't trust anyone over thirty!" (*Hannah Montana, True Jackson VP,* and even Schneider's own *Victorious* are another matter).[17] These sitcoms posit that "adults are best who govern least," and provide ethical and ideological lessons around self-governing teenagers and their self-regulating communities which run better on their own rather than the dictates of institutional adult power structures imposed on them (parents, teachers, businesspeople, police, etc.). In terms of neoliberalism, the metaphor is how to maintain a workable liberal democracy without "big government."

If adults largely control the production of teen culture, Schneider's comments suggest an additional contradiction. As a multiplicity of discourses, teen culture can overtly presents itself as "speaking for the kids" and offer representations of "teen empowerment" while it can also impose adult lessons and values as to what constitutes acceptable or unacceptable modes of social behavior, such as *True Jackson, VP* (see Chapter 7). Rock music quite loudly celebrates freedom, non-conformity, and rebellion, be it the hardcore punk of the Circle Jerks' "Wild in the Streets" and Black Flag's "Rise Above" or the teen pop of Hannah Montana's "We Got the Party" and Miley Cyrus's "Robot." Sitcoms often negate the agency of teenagers with lessons that reinforce obedience to a status quo where *the adults* are "the ones in charge." With the intersection of teen pop and teen sitcoms the tension becomes especially pronounced. As far

Cross-marketing rock ideology: *School of Rock* promotional image modeled on a *Rolling Stone* magazine cover (Photofest).

as ideology marketing, Hannah Montana becomes ensnared in the contradiction between individuality and agency (the message of teen pop) versus community and conformity (the message of teen sitcoms) which ultimately reaches an untenable crisis in *Hannah Montana: The Movie* and cannot be rectified underneath the film's superficial sappiness; conversely, *Big Time Rush* champions individualism while community becomes the byproduct of domination (respectively discussed in Chapters 11 and 12).

Specific political messages aside, teen culture is *itself* a form of identity politics. While teen culture is *produced for teenagers by adults*, teen culture is *consumed by teenagers* and through their consumption they define their particular generation. Put differently, while teens may be forced to order from the menu of the teen culture industry, they also decide what "chiz" they won't eat.[18] Nevertheless, the demonization of teen culture is still rooted in critical positions that it is all derivative swill that preys on naïve waifs. A more famous example was the 2001 documentary "The Merchants of Cool" aired on PBS *Frontline*, a blanket attack on the Big Five and how they "exert unprecedented power in marketing messages to young people, capitalizing on the lifestyle of 'cool' and incorporating what have historically been subversive and anti-establishment ideologies as the very center of marketing strategies."[19] Again, this is a valid but limited assessment of teen culture, and "The Merchants of Cool" need be qualified around its own political agenda. Increasingly a niche network for middle-aged, middle-class liberals who were teens or young adults in the 1960s and 1970s, PBS has become a bastion for perpetuating the myths of the 1960s as the apex of American progressivism and youth counterculture (in November 2010, PBS premiered documentaries on Hubert H. Humphrey as well as John Lennon). The 2010 *American Masters* documentary on the Doors was one particular example, with the closing statement asserting the Doors remain oppositional culture because they have never licensed their songs for car commercials. In "The Merchants of Cool," contemporary teen culture is reduced to crass corporate profiteering. In the *American Masters* documentary on the Doors, authentic youth culture in all of its supposed subversive glory is found in the 1960s counterculture that always was, is, and will be "anti–Establishment."

Since World War II, each successive generation has grown up around the cultural discourses of cinema, comic books, TV, and rock music as increasingly legitimized forms of culture (for instance, the comic book that is now the "graphic novel"). When teen culture versus adult culture first emerged in the 1950s, it was a fairly clear binary between high culture versus low culture and unambiguously expressed in Chuck Berry's hit song "Roll Over, Beethoven" (1956). After 50-plus years, the debate is no longer high culture versus low culture and whether and why kids should be listening to Beethoven instead of Chuck Berry. The debate now is over "high popular culture" versus "low popular culture" and whether and why kids should be listening to the Beatles instead of Britney Spears.

There is much to be critical of as far as the production and consumption of teen culture as there is the production and consumption of adult culture — *and each on its own terms.* Teens in the 1960s and 1970s demanded their own counterculture and not the culture of their parents. As adults, they now insist on imposing their youth culture on teenagers in the twenty-first century, exemplified in cultural discourses ranging from PBS, *Rolling Stone,* and *School of Rock.* The contradiction of the Woodstock generation of the 1960s and the classic rock generation of the 1970s is that they have become the middle-aged Establishment as much as they wish to define themselves as the older and more sophisticated version of their rebellious anti–Establishment teen essence — painfully signified by the remaining members of the Who, now in their sixties rather than being part of the 1960s, trotting out "My Generation" at the 2010 Super Bowl halftime show. Almost inevitably, each generation dismisses the teen culture of the subsequent generations while it nostalgically and more desperately clings to its own teenage cultural canon well into adulthood. Even though teen culture is a product of specific historical pressures, political tensions, and social conditions, adults insist their particular era of teen culture has a timeless significance that not only defined their generation but should define all generations to come. Pity the poor teenager in the twenty-first century who doesn't appreciate the eternal quality and metaphysical wisdom of *Star Wars* or "Stairway to Heaven," and also pity the poor parent who failed as cultural mentor in the process.

It is not that there is "much less of a generation gap" as cultural theorist Bret Michaels would have it. Rather, the generation gap has been *obscured* by the fact that since the 1950s the popular culture of movies, TV, and popular music — especially rock music — are not only "dominant culture" but *mainstream* cultural discourses. The struggle between adolescent autonomy and adult authority remains the central aspect of generational politics. Indeed, the drive to canonize the generational signifiers of past decades as an authentic and superior culture to the inauthentic and inferior teen culture of the present is as much evidence of this ongoing struggle as any proof it has diminished in the twenty-first century. In this respect, the crisis in American popular culture, to paraphrase Antonio Gramsci, can be assessed as one where "the old *refuses to die* and the new cannot be born."

# 2

# On the Importance
# of Being Hip

## White Hipness

> Our skin might be white, but our souls are black!—*Tracy Turnblatt,*
> Hairspray

In the 1950s, rock music became a primary cultural outlet for the angst
and aspirations of the younger generation in America. During a decade when
racial segregation was stridently contested and staunchly defended, rock and
roll was an unprecedented merging of rhythm and blues ("black music") and
country-western ("white music"). Simon Frith contended, "The shock was not
musical ... but ideological: it was the overt, assertive, *social* intermingling of
black and white."[1] However, what has become more problematic over the
decades is the cultural construction of race and "Otherness" as a key signifier
of Hipness.

Norman Mailer's essay "The White Negro" (1957) advanced an argument
for the liberation of white, middle-class males through embracing "black culture" and rejecting "white culture." As Mailer proclaimed, "*One is Hip or One
is Square*, (the alternative which each new generation coming into American
life is beginning to feel), *one is a rebel or one conforms*, one is a frontiersman in
the Wild West of American night life or else a Square, trapped in the totalitarian
tissues of American society."[2] While Mailer's essay now reads as a backhanded
compliment (at best) and hopelessly stereotypical (at worst), its influence was
substantial as far the formation of youth culture ideology. Dick Hebdige argued:

> All the classic symptoms of hysteria most commonly associated with the emer-
> gence of rock 'n' roll a few years later were present in the outraged reaction with
> which conservative America greeted the beat and the hipster, and at the same
> time a whole mythology for the Black Man and his culture was being developed
> by sympathetic liberal observers.... The Black Man, mistily observed through the
> self-conscious prose of Norman Mailer or the breathless panegyries of Jack Ker-
> ouac (who carried the idealization of Negro culture to almost ludicrous extremes
> in his novels) could serve for white youth as the model for freedom-in-bondage.[3]

Timothy D. Taylor suggested, "The embrace of blackness was a way for whites to rebel in the 1950s and 1960s, and while the present moment is different in many ways, it is also quite similar.... The hip was black; the square was white, and it was also southern (and Midwestern, and lower-middle and working-class, and rural)."[4] *Footloose* (1984) constructed a Hip-Square conflict where Hip was personified by a non-conformist white male from a Northern city (Chicago) while Square was represented by the fundamentalist conservative community of a white, rural town in the South where rock music is banned and dancing is illegal. In the historical context of the 1980s (Reaganism and the Moral Majority), *Footloose* was ostensibly a "liberal" film attacking right-wing morality politics.[5] With the exception of two African-American performers (Deniece Williams and the band Shalamar), *Footloose* also placed a decided emphasis on white stadium rock such as Foreigner, Sammy Hagar, Quiet Riot, a duet by Ann Wilson (Heart) and Mike Reno (Loverboy), and the title song by 1970s holdover Kenny Loggins.

*Hairspray* (1988) was set in Baltimore in 1962 and politics surrounding *The Corny Collins Show*, a local teen-dance TV show with a racially segregated policy.[6] White teenagers learned to be Hip as well as politically progressive citizens through identification with black culture; given the film's time frame, the popular music of rebellion is 1950s and early 1960s rock and R&B music. Moreover, *Hairspray* took place in an East Coast milieu where black inner-city neighborhoods are dangerously Hip and the white residential areas are stiflingly Square: all very much consistent with Mailer's "White Negro" essay. However, *Hairspray*'s Hip protagonist was Tracy Turnblatt, a white, lower-middle class teenage girl; the film's Square antagonist was Amber von Tussle, a white, upper-middle class teenage girl. As much as race, the Hip-Square dialectic was also constructed around women and class strata.

Both *Footloose* and *Hairspray* represented Hipness around *competing* identity politics of race, gender, class, geography, and *music*. *Footloose* constructed the Hip versus Square conflict around Northern-urban versus Southern-rural geographic politics with mainstream rock the sound of individualistic rebellion while race, gender, and class politics are largely and conveniently "sidestepped."

*Hairspray*'s configuration of Hip occurred within a Northern-metropolitan setting and through a collation of the marginalized elements of American society — African-Americans, women, and lower-middle class whites — united by R&B and early rock and roll. In this context, and as much as Taylor's observation is perceptive, it cannot be taken as an all-purpose "formula" to categorize representations of Hip versus Square in American popular culture. Particularly in rock ideology, "upper class" and high culture is often deemed Square as opposed to "lower class" and popular culture being the domain of Hip. Among the many reasons English progressive rock bands in the 1970s were castigated by American rock critics was the predominant influence of bourgeois classical music and high culture (Square). In contrast, Bruce Springsteen's authenticity and Hipness was and remains built around an urban, East Coast, white "working class hero" liberal-populist image along with his merger of R&B, folk, and early rock and roll. "Southern Hipness" as a kind of anti-authority, rebellious, lower class, more conservative (or less liberal) "white trash Hipness" was manifest during the 1970s in cultural discourse ranging from the film *Smokey and the Bandit* (1977), the TV show *The Dukes of Hazzard* (CBS, 1979–85), and popular music with "Southern Rock" like Lynard Skynard and the Charlie Daniels Band as well as "Outlaw Country" (Johnny Cash, Willie Nelson, etc.).[7] While the popular permutation has become "redneck comedy" (e.g., Jeff Foxworthy and Larry, the Cable Guy), the teen drama *Hellcats* (the CW, 2010–11) was set at a college in Memphis and reconfigured Southern Hip-Square binaries through the main characters Marti Perkins and Savannah Monroe.[8] Marti was Hip: white, lower class, non-conformist, a rock musician as well as a liberal pre-law student. In order to retain her scholarship, Marti reluctantly joined the college cheerleading team, introduced raunchy dance moves to the routines, and became romantically involved with an African-American male on the squad. Savannah Monroe struggled with urges for Hip "liberation" versus her Square lifestyle and strict upbringing in a conservative, religious, upper-class white environment. A dedicated cheerleader, she was socially proper and sexually prudish (the character's name sounding like an adult-film star pseudonym notwithstanding).

Teen sitcoms also express similar yet different tensions as far as representations of Hip versus Square. Hip is urban, less Hip is suburban, and Square is rural; not unrelated, East Coast and West Coast is Hip, Midwestern is Square, and Southern is especially Square. In the *Victorious* episode "Sleepover at Sikowitz's" (2011), Hollywood Arts High School drama teacher Mr. Sikowitz (an acid casualty hippie whose name is pronounced "Psycho-witz") devised a method-acting exercise wherein the class assigned each other a character to play for an entire evening at his home. Tori Vega decided the character for her primary antagonist, the Goth/punk "mean girl" Jade West, and made Jade play a farm girl from Alabama — *much* to Jade's displeasure. The *iCarly* episode "iDo" (2010) involved Seattle residents Carly Shay and her friends reluctantly agreeing to be in the wedding party for fans of their "iCarly" webshow in Milwaukee. Midwestern and Southern stereotypes were conflated into a representation of "Middle America" where everyone was "thick" both physically and mentally. A transitional shot using stock footage of a jet airliner was accompanied by voiceover dialogue. The pilot announces they are about to land in Wisconsin, the news of which is received with a collective groan by the passengers. The pilot sighs, "Yeah ... I know." In this context, the following is a list of the ten primary and secondary teen sitcoms discussed in this project and their locales:

*Saved by the Bell* — Los Angeles (Pacific Palisades)
*Clarissa Explains It All* — suburban Ohio

*Drake and Josh*—suburban San Diego
*Zoey 101*—Los Angeles (Malibu)
*Hannah Montana*—Los Angeles (Malibu)
*iCarly*—metropolitan Seattle
*Wizards of Waverly Place*—New York City (Greenwich Village)
*True Jackson VP*—New York City (Manhattan)
*Big Time Rush*—Los Angeles (Hollywood)
*Victorious*—Los Angeles (Hollywood Hills)

Nine are set within an East or West Coast city, residential area, or suburb; five are L.A. (city or county) specific and two NYC. One took place in the Midwest and none in the South.[9] Moreover, as far as the earlier teen sitcoms, *Saved by the Bell* was a considerably revised version of a short-lived Disney Channel sitcom *Good Morning, Miss Bliss* and one component of the makeover was changing the locale from Indiana (Midwest Square) to Pacific Palisades (West Coast Hip). On *Clarissa Explains it All*, the series ended with Clarissa Darling leaving Ohio (Midwest Square) for NYC (East Coast Hip) to embark on a career in journalism.[10]

Conversely, *Hannah Montana* took place in Malibu but the main character, Miley Stewart, was a white teenage girl from Tennessee—the equivalent of "three strikes and you're out" as far as the politics of Hipness—who had a double-life as teen pop star Hannah Montana. The Stewart family possessed a Southern Hipness manifest in "down home" demeanor and traditional values versus the pretense of "high society" and West Coast lifestyle.[11] The stars of *Big Time Rush* are four teenage males (three white, one very uncool Latino) from Minnesota pursuing pop stardom as a boy band in Hollywood with their "down to earth" Midwestern values—or, more correctly, *attitude*—constituting a Middle American Hipness. The inconveniences of hard work, humility, and responsibility championed by *Hannah Montana* become another matter on *Big Time Rush*, where success is achieved through continual male adolescent irresponsibility and not despite it.

As far as socioeconomic status, teen sitcoms are middle-to-upper class, with few exceptions.[12] On *Wizards of Waverly Place* the Russo family lived in an apartment above a Greenwich Village deli they owned and operated. Their life as unassuming middle-class entrepreneurs was modest by design; the Russo children had magical powers and their parents instilled values of hard work and self-discipline rather than the lure and inevitable pitfalls of using the supernatural to conjure up anything and everything they might want. On *Hannah Montana*, the Stewart family was rich and lived in a large beachfront house in Malibu. However, the Stewarts did not "show off" their wealth as much by choice and adhering to their old-fashioned values as well as the necessity of protecting Miley Stewart's dual-identity as Hannah Montana. Like *Wizards of Waverly Place*, the message of *Hannah Montana* was contended living within the boundaries of a humble, middle-class, "average" lifestyle.[13]

As far as Nickelodeon's recent teen sitcoms, middle-upper class is the norm. On *Drake and Josh*, the family lived comfortably in suburban San Diego. *Zoey 101* was set at Pacific Coast Academy in Malibu, a private and presumably expensive boarding school. On *True Jackson, VP*, True Jackson worked in Manhattan, went to a public high school in Brooklyn, but lived in a large house in what appeared to be an upscale residential neighborhood. *Victorious* takes place in Hollywood Hills where Tori Vega, her sister Trina, and her friends live in relative affluence and attend a private performing arts high school. In the *Victorious* episode "Jade Dumps Beck" (2010), a relationship crisis between the perennially debonair Beck Oliver and pathologically jealous Jade was prompted by Beck's friendship with a girl in his yoga class who is also a rich socialite. Tori learned Beck lives in an old RV trailer and, as Beck put it, by "my rules" rather than the dictates of his parents. In fact, Beck's RV is parked his parent's driveway and he even has a maid; a subsequent episode explained that Beck's father bought the trailer for him, and the previous owner was a rap star. Hence, Beck can slum it as far as projecting a lower-class "bohemian" rebel Hipness while at the same time enjoying the perks of upper-class Hipness as far as celebrity friends and living off the family dime. This idealized representation of independent teen living is even more pronounced on *iCarly* in which Carly Shay is a teenage girl who effectively lives on her own in downtown Seattle, produces her own highly popular webshow, and yet is entirely free of any and all economic responsibilities (an issue returned to in Chapter 6).

Within the prevailing middle-upper class and metropolitan-coastal geographic representation, teen sitcoms are predominantly *white*. Out of the previous ten teen sitcoms listed, seven feature white main characters, one an African-American main character (*True Jackson, VP*), and two white-Latina main characters (*Wizards of Waverly Place* and *Victorious*).[14] On *Victorious*, "whiteness" is frequently addressed. In one episode, when Tori's friend André jokingly referred to her as a "white girl," Tori less jokingly pointed out that she is "half-Latina"; however, Tori's occasional attempts to act "urban" (read: black) inevitably end with her embarrassment. André is the only African-American in the main cast of characters and the hippest of the Hip characters. Conversely, Robbie Shapiro is hopelessly Square, an utter failure with girls, and a geek. He is played as a "neurotic Jew" stereotype to the point that Robbie totes a ventriloquist puppet named Rex Powers (or "wrecks powers") to verbally express his repressed thoughts. Rex speaks in a strained African-American dialect and much of his repertoire consists of sarcasm and sexist comments. In the *iCarly-Victorious* crossover movie "iParty with Victorious" (2011), Robbie mentions he is a big fan of the Spice Girls while Rex is a passable free-style rapper. To be sure, Rex is frequently obnoxious while Robbie is merely annoying; the issue is how Robbie attempts to project Hipness through Rex around stereotypes of "blackness" or, more correctly, the White Negro.

The dominant societal representation in teen sitcoms becomes ideological as far as constructing a normative teenage experience around an idealized Hip lifestyle that is predominately metropolitan, Northern, Coastal, middle-to-upper class, and white. Within this environment, "diversity" is contained, with "contained" being used in *both* senses of the word. In short, the teen sitcom is largely a world comprised of bourgeois teenagers. However, the complexities of Hipness become configured and reconfigured around other forms of identity politics with particular emphasis on Americanism, gender, and age.

## One Nation Under the Hip

The cultural clash between America versus Europe, and usually the inherent superiority of the former, is a recurring theme in American cultural texts dating back to Henry James's *The American* (1877) and Mark Twain's *A Connecticut Yankee in King Arthur's Court* (1889). *Black Knight* (2001) was a film adaptation of *A Connecticut Yankee in King Arthur's Court* starring Martin Lawrence that added the "Hip-black/Square–white" dynamic to the America-versus-Europe cultural struggle. Recent teen culture is no exception, and the framing of Hip as American and Square as European, specifically England, was central to the film *What a Girl Wants*. The antagonist in *Hannah Montana: The Movie* is Oswald Granger, a sleazy English tabloid reporter seeking to reveal the truth behind Hannah Montana and destroy "the dream" (which is to say "American Dream") that Hannah Montana represents.

Negative depictions of the English are also common on *iCarly*.[15] One of the recurring skits on the "iCarly" webshow within *iCarly* episodes is called "Pathetic Plays" and centers on a moronic British family. In "iPromise Not to Tell" (2007), Mr. Devlin, who is English as well as a typically authoritarian teacher, gave Carly an arbitrary B on a history report because he didn't like the three-hole punch paper she used. In "iHeart Art" (2008), Spencer Shay, an aspiring Pop-Art sculptor, met his main artistic influence, Harry Joyner, a pompous Englishman as well as pretentious artist stereotype; Joyner ridiculed Spencer, although eventually confessed he criticized Spencer because he was jealous of his work. The situation of "iRocked the Vote" (2009) entailed Carly and her friends making a music video for insufferable English pop singer Wade Collins, who made it emphatically and repeatedly clear that he "hates Americans." Indeed, "iRocked the Vote" manifested how popular music has historically been a highly contentious battlefield in the America-Europe cultural conflict. Rock critic Lester Bangs was an ardent proponent of Mailer's "White Negro" thesis as well as a fervent supporter of punk and the more extreme avant-garde strains of punk rock practiced by NYC "No Wave" bands. Nonetheless, in a highly controversial essay "The White Noise Supremacists" (*The Village Voice*, 1979), Bangs criticized the whiteness of punk and No Wave:

> The Contortions' James Brown/Albert Ayler spasms aside, most of the [No Wave] bands are as white as John Cage, and there's an evolution of sound,

rhythm, and stance running from the [Velvet Underground] through the Stooges to the Ramones that takes us farther and farther from the black stud postures of Mick Jagger that Lou Reed and Iggy [Pop] partake in but Joey Ramone clearly doesn't ... Joey is a white American Kid from Forest Hills, and as such his cultural input has been white, from "The Jetsons" to Alice Cooper. *But none of that cancels out the fact the greatest, deepest music America has produced has been, while not entirely black, the product of miscegenation.*[16]

In the same essay, Bangs took Nico to task for offensive racist remarks she made in the rock press and then referred to her as "a dumb kraut cunt."[17] While the comment speaks volumes for the sexism of rock ideology (to be returned to shortly), it also betrays the nationalism. In 1956, Chuck Berry threw down the gauntlet with "Roll Over, Beethoven," which not only championed the low culture of rock music against the high culture of classical music but American culture versus Continental culture. Berry's 1959 hit "Back in the U.S.A." was a celebration of American life, as was Jay and the American's 1963 hit "Only in America." Numerous rock songs since have made rock and roll synonymous with an exercise of personal freedom in America; examples range from the traditionalist rock of John Mellencamp's "R.O.C.K. in the U.S.A.," the stadium rock of Night Ranger's "You Can Still Rock in America," or the teen pop of Miley Cyrus's "Party in the U.S.A."[18]

As briefly noted, in the early 1970s progressive rock emerged as a highly popular genre. Primarily English bands, they merged American rock and jazz with European classical and folk influences; the most famous were Emerson, Lake, and Palmer (ELP), Genesis, King Crimson, Jethro Tull, and Yes. Progrock was reviled by American rock critics as a complete bastardization of rock and roll; not only was it white and Continental, it aspired to make rock music respectable "bourgeois culture."[19] Punk exploded onto the popular music scene in the mid–1970s. When it became apparent that rock history would be defined thereafter as "before punk" and "after punk," a battle broke out between American and English rock critics over who invented punk and, more importantly, whether the Ramones or the Sex Pistols did it better.[20] In the early 1980s, the "New Pop" movement emerged out of England and commercially successful bands included Culture Club, Duran Duran, Frankie Goes to Hollywood, and the Human League. New Pop combined black popular music genres (R&B, funk, disco, soul) with white popular music genres (bubblegum, MOR, New Wave); it was topped off with an emphasis on stylish and stylized visual image apropos for the advent of MTV and music videos quickly becoming the primary means of marketing bands (Madonna being the concurrent American equivalent to New Pop). Simon Reynolds argued:

> In rock, the opposition between modernism and postmodernism corresponds neatly to the after-punk vanguard.... [Post-punk] driving strenuously for total innovation versus the [New Pop] retro-eclectic approach.... Postmodernism also

eroded the certainties and knee-jerk reflexes of a certain kind of rock think rooted in binary oppositions like depth versus surface and authentic versus inauthentic.... Journalists such as [Paul] Morley celebrated the "transient thrill" of disposable pop. *They trashed well-meaning and meaningfulness if favor of hedonistic pleasures and polished product.* And they challenged the implicitly masculine critical hierarchies that despised the synthetic and mass produced. This gender-coded shift from "rock" to "pop" was in many ways a flashback to glam.... New Pop involved a renaissance of glam's interest in artifice, androgyny, and all the delicious games you could play with pop idolatry.[21]

While glam and its relationship to rock ideology and gender politics will be returned to shortly, the immediate issue is the critical debate that erupted over New Pop. Traditionalist American rock critic Dave Marsh roundly condemned New Pop as cultural imperialism which "imports a rare and precious commodity — usually some form of black music — and sells it back, in 'improved' processed form."[22] In response, Reynolds seemed to take a degree of pride in the accusations of musical colonialism. "African American production sounds (Chic, P-Funk, the Michael Jackson/Quincy Jones sound, the New York electro and synthfunk sounds of the early 1980s) had been assimilated by the perennially quicker-off-the-mark Brits and then sold back to white America."[23] The debate between Marsh and Reynolds amounts to indignation versus conceit over the buying and selling of national musical "property" and territorialism masked in the politics of Hipness and race.

Moreover, Reynolds took particular exception to Simon Frith's negative appraisal of New Pop as "mall music, shiny but confined.... There is a limit to how long people can look like they are having fun."[24] Reynolds bristled, "That's a little unfair to the millions who loved New Pop and *weren't* pretending to have fun (*not all of them teenage girls*)."[25] The second emphasis has been added deliberately in that Reynolds, perhaps unwittingly, raised a crucial issue. *Nowhere* in the cited quote did Frith mention any assumed audience of New Pop unless "mall music" somehow necessarily implies teenage girls. Given that Reynolds championed New Pop because it challenged the masculine and heterosexual dominance in rock ideology, it is striking he added the disclaimer that he and other like-minded New Pop aficionados should *not* to be mistaken for the worst form of pop music fans: "teenyboppers."

## This Music Fan Which Is Not One: Teenyboppers

Nigel Tuftnell: What's wrong with being "sexy?"
Bobbi Fleckman: —Ist! Sex*ist*! —*This is Spinal Tap*

While the 1960s counterculture prided itself on being anti–Establishment, the contradiction was it shared many of the sexist and heterosexist views of the

Establishment. As historian William L. O'Neill argued, the 1960s counterculture mirrored the gender and sexual politics of the Establishment: "New Leftists did not automatically shed their masculine personalities by becoming revolutionaries. Sometimes they were even worse.... This spurious *machismo* was most readily taken out against movement women."[26] Putting it more bluntly, MC5 guitarist Wayne Kramer recounted, "We were sexist bastards.... We had all this rhetoric of being revolutionary.... The boys get to go out to fuck and the girls can't complain about it. And if they did complain, they were being bourgeois bitches ... counterrevolutionary."[27] The contradiction of rock ideology is that while it valorizes racial otherness, it vilifies gender otherness, as pointed out by Norma Coates:

> Although rock culture, as it emerged in the late 1960s, was largely populated by upwardly-mobile white middle-class youth, it embraced and honed an oppositional relationship to mainstream culture. It was not enough to designate women as low Others.... They had to be actively distained and kept in their place. At the same time, women were very necessary for the maintenance and coherency of rock masculinity, as sexual objects [groupies] as well as adoring subjects [teeny-boppers].[28]

The equation of masculinity and rock can be traced to Elvis Presley and his suggestive hip-shaking stage moves, earning him the nickname "Elvis, the Pelvis," in some ways a euphemism for "Elvis, the Phallus." Mick Jagger mined the White Negro myth to the hilt in his self-conscious appropriation of black-coded dance moves and physical mannerisms along with a swaggering masculinity; the lyrics of Rolling Stones songs could easily tend towards male chauvinism and outright misogyny (e.g., "Under My Thumb"). An iconic rock image remains a photo of a shirtless Jim Morrison looking sullenly at the camera. As Coates suggested, such images in rock culture are mystified and mythologized as "symbolic of ... authentic phallic power rather than a site of homoerotic fetishism."[29]

In this respect, it is not only women that are marginalized in rock culture, but any threat to normative masculinity, namely homosexuality. There were no openly gay men or women in rock music prior to the 1970s, when "bisexual" became an operative code word in rock culture.[30] Amid the gender and gay identity politics of the 1970s, glam emerged and utilized elements of androgyny, camp, gender-bending, homoeroticism, and even gay subculture. As Al Spicer noted, "[David] Bowie completely redefined the term 'star' as applied to men in rock 'n' roll ... Rock 'n' rollers were mean, out-and-out heterosexual[s].... They certainly never wore dresses, never appeared in make-up off-stage or wrote songs with titles like 'Queen Bitch.'"[31] Glam was much more of stylistic approach to rock than a specific musical genre, characterized by *image* in the extensive use of make-up, outrageous stage apparel, and even adopting "personas" (for instance, Bowie's androgynous spaceman/rock star "Ziggy Stardust"). It encompassed an array of bands ranging from art rock (Bowie, early Roxy Music), hard rock (T. Rex, Mott the Hoople, Queen, Slade), power pop (Sweet), proto-punk (Lou Reed's glam phase in the early 1970s and the New York Dolls), and heavy metal (Kiss). In the 1980s and the aftermath of punk, glam experienced a resurgence in the British New Pop movement as well as American metal bands like Twisted Sister, Poison, and Warrant.

While glam problematized and even jeopardized images of rock masculinity, a competing discourse was "cock rock," exemplified by the clichés of hard rock and heavy metal music and performance that boarded on self-parody — intentionally or not remains debatable — with bands like Led Zeppelin, Bad Company, Van Halen, and Whitesnake (no comment necessary). Simon Frith described cock rock as "a masturbatory celebration of penis power."[32] Masculinity is a cultural construct as much as rock music is a cultural discourse, and the two engaged to mutually support each other as a synthetic "truth." Ultimately, the Other in rock ideology became "femininity," and the equation of Hipness to masculinity has increasingly become central in American popular culture as a whole.

## You're Not Getting Older, You're Getting Hipper: Enter the Tween

While a function of sexism and heterosexism, the construction of the teenybopper also becomes inseparable from generational politics. Norma Coates argued, "It doesn't matter whether the teenyboppers in question are nine or 17. What unites them is their bad taste, as perceived by the critics and scholars who 'know better'.... [This] typifies the continuing power of discourses that feminize mass culture in general and valorize the 'authentic masculine' in rock."[33] In fact, it increasingly *does* matter if the teenybopper is nine or 17, at least as far as the teen culture industry and niche marketing. A crucial demarcation point in teen culture is now *the teen* versus *the tween.*

While nebulous categories, a teenager is 13–19 (as designated by the suffix "teen"), although 18 is legal adulthood and 17 has become the standard of "cultural adulthood." The tween is generally around eight-14 years of age. Another way to define the distinction is that a teen is a high school student whereas a tween is a late elementary or middle-school student. While less gender specific than the teenybopper, tweens are frequently associated with a *female* consumer demographic. As far as differentiating tween-versus-teen cultural consumers, the separation is constructed around *content.* The music industry does not have an official rating system and employs a "Parental Advisory" blanket warning. However, the film and TV industries developed specific rating systems for intended audiences based on content appropriateness and age groupings:

*Films:*
G (children); PG (tween); PG-13 (teen); R (adult); NC-17 and X (adults only)
*TV:*
TV-Y (preschool); TV-Y7 (children); TV-G (children and tweens); TV-PG
(tweens and teens); TV-14 (teens); TV-MA (adults)

The intent of these ratings is offering guidelines for parents, and, at least
in theory, even restricting the access of certain cultural products to the adolescent consumer. However, also built into these ratings systems are hierarchical
levels of tween, teen, and adult cultural consumption as points of cultural status
where an adolescent "graduates" and can independently access more "mature"
culture. In this respect, Coates suggested that "contemporary critics do not
care to acknowledge that teenybopper taste is not 'bad,' *but more likely underdeveloped* (who amongst us does not have aesthetic skeletons in our [pre-
]pubescent musical closet)."[34]

This still implies inferiority and even a kind of shame as far as teen culture
consumption, but reconfigured around *age* rather than *gender*. To be sure, adolescent taste changes, often frequently, with exposure to new forms and brands
of culture. As cultural consumers, adolescents also want to demonstrate upward
cultural mobility rather than show signs of cultural "regression" as far as taste.
The issue is when "changing taste" becomes equated with "maturing taste" as
code for "better taste."[35] A tween "should" watch *High School Musical* or *Sonny
with a Chance* while the teen "should" watch *Glee* or *30 Rock*. The tween who
watches *Glee* or *30 Rock* demonstrates premature cultural sophistication with
"underdeveloped taste" accordingly developing into "good taste" because they
can appreciate the same cultural products as teens and adults. The teen, yet
alone adult, who watches *High School Musical* or *Sonny with a Chance* demonstrates severely stunted cultural "maturity." Likewise, a tween who starts listening to ABBA is not expected to "grow out of it" in the same way as a tween
who starts listening to Hannah Montana, and certainly not expected to "revert"
and start listening to Hannah Montana again after they start listening to ABBA.

At the moment, the issue is not assessing the emergence of a "mature mass
culture" from the *production* standpoint (an area discussed in the next chapter).
The question is *consumption* and how maturity becomes a critical means to
classify texts as a struggle between different taste formations: adult versus teen,
teen versus tween, tween versus toddler, etc. In the *Victorious* episode "The
Diddley-Bops" (2010), Tori and her friends accept $1,000 to perform a one-
time show as the Diddley-Bops, a children's musical group dressed in food costumes. In short, they "sell out." A major record label is interested in signing
André, but rejects him after company executives see a video of him performing
as a Diddley-Bop and determine he has no integrity as a "serious" musician.
André's credentials are reestablished when he and Tori perform a pop-soul ballad that impresses the record executives. Whether or not André was signed is
left unanswered. What matters is André regained his musical credibility after

it was jeopardized by being tagged as a kiddie performer with a pre-tween fan base as opposed being a potential teen idol with a teenybopper fan base. To prove his musical worth, he has to earn the respect of *adults*.

Similarly, in the *iCarly* episode "iDate a Bad Boy" (2009), Carly is horrified when she learns that her new juvenile delinquent boyfriend, Griffin, is a vociferous collector of "Pee Wee Babies" dolls. As much as Griffin's obsession with Pee Wee Babies signifies effeminacy that contradicts his rebel Hip masculinity, it also signifies immaturity; it is not only "girlish" as far as what is culturally acceptable for a boy (and a "bad boy" to boot), but something "childish" as far as what is acceptable for a teenage cultural consumer. When Carly asks Freddie what he thinks of someone who collects Pee Wee Babies, he answers, "It depends ... how old is she?" The *gender* of the collector is a given; *age* becomes the marker of appropriateness.[36]

## Teen Culture/Mass Culture: Gender Gaps and Generation Gaps

Over the decades, the potential space for women as cultural producers has increased considerably; the stereotypes as cultural consumers may be another matter. On TV, comedies and dramas with women as the main characters are now common; referring back to the previous list of ten teen sitcoms, seven have girls as the title or main character. In popular music, the punk/post-punk explosion of the latter 1970s heralded a proliferation of bands with women acting as the "front men" (the Patti Smith Group, Blondie, Siouxsie and the Banshees), mixed gender bands (the Talking Heads, the B-52s, Au Pairs) and all-women bands (the Runaways, the Slits, the Raincoats, the Go-Go's).[37] Joan Jett and Lita Ford emerged out of the Runways to have successful solo careers since the 1980s. During the 1990s, notable performers in alternative rock included PJ Harvey, Juliana Hatfield, Liz Phair, and Gwen Stefani (as lead singer of No Doubt as well as a solo artist). First Wave Teen Pop stars included the Spice Girls, Britney Spears, and Christina Aguilera; among the Second Wave Teen Pop stars are Hannah Montana (as such), Miley Cyrus, Selena Gomez, and Demi Lovato. Writing in 1986, Andreas Huyssen claimed:

> After the feminist critique of the multilayered sexism in television, Hollywood, advertising, and rock 'n' roll, the lure of the old rhetoric does not work any longer. The claims that the threats (or far that matter, the benefits) of mass culture are somehow "feminine" has finally lost their persuasive power.... After all, it has always been men rather than women who have controlled mass culture production.... It is primarily the visible and public presence of women in high art, as well as women the emergence of new kinds of women performers and producers in mass culture, which make the old gendering device obsolescence. The universalizing ascription of femininity to mass culture always depended on

the very real exclusion of women from high culture and its institutions. Such exclusions, for the time being, are a thing of the past. Thus, the old rhetoric has lost its persuasive power because the realities have changed.[38]

By 1986, Madonna was at the forefront of "reinventing" the role of women as producers in mass culture, and there was a great degree of critical interest and even optimism connected with Madonna's project as a consumerist, feminist, postmodern approach to "subversive culture." The specific critique of Madonna set aside (discussed further in Chapter 9), over the course of 1986–2011 it becomes more and more difficult to claim that the gendering of mass culture is obsolete. The morbid symptoms of previous historical eras and their ideological residue very much remain within American popular culture, and the "old rhetoric" is indeed still relevant around questions of representation. Two examples from TV advertising in 2010 offer brief case studies.

One was a Verizon cell phone commercial in which a mother and her tween daughter are at the shopping mall. The mother is allowing her daughter to shop for the first time with her friends without parental chaperone, in that the Verizon phones they both own offer GPS tracking between the people on the line. I saw this commercial in two distinct settings. One was during a late-night rerun of *Law and Order: Special Victims Unit* (coincidentally or not, the episode's focus was pedophilia). In this context, the target audience was the parent consumer with the message that the mother can be a "cool parent" and grant her daughter independence but still "keep an eye on her" with the phone. The other time was during an afternoon of teen programming on Nickelodeon. Here, the target audience was the adolescent consumer. The message is that the daughter can be a "cool kid" and that increased adolescent autonomy can be achieved while still conceding parental authority through cell-phone surveillance technology. As important is the milieu where this pseudo-freedom is actualized. The mother-daughter "rite of passage" and the daughter's initial foray into "womanhood" occur at the shopping mall.

The second example was one of a series of Allstate Insurance TV commercials featuring a bruised, burly, gravel-voiced man in a black suit known as "Mayhem." In this particular commercial, Mayhem explicitly states, "I'm a teenage girl," and does a hit and run in a shopping mall parking lot while driving a pink compact SUV because Mayhem is distracted by a text message from another teenage girl. Mayhem is a highly masculine, almost metaphysical force of chaos and unrest underneath the surface of society: something brooding, dangerous, intimidating, violent, and *manly*. However, in social reality, Mayhem takes on the form of *the female* as an idiotic teenage girl who brings calamity and obliviously goes on her way to inevitably create more chaos.[39]

In summary, the emergence of a youth culture defined around teenagers in the 1950s was tied to the popularization of the Hip versus Square binary. Race was the initial demarcation point, namely the identification with/appropriation of black culture by whites. The 1960s further configured Hipness around gender and sexuality by valorizing masculinity and heterosexuality through rock ideology. Over the decades, representing Hipness has entailed numerous juxtapositions of other identity politics including class, ethnicity, generational difference, and geographic distinctions. In this context, Part Two examines the teen sitcom genre, and how such representations are both utilized and subverted as far as the production and consumption of ideology as well as culture.

# PART TWO

## THE SOCIETY OF THE TEEN SITCOM

In democratic countries knowledge of how to combine is the mother of all other forms of knowledge.—*Alexis de Tocqueville,* Democracy in America *(1835–40)*

In the liberal system, freedom is destroyed by mutual interference: one person's liberty begins where the other's ends.—*Raoul Vaneigem,* The Revolution of Everyday Life *(1967)*

# 3

# The Form and
# Function of the Sitcom

## Standardizing TV Comedy: Classical Sitcoms
## and Contemporary Sitcoms

In TV's early years, the live comedy-variety show was the dominant genre and among the most famous were *The Milton Berle Show*, *The Jackie Gleason Show*, *The Red Skelton Show*, and Sid Caesar's *Your Show of Shows*.[1] However, as David Marc observed, "Spontaneity and uniqueness of occasion and performance — precisely those qualities that were potentially most satisfying in a comedy-variety show — came to be viewed as liabilities. Seed money was attracted by the rationalized system of film production.... This meant the sitcom."[2] While the sitcom's origins owe considerably to the methods and style of Classical Hollywood cinema, TV and the sitcom also need to be considered in its relationship to *radio*. Like radio, the audience experiences TV at home as opposed to going out to satisfy the demand for culture. John Ellis noted that TV is watched indifferently (the "glance") while films are watched intently (the "gaze"); *sound*, and especially *the voice*, becomes a primary means of TV identification for the audience as far as character dialogue, news announcers, or documentary narrators.[3] TV is listened to as much as watched, often in conjunction with other home activities (eating, reading, spending an evening with friends, working on a computer, etc.). Indeed, it tends to be much more difficult to watch TV with the sound muted versus listening to TV without watching the screen.

Like many of the early sitcoms, *I Love Lucy* (CBS, 1951–8) was adapted from a radio show, Lucille Ball's *My Favorite Husband*; other radio shows converted into sitcoms in the 1950s included *The Adventures of Ozzie and Harriet*, *Our Miss Brooks*, and *Father Knows Best*. *I Love Lucy* also pioneered the *classical sitcom* format. Classical sitcoms employ a multi-camera arrangement (usually three cameras) and obey the 180-degree rule where the camera stays on one side and the performers on the other; a fairly limited number of recognizable sound-stage sets are used (an apartment, rooms in a house, a local hangout, the workplace, school, etc.). They are either performed in front of a live studio

39

audience providing laughs and other responses, or in closed studio settings with laugh tracks added in postproduction. Characters stay in character and rarely, if ever, directly address the camera or the studio audience. In that TV is an audio as much as visual medium, verbal comedy is usually emphasized over physical comedy; however, teen sitcoms in the classical mode tend towards physical comedy more than primetime network counterparts. Examples of classical sitcoms over recent decades include *Family Ties, The Cosby Show, Home Improvement, Everybody Loves Raymond, The King of Queens, According to Jim, My Wife and Kids, George Lopez,* and *Two and a Half Men.* With some occasional deviations, the classical sitcom format is utilized on Nickelodeon teen sitcoms such as *Drake and Josh, iCarly, True Jackson, VP,* and *Victorious* as well as the Disney teen sitcoms like *Hannah Montana* and *Wizards of Waverly Place.*

The increasingly popular alternative is the *contemporary sitcom* format. Contemporary sitcoms often use a single camera and various location settings as well as the familiar set surroundings, sometimes adopting a "mockumentary" style (*The Office*), and they usually eschew studio audiences and laugh tracks altogether. Unlike the unobtrusive camera work of the classical sitcom, contemporary sitcoms incorporate an array of rapid pans and zooms. The contemporary sitcom's brisk pace of non-continuity editing, jump-cuts, cutaways, and cross-cutting between scenes is also markedly different from the moderate pace and conventional editing structures of classical sitcoms. Contemporary sitcoms can and do utilize an array of audio and visual effects (music cues, sound effects, CGI, slow and fast motion). They also might include non-diagetic inserts (*Everybody Hates Chris* occasionally used stock footage to visually punctuate jokes). As opposed to "dream sequences," "subjective sequences" might depict events as the characters imagine or perceive them rather than reality per se. For instance, the *Big Time Rush* episode "Big Time Girlfriends" (2010) opened with Carlos commenting on a girl he'd like to date, cross-cutting with a shot of the girl nonchalantly sitting in lawn chair. When his friends discouraged the idea because she has a reputation for "anger issues," the shot cut back to the girl wearing a hockey mask and holding a chainsaw (the joke is also indicative of *Big Time Rush*'s gender politics).

In contemporary sitcoms, characters can and do directly address the camera, although they do not "break character" as in the theater of Bertolt Brecht. On *Malcolm in the Middle*, Malcolm regularly addressed the camera as Malcolm and provided the character's perspective on the events in the episode; Frankie Muniz, the actor playing Malcolm, did *not* break character and comment on the representation as a whole. The main character may also provide voiceover narration and commentary (the wisecracks of Chris Rock on *Everybody Hates Chris*) or there may be a third-person narrator (*Arrested Development* and the sardonic observations of executive producer Ron Howard).[4] As well as extensive cultural referencing, there is much more exaggerated and "ironic" self-awareness around acting, characterization, directing, and writing. *The Monkees* pioneered the contemporary sitcom format, with more recent examples including *Arrested Development, Everybody Hates Chris, Malcolm in the Middle, Scrubs, The Office,* and *My Name is Earl.* As far as teen sitcoms, the contemporary sitcom style was evident in Nickelodeon's early "girl power" sitcom *Clarissa Explains It All* and, more recently, *Ned's Declassified School Survival Guide* and *Big Time Rush,* both created by Scott Fellows.

From a critical standpoint, there are two problems. One is that the classical sitcom can be assessed as "dated" or "old-fashioned" whereas the contemporary sitcom style is thought of as "innovative" and "modern" or, more correctly, "*postmodern.*" In short, the contemporary sitcom becomes Hip whereas the classical sitcom is Square. The contemporary sitcom is also deemed a more "evolved" or "mature" brand of sitcom defined by increased artistic sophistication, advanced stylistic/visual techniques, and greater cultural literacy.[5] By extension, it requires the manufacture of a more sophisticated audience than the average dullard glued to the idiot box. The classical sitcom becomes synonymous with older viewers unwilling or unable to grasp the sitcom beyond the long-established and highly predictable genre conventions affirming a status quo of family, gender, and generational order. To be sure, this becomes crucial in assessing the early pop-music sitcoms. *The Monkees* element of "subversion" owed as much to its assault on classical sitcom form through contemporary sitcom techniques as well as the anti-authority content; *The Partridge Family*'s conservatism relied as much on the classical sitcom conventions as well as content instilling messages of good teenage behavior. As touched on in the previous chapter, this construct of "mass culture maturity" becomes equally, if not *more,* pronounced as far as differentiating adolescent-versus-adult cultural consumption. The majority of teen sitcoms are well within the classical sitcom conventions, which becomes tied to an overall view of younger viewers whose cultural and intellectual capacity is such that they can only understand a "dumbed-down" sitcom form and passively consume the same messages. However, *iCarly* uses the classical sitcom form and offers a highly ambivalent critique of American society, whereas *Big Time Rush* quite consciously utilizes the contemporary sitcom style to the point of overkill while its politics are extremely conservative. This becomes the second problem. The error is assuming contemporary sitcoms inherently contain "liberal" political messages and the classical sitcom "conservative" political messages. In fact, the drive of the sitcom — be it in classical or contemporary mode — is sustaining dominant ideology.

## "Ethical Form": Deleuze, Adorno, and the Sitcom

TV sitcoms owe most to Classical Hollywood cinema through what Gilles Deleuze defined in *Cinema 1: The Movement-Image* as the difference between "large form" and "small form." The large form is a trajectory from *situation to transformative action to modified situation* (SAS′) and the small form *action to transformative situation to modified action* (ASA′). In terms of literature, Deleuze differentiated the crime novel as large form and detective novel as small form: James M. Cain's *Double Indemnity* and *The Postman Always Rings Twice* are large form with situation (adultery) → action (murder) → situation (the aftermath of the crime); Dashell Hammett's *The Thin Man* and *The Maltese Falcon* are small form with action (murder) → situation (investigation) → action (revelation of the murderer's identity).[6]

TV genres operate through large and small forms as well. The small form (ASA′) corresponds to the various permutations of TV dramas. On medical shows such as *Marcus Welby, M.D.* or *House* there is action (the onset of illness) → situation (diagnosing the illness) → action (curing the illness). Police dramas like *Dragnet* and *CSI* or legal dramas like *Perry Mason* and *Boston Legal* are also examples of small form with action (a crime or litigation) → situation (police investigation or courtroom maneuverings) → action (solving the crime or resolving the case in question). For Deleuze, the Westerns of John Ford were examples of the large form of situation (disturbance in the social fabric) → action (the behaviors of the characters within their milieu) → situation (the resolution of the crisis and restoration of order). In spite of their grandeur and immense scope, Ford's Westerns were fundamentally concerned with a simple if ambitious goal: establishing or maintaining an orderly community through the actions of its inhabitants. As Deleuze stated, "It is *ethical* rather than an epic form."[7] The sitcom as *situation comedy* corresponds to the large form (SAS′) and similarly functions as an "ethical form" (again, whether it operates within the classical or contemporary modes of presentation).

"A Question of Ethics," an episode of *Saved by the Bell: The College Years* (NBC, 1993–4), offers a convenient example to discuss the sitcom ethical form as well as contextualize the analysis of *Saved by the Bell* in the next chapter. Zack Morris is taking a philosophy course from a notoriously difficult professor and obviously has no interest in the topic of Kant's "Categorical Imperative," preferring instead to crack jokes and doodle in his notebook. When he inadvertently acquires a copy of the pending midterm examination, and always the opportunist, Zack looks directly at the camera and glibly announces that his ethical dilemma is whether to sell copies of the exam to his fellow students or benevolently give them away for free (i.e., profiteering or philanthropy). After his copy is thrown away, Zack and his friends resort to digging through a dumpster to retrieve it, although Zack is the only one clearly bothered by the depths to which they have sunk to pass the midterm. On the day of the scheduled test, the professor announces that the class *already* took his exam. He purposely made copies of the midterm available throughout the week, and the students should now grade themselves on how they responded. Several students admit they cheated and they deserve an F. However, Zack announces he did *not* cheat because that would have compromised his ethics; Zack then points out that the professor's entire test is based on dishonesty and manipulation and, therefore, "unethical." Impressed, the professor tells Zack he deserves an A. Zack becomes the classroom standard bearer of community ethics in everyday practice rather than the academic expert who specializes in philosophical theories but cannot put the Categorical Imperative where his mouth is. Hence, the ethical form of the episode is situation (Zack and the other students have the opportunity to cheat on the ethics test) → action (everybody cheats except for Zack) → situation (Zack is the only one who passes the real ethical test, including the teacher).

While Deleuze would probably take exception to the terminology, the ethical form can also be described as an *ideological* form. From the perspective Adorno and his condemnations of the Culture Industry, the sitcom genre is a means to standardize the production and consumption of culture and ideology. Sitcoms offer predictable, teleological narrative patterns of conflict and resolution through a parade of characters that are both stereotypical and yet "slice of life" so the viewer can immediately identify with them. Above all, the sitcom provides comedic predicaments that house ideological lessons though a juxtaposition of overt and hidden messages:

> The script does not try to "sell" any idea. The "hidden message" emerges in the way the story looks at human beings; thus the audience is invited to look at them in the same way without being made aware that indoctrination is present.... This latent message cannot be considered unconscious in the strict psychological sense, but rather as "unobtrusive"; this message is hidden only by a style which does not pretend to touch anything serious and expects to be regarded as featherweight.[8]

Despite its reputation as the acme of subversive TV comedy, *The Simpsons*'s overt liberal satire and cultural referencing frequently contains hidden conservative messages, in particular gender politics.[9] Homer Simpson represents the bumbling, unintelligent, but always lovable American male who is lovable because he is bumbling and unintelligent (read: infantile and anti-intellectual). Marge Simpson represents the dutiful domestic servant whose fulfillment in life revolves around her slavish devotion to her role of wife and mother, as annoyed as she might become with her position. In "Ice Cream of Marge (with the Light Blue Hair)" (2007), Marge wants to establish an individual "lega-*she*" after watching a female empowerment episode of *Opal* (an obvious Oprah Winfrey parody). She becomes a successful Popsicle stick artist, causing marital friction with Homer (disordered situation). At the end of the episode, Marge unveils her final masterpiece in front of city hall: a gigantic Popsicle statue of Homer in his underwear (transformative action). Without a hint of irony, Marge proclaims it is her testament to "my sweet, imperfectly perfect you. My most enduring creation is the life I've sculpted with you ... now I know that my 'lega-*she*' is really a 'lega-*we*.'" This cuts to a flash-forward to the future and the ostensive joke that iPods have taken over the world. The statue of Homer, the monument to the "imperfectly perfect" man created by the adoring and supportive wife, is the last remaining piece of culture from the Modern Age (order restored with male authority sustained throughout time).

Likewise, Bart Simpson's "boyish" approach to life is individualistic *joie de vivre* whereas Lisa Simpson's "girlish" approach to life is a liberal social consciousness and humorless intellectualism. In "Girls Just Want to Have Sums" (2006), Lisa is thrilled that Springfield Elementary plans to segregate classes along gender lines in order to make the learning process more equitable between the boys and the girls (i.e., "affirmative action"). However, she is bitterly disappointed when the boys are efficiently taught math by a hard-nosed drill instructor and the girls are inefficiently taught by a liberal-feminist who emphasizes feelings and relating emotionally to math. To gain access to the male math classes, Lisa masquerades as a boy and, with coaching from Bart, learns how a "real boy" behaves. In the conclusion, Lisa wins the school's math award, and uses the opportunity to proclaim that girls are as smart as boys. Bart, quite seriously, corrects her by noting she won the award not because girls are as smart as boys, but because she "learned to think like a boy." In fact, Lisa not only learned to think like a boy, but *act* like a boy. The following award is presented for "best flautist" and the winner is none other than the school's resident boy-genius, Martin Prince. Dressed in Shakespearean garb, his acceptance speech is reciting the opening lyrics from progressive rock band Jethro Tull's "Thick as a Brick" (as noted in the previous chapter, a rock subgenre critically deemed as Square). To provide the rather literal punch line, Lisa ends the flowerily display by whacking Martin with a folding chair and does what any real boy would do in similar circumstances by beating up the sissy.

## From Men to Boys (or, Jung as You Feel): Masculinity and the Sitcom in the 1990s

In 1991, Robert Bly's men's movement manifesto *Iron John* was published, built around a Jungian reading of the Grimm Brothers fairy tale "Iron John" which Bly contended provided universal lessons about the male experience. In what amounted to a neo-1960s counterculture political tract for the 1990s in response to the competing brands of neoliberalism being offered by the Democrats and Republicans, *Iron John* attacked corporate conformity and militarist mentality while championing environmentalism and multiculturalism. Above all, Bly's strident defense of the masculine and patriarchal order cannot help but be read as anti-feminism. Bly extolled the purely mythic concept of "Zeus Energy," which Bly claimed was the coalescing force in ancient society and continually undermined in American culture:

> The Greeks understood and praised positive male energy that has accepted male authority. They called it Zeus energy ... *Zeus energy is male authority accepted for*

*the sake of the community* ... Zeus Energy has been steadily disintegrating decade after decade in the United States. Popular culture has been determined to destroy respect for it, beginning with the "Maggie and Jiggs" and "Blondie and Dagwood" comics ... in which the man is always weak and foolish.... The image of the weak adult man went into animated cartoons.... In situation comedies, *The Cosby Show* notwithstanding, men are devious, bumbling, or easy to outwit. It is the women who outwit them, or teach them a lesson, or hold the whole town together all by themselves.[10]

Referring back to *The Simpsons*, the ethical form is completely overlooked by Bly who can only wax indignant about negative and overt representation of men on sitcoms (save *The Cosby Show*). To be sure, Homer Simpson is "weak and foolish" and Marge is the force who "holds everything together." Yet she does so by conforming to the conservative and traditional role of subservient wife and mother who accepts and sustains Homer's "Zeus Energy" as a continual pattern of infantile male behavior no matter how flawed or irritating it may be. Moreover, what has become commonplace on American sitcoms is a representation of women who are actively engaged in undermining supposed Zeus Energy that is the metaphysical glue of all social order. As the most conspicuous example, on *Two and a Half Men* women are uniformly represented as nothing short of manipulative psychopaths with their sole purpose in life emasculating men. The ideal woman, a gorgeous, empty-headed slut who knows her proper place in the male order, is as a one-night stand.

The fundamental problem of Jungian psychoanalytic theory is the essentialist view of gender. As Carl Jung summarized, "I have tried to equate *masculine consciousness with the concept of Logos and the feminine with that of Eros. By Logos, I mean discrimination, judgment, insight, and by Eros I mean the capacity to relate.*"[11] Stating it another way, Jung contended, "The anima has an erotic, emotional character; the animus has a rationalizing one."[12] As much as Jungian psychology claims its gendering terms are purely "descriptive" or "symbolic," its universal archetypes and gendered binaries are inseparable from cultural stereotypes and gender politics in practice, and to diagram the structure as it is typically represented in recent American sitcoms:

|              | Men          | Women           |
| ------------ | ------------ | --------------- |
| Logos/Animus | common sense | intellectualism |
| Eros/Anima   | passions     | feelings        |

Premiering on ABC in 1991, *Home Improvement* was a fixture in the Nielsen Top Ten throughout its run, which concluded in 1999. A competing discourse to *Iron John*, *Home Improvement* retained the most conservative aspects of Bly — Zeus Energy and patriarchy — while consciously and conspicuously scrapping Bly's intellectual, liberal, New Age sensitive rest.[13] Tim "the Tool Man" Taylor was the Logos of common sense *balanced* by the Eros of all-American manly passions for sports, automobiles, industrial arts, and power tools, the last of which became comical signifiers of masculinity and phallic power. The femininity of Jill Taylor was the Logos of pretentious intellectualism *unbalanced* by the Eros of maudlin sentimentality.[14] Tim's sidekick Al Borland epitomized the "soft male" as a blubbering man with a severe Oedipus complex. While Tim was a man's man (and a "guy's guy"), Al was a woman trapped in a burly man's body, and Jill suffered from a severe case of animus poisoning.

Indeed, Jung may have well been summarizing *Home Improvement* when he made one of his typically suspect claims that "the woman possessed by the animus is *in danger of losing her femininity*, her adapted feminine persona, *just as man in like circumstances runs the risk of effeminacy*."[15] Moreover, as Jung quite outrageously put it, "Often the man has the feeling — and he is not altogether wrong — that only seduction or a beating or rape would have the necessary power of persuasion.... No man can converse with an animus for five minutes without becoming the victim of his own anima."[16] This became a running joke on *Home Improvement* when Tim Taylor's arguments with women prompted him to adopt a sarcastic, effeminate voice and accompanying gestures in retaliation — in effect acting like a gay stereotype — as in the aptly titled "Forever Jung" (1992) and Tim's ongoing arguments with Jill's friend Karen, a feminist and "animus-woman" *par excellence*. Indeed, the battle in recent sitcoms is between "real men" against an array of "feminists" and "femmes," represented in *unintentionally* hilarious extremes on *According to Jim* and *Two and a Half Men*.

As *Home Improvement* neared the end of its run, *The King of Queens* (1998–2007) premiered on CBS, starring Kevin James as Doug Heffernan, an "everyguy" who worked as a delivery driver and was locked in perpetual male adolescence against the feminine of discipline (in both senses of the word) represented by Carrie Heffernan: an acid-tongued, emasculating, animus-woman who acted as much like Doug's killjoy mother as his killjoy wife. Another one of Jung's archetypes is the Puer Aeternus ("eternal boy"), and the irony steeped in Jung's comments need be kept in mind: "The Puer Aeternus is simply the personification of the infantile side of our character, repressed because it is infantile. If the dreamer allows that element to come in, it is though he himself has disappeared and become a little naked boy. *Then if his wife could accept him as such, everything would be all right*."[17]

For Jung, the Puer Aeternus was an impediment rather than a boon to self-individuation; if the Puer Aeternus is useful, it is only that the immature infant becomes a stepping stone to adulthood and maturity. As Jung tersely put it, "The little boy ought to be brought up, educated, [and] perhaps spanked."[18] Likewise, Bly contended, "The Wild Man can only come to life inside the man who has gone through serious disciplines.... The Wild Man is a better guide ... than our inner child, *precisely because he is not a child*."[19] American popular culture has gone the opposite route, translating the "inner child" into a glorification of the undisciplined and self-indulgent "eternal teenager" within the adult male as Hipness suppressed by societal responsibilities and institutional constraints almost inevitably signified by the adult female as Square. To be sure, gender politics are prevalent in sitcoms as early as the 1950s. Since the 1990s, it is not so much that the message has changed but the representations have been reconfigured as well. Masculine is the realm of Hip, feminine is domain of Square. Teen sitcoms are very much consistent with this representation as well, with *Saved by the Bell* one of the more overt examples.

# 4

# Free, White, and Teenage Male:
# (or, How to Con Friends and
# Manipulate People):
# Saved by the Bell

## Zack Attack

If not the first teen sitcom as such — *Square Pegs* (CBS, 1982–3) and *Head of the Class* (ABC, 1986–91) could be seen as precursors— one the most influential was *Saved by the Bell* (henceforth *SbtB*). Running on NBC Saturday mornings from 1989–93, the success of *SbtB* prompted NBC to replace the traditional Saturday morning fare of cartoons with blocs of various teen sitcoms under the slogan "Teen NBC" (a.k.a. "TNBC"), a format that lasted until 2002. However, *SbtB* began as a short-lived, school-based sitcom *Good Morning, Miss Bliss* (1988–9, henceforth *Miss Bliss*), starring Hayley Mills in the title role. *Miss Bliss* was essentially a remake of *Our Miss Brooks* as a throwback to the Golden Age sitcoms of the 1950s in the era of Reaganism, with the dominant sitcom at the time being *The Cosby Show* as an update of *Father Knows Best*. While a pilot aired on NBC, the network passed and Disney Channel subsequently purchased *Miss Bliss*, running 13 episodes before canceling it.

NBC expressed renewed interest in the show, which was drastically reconfigured in the process. Retitled *Saved by the Bell*, the location was shifted from John F. Kennedy High School in Indiana (middle-class, Middle America Square) to Bayside High School in California (middle-upper class, West Coast Hip). While *Miss Bliss* seemed like it was actually made in the 1950s, *SbtB* adopted a more contemporary post–MTV visual style but largely stayed within classical sitcom conventions with multi-camera set-up, studio sound-stage locales, and a hyperactive laugh track. Most importantly, much of the original cast of characters were replaced, excepting Zack Morris, Samuel "Screech" Powers, Lisa Turtle, and the school principal Mr. Belding.

Rather than saying *SbtB* became more teen-centered and less teacher-centered, it is more correct to say that *SbtB* became Zack-centered. One of *SbtB*'s "innovations" was that Zack addressed the camera directly, usually in the cold opening of the show; it was also common for Zack to offer verbal or visual asides (e.g., looking at the camera and rolling his eyes when Screech made an asinine comment or smiling and winking after he delivered a zinger to Mr. Belding).[1] As noted in the previous chapter, this "breaking the fourth wall" is not the same as "breaking character." The direct address from character to audience via the camera, as with sitcoms like *Clarissa Explains It All* or *Malcolm in the Middle*, had the effect of constructing a primary identification, especially since the main characters (Zack, Clarissa, Malcolm) assumed a privileged status of being the *only* character who interacted with the viewer while the rest of the cast obliviously carried on within the show's pseudo-reality. In the case of *SbtB*, this tactic served a political purpose as well. The Zack-viewer relationship manifest in direct address was anything but an attempt to construct a "critical distance" between Zack and the audience by which they might objectively examine his and their conduct. The assumed audience of adolescents were encouraged to personally relate to Zack as he cavalierly coasted through life at Bayside and manipulated people and situations to his liking while, at the same time, the viewers gleaned the ethical lesson Zack learned — as phony as that lesson often was.

Indeed, Zack was the image-ideal of and for the American teenage male. As well as living in middle-upper class comfort, Zack was Bayside's most popular kid, the school heartthrob, a star athlete, and the resident rebel. He was concerned with enjoying the present over the pressures of impending adulthood. If he had any sort of career goal, it was becoming a rock and roll star with his band "Zack Attack." The line-up consisted of Zack on lead guitar and lead vocals, Lisa on bass, Screech on keyboards, A.C. Slater on drums, and Kelly Kapowsky as second vocalist; it was not coincidental that Jessie Spano was "excluded" from membership in Zack Attack ( Jessie's status on *SbtB*, or decided lack thereof, to be addressed shortly). However, as much as Zack possessed rock rebel spirit, he was hardly immature. Zack personified "13 going on 30" whereas the most infantile and effeminate male on *SbtB* was also the school's biggest geek, Screech Powers.

While Zack was eminently disinterested in school, he trounced his classmates on the SAT without studying or even putting any effort into the actual test ("S.A.T.S.," 1991). Zack possessed "natural" (read: male) intelligence which was most clearly expressed in his passion for all things "business" rather than the miasma of the liberal arts.[2] In a *Miss Bliss*-era episode "Wall Street" (1988), Miss Bliss invests a small amount of her money in the stock market for the class to track as a school project. Immediately enthralled with the fast money profits of the stock market, Zack wants to learn more about economics at the library, but first needs to know where the library is actually located. Zack then convinces the class to take the money out of stable airline stock and reinvest it on margin in potato futures without telling Miss Bliss. The move ends up costing Miss Bliss over $1,500. After her initial rage, Miss Bliss forgives the whole class even through Zack is largely responsible for the whole debacle. Her "equitable" solution is requisitioning the potatoes she now owns and putting everyone in class to work on a liquidation sale. The overt message was that Zack learned the importance of ethical capitalism, but the hidden message was that the ambitious individual pursing monetary profit (Zack) can create a financial disaster that becomes the brunt of the community to handle (Miss Bliss and the rest of the class). The lesson was put into practice two decades later with the stock market collapse and federal bailouts of Wall Street in 2008.

The ethical form became the standard operating procedure of *SbtB*. Zack conceived numerous academic, economic, and romantic schemes designed to reap the maximum amount of profit with a minimum of effort. However, these endeavors were always presented as the mischief of a charming rogue rather than the machinations of a self-centered jerk with the loophole being that Zack learned something about himself that made him a "better person." Many *SbtB* episodes entailed a Zack scheme becoming the basis for the disordered situation, the transformative action Zack realizing the ethical failings of what he was doing, and the reordered situation Zack usually getting what he wanted in the beginning while learning and voicing a bogus life lesson about fair play, honesty, and/or responsibility — at least until the next episode and the next scheme.

## Some Guys Have It, Some Guys (and Girls) Don't

Screech and Slater served as the masculine counterpoints to Zack. Screech was an annoying geek whose skill in academic and intellectual pursuits could not conceal a basic immaturity and ineptitude when it came to dealing with everyday problems and situations. While the general thrust of *SbtB* was ridicule of anyone and anything outside the norm, *SbtB* specialized in a uniform and almost vindictive representation of nerds and geeks as pathetic, lowly cretins, neither Hip nor masculine, that is now the routine representation on both adult and teen sitcoms: as far as the former, *The Simpsons*, *The King of Queens*, *Still Standing*, *The War at Home*, and *The Big Bang Theory*; in terms of the latter, *Drake and Josh*, *iCarly*, *Wizards of Waverly Place*, and *Victorious*.[3] While Zack was the school's "chick magnet," Screech was pure "chick repellant." Conversely, Slater was an egotistical, hunky jock who projected an off-putting air of macho arrogance and sexist conceit. Although Slater and Zack were good friends, the two often engaged in less-than-friendly competition over alpha male status of Bayside High School. In the end, Slater's masculinity was often "too much" and Screech's masculinity always "too little," whereas Zack's masculinity was constantly "just right."

This carried over to the main trio of female characters. The "just right" character was Kelly. She was the head cheerleader, the captain of the volleyball team, and the girl-next-door stereotype of male fantasy. If Zack was represented as what a teenage boy wanted to be, Kelly represented what every teenage boy wanted to have.[4] Lisa was "too much" the teen girl stereotype: she was shallow, self-obsessed, and focused on fashion and other trendy pursuits to advance her popularity. In this sense, *SbtB* offered a subtle but important reframing of Hipness in relation to its historically constructed connection to ethnic and racial otherness. While the only African-American in the primary cast of characters, Lisa functioned as the stereotype of a consumerist, middle-upper class, suburban "white valley girl." Slater was Latino and his *machismo* most overtly expressed as unapologetic male chauvinism as opposed to Zack's natural "sex appeal." In "Running Zack" (1990) a history assignment required the student to trace their ancestry, and Zack discovered he was the descendant of Native Americans. While defined as a Bayside "Other" just as much as Lisa and Slater, Zack also represented the normative ideal of the white, male, middle-class teenager as the conquering Bayside "ought" to the inferior Bayside collection of "is" that surrounded him. As a metaphor of liberal democratic society, the implications for "empowerment" become ominous. As Brian Massumi argued:

> Labor, women, Blacks, and at times sexual minorities, may be admitted into positions of power, but only to the extent they become, for all practical purposes, capitalist, white male, and straight — honorary members of the majority. The "Other" (the outside) is interiorized by being identified, and all identification is set against the Standard of the European White Male Heterosexual as the embodiment of good/common sense, in politics as well as personal conduct. Minorities are expected to become equal-in-theory but less powerful versions the Same [the Standard].... The staying power of the liberal nation-state rests on its adaptive ability to ability to *represent* the "Other"/ the outside — but only represent it.[5]

The "too little" as far as the teenage girl stereotype was Jessie Spano. If antagonistic animus-women have become the common representation in sitcoms since the 1990s, Jessie was an "animus-woman in training" as well as a pedantic feminist and overbearing activist for a variety of liberal causes. A driven student, one episode's cold opening depicted Zack partnered with an intently concentrating Jessie in science class. Zack looked at the camera and told the audience they make a great team because she "works hard" and he "hardly works." In the aforementioned "S.A.T.S.," Zack hardly worked to get an astounding 1500 while Jesse worked hard to earn a meager 1200 on the SAT, guaranteeing Zack his choice of any college in America, while Jessie would have to take what was offered. In another gendered academic embarrassment, Jessie was runner-up as the class valedictorian to Screech. While this amounted to Zack and Screech being "naturally smarter" than Jessie, the ultimate insult occurred in "Running Zack." While her friends shared a lineage of oppression (Lisa's ancestors were slaves and Zack's ancestors displaced to reservations), Jessie learned she was the descendant of white European slave traders. Her white

A boy and his duck: Zack Morris (Mark-Paul Gosselaar) and ill-fated feathered friend about to earn a lesson in ethical capitalism in the episode "Pipe Dreams" (NBC/ Photofest).

liberal guilt was only matched by her white liberal resentment that she was not "the Other" she desperately wanted to be. More correctly, on *SbtB* Jessie represented "the Other" to Zack as Bayside's teenage embodiment of Zeus Energy.

In this context, "Pipe Dreams" (1991) was one of *SbtB*'s most "political" episodes, with the politics extending far beyond the superficial message. The students are engaged in a science project on environmentalism studying animals in a nearly pond, and Zack becomes particularly attached to an injured duck he helps nurse back to health. The disorder occurs when what is initially thought to be a leaking pipeline reveals Bayside High School was built over an untapped oil deposit. Most of the students, and especially Zack, are thrilled about the prospect of an oil company contracting with the school board, which entails a complete renovation of Bayside High and a sizable boon for the school budget. The leading dissenter is Jessie, who voices her various protests, much to the annoyance of Mr. Belding and her fellow students. When a preliminary drilling mishap causes a minor oil spill around the school, the pond is severely polluted and Zack's beloved duck is killed. The remorseful Zack tells Jessie she was right, and joins her crusade against big oil.

As far as the Bayside community, Jessie's stance against the oil company is largely ridiculed, with the possibility of economic profit trumping her liberal political objections. However, once Zack and the others are personally affected by the oil company's negligence, there is a turnabout on the issue. The overt message of "Pipe Dreams" is that the individual has to be as concerned with long-term community consequences rather than focus on the immediate individual advantage; one could even argue that there is an anti-big business message. The hidden message is expressed in the transformative action. At the school board meeting set to authorize final approval of the Bayside-oil company merger, *Zack* serves as the spokesman for the cause. His impassioned speech sways everyone when he says that he wanted a "bigger and better Bayside" but the ultimate cost is not worth it. Mr. Belding, speaking for the school board, responds that "we already have a better Bayside; *we just didn't know it until now*" (emphasis added). The hidden message is that it is not so much the *message* but the *messenger*. As an environmentalist and opponent of big business as part of her overall liberal-feminist world-view, Jessie was viewed as the pain in the posterior of Bayside progress. Zack, who fully supported the oil company until their actions negatively affected him personally, is not motivated by any sort of ideology but, as usual, how the issue directly pertains to him at the moment. Yet in the end, Zack is hailed for making Bayside a better place by providing community enlightenment.

In "Save the Max" (1990), the students were surprised to learn that Mr. Belding not only went to Bayside High School in the 1960s, but was a teenage hippie activist and the school's "anti–Establishment" hero. As Jessie exclaimed, "Mr. Belding was the Zack Morris of the 1960s!" However, Zack Morris is anything but representative of the 1960s. While it was not a teen sitcom *per se*, *Family Ties* (NBC, 1982–9) featured one of the most popular teenage characters on TV during the 1980s, Alex P. Keaton (Michael J. Fox). A devout conservative, Alex served as the young Hip voice of Reaganism against the liberal viewpoints espoused by his counterculture parents who still retained their antiquated 1960s idealism. As *Family Ties* ended its run in 1989, *Miss Bliss* was resurrected and reconfigured into the Zack-dominated *SbtB* to seemingly fill the conservative void and target a younger audience for whom the Reagan Revolution would be

history within a few years.[6] The difference was that Alex P. Keaton was an ide-
ologue. Zack was simply out for himself.

  *SbtB* was both product and producer of the political and ideological shifts
that occurred during the show's run from 1989–93. It emerged out of the decade
of Reaganism (*Family Ties*) and coincided with the advent of the men's movement (*Home Improvement*). On *SbtB*, Zack Morris represented Hip as the white,
middle-class teenage male where rebellion was unrestrained self-interest coated
with a veneer of slick non-conformity, individuality was the embrace of ambition and manipulation, and community was constructed by and through specious ethics. Far removed from slacker alienation and apathy, Zack's
lackadaisical approach was a guise for effortlessly putting forth his best efforts
to dominate his social circle, orchestrate his peers, and run Bayside High School
on his own terms and for his own benefit. And just like capitalist society, Bayside
High School was not made up of successes and failures, but winners and losers.
The winner was always Zack Morris. While the loser may have appeared to be
Screech Powers, the real loser was ultimately Jessie Spano.

# 5

# *Nickelodeon Nation Building: From* Clarissa Explains It All *to* Zoey 101

## *For Kids Only: Nickelodeon and "Children's TV"*

Nickelodeon's brand identity is not without contradictions. Sarah Banet-Weiser pointed out that "[Nickelodeon] can claim to be for 'kids only,' challenging both the authority of both adults and advertisers, as the network simultaneously delivers an audience of millions to advertisers."[1] To be sure, Nickelodeon features a daily barrage of outside sponsor advertising.[2] However, the product most often advertised on Nickelodeon is Nickelodeon and its own lines of "in-house" cultural products; the marketing of Big Time Rush (sitcom, CDs, DVDs, fan merchandise) was as much a staple of Nickelodeon's daily teen programming as *iCarly* and *SpongeBob SquarePants* by 2011. Not unrelated, Nickelodeon is engaged in ideology marketing towards a "Nickelodeon Nation" niche audience of tweens and teens, be it through the "role models" offered in teen sitcoms, issue awareness with *Nick News*, and the Big Help public service campaigns. As much as entertainment, Nickelodeon programming provides a civic education to the adolescent viewer. In this respect, John Hartley contended:

> Broadcasters have to maintain an uneasy equilibrium; without striving to be too populist or nationalistic, they must drive to be popular, and speak to, for and about the nation. In addition, their popularity is not organized around citizenship or jingoism, but primarily around pleasure.... Broadcasters tend not to insist on allegiances and identities that might be constructed on other sites, but, on the contrary, to persuade audiences to abandon any such allegiances and identities, especially those of class (rendered as "demographics" in television, of course), ethnicity, and gender. Other "variables," like region, age, education, family structure, even nation itself, may be significant, *but the whole point of popular television is to cut across such divisions and reconstitute the people into one unified constituency: the audience.*[3]

Hartley's claim that TV seeks to neutralize the political and factionalism in order to manufacture "one unified constituency" of viewers proves tenuous. Rather, TV networks increasingly manufacture *competing constituencies* as far as target audiences that exclude as much as include disparate segments of the TV viewing public. Put differently, TV networks do not evade but *forge* allegiances and identities through daily programming, which encompasses specific shows and the accompanying advertising (commercials, infomercials, network promos, public-service announcements, etc.). Especially with the advent of cable/DBS TV and the proliferation of niche networks, TV audiences are imagined and manufactured *through* various allegiances and identities: gender identity with Spike versus Lifetime, political identity with FOX News versus MSNBC, or adolescent identity with Disney Channel versus Nickelodeon. In short, niche networks not only construct brand identity in the programming but ferment brand *loyalty* in the audience.

What could be termed "post-cable TV programming" suggests a further affinity to radio, which has a long history of programming around niche audiences with specific and *definite* listening preferences as far as talk radio (politics, sports, or general interest) and music (pop, oldies, classic rock, Alternative, classical, country, jazz, hip-hop, etc.).[4] Nickelodeon's approach to teen TV is not so much based on "regularly scheduled programming" like most TV networks (*x* program at *y* time on *z* day) but a system of "heavy rotation" akin to Top 40 radio, where reruns of popular shows (*iCarly* and *SpongeBob Square-Pants*), the newer shows (*Big Time Rush* and *Victorious*), and especially the newly released episodes, are shown daily or almost daily in shifting time slots.[5] As examples, the *Victorious* hour-long special episode "Freak the Freak Out" premiered on November 26, 2010, after considerable network promotion. Over the course of the next week (11/28–12/4/10) it was rerun *six* times; moreover, a Victoria Justice performance of her song "Freak the Freak Out" was also written into the episode with her character, Tori Vega, singing it at a karaoke bar. The heavily promoted 90-minute *iCarly-Victorious* crossover movie "iParty with Victorious" premiered on June 11, 2011 at 7 p.m. (CST).[6] It was immediately rebroadcast at 8:30 p.m. and aired an additional *five* times, from June 12–17.

Hartley argued, "For the industry, television is a *paedocratic regime*. The audience is imagined as having childlike qualities and attributes. Television discourse addresses its viewers as children."[7] While this could easily be read as Adorno, Hartley also contended, "This isn't to say that television is infantile, childish, or dedicated to the lowest common denominator — those would be certain mechanisms for losing the audience.... Broadcasters paedocratize audiences in the name of pleasure. They appeal to the playful, imaginative, fantasy, irresponsible aspects of adult behavior."[8] Yet Hartley is equally clear that paedocracy becomes a means to unify audiences around "a *fictional version of everyone's supposed childlike tendencies*."[9] What becomes problematic is Hartley's own formulation of an imagined audience of TV viewers that are treated like children in need of paternalistic institutional guidance, not as intelligent adults capable of making informed decisions. Yet the audience is manufactured into children by the industry with TV serving as the teacher, if not the babysitter. Ultimately, Hartley's argument reiterates Adorno's position on mass culture as much as achieving any critical alternative:

> Television audiences are subject to a *pedagogic* regime of pleasure ... they do not live, while acting as audiences, in a democracy. But they do not live in a paedocracy either, since a pedagogic regime cannot be governed *by* childlike qualities but on the contrary constitutes government *over* them.... Paedocracy too often functions within the industry not to explain the audience, but to explain them away, to contain their potential threat, to render obvious their need for protection, regulation, rule.[10]

The contradictions of recent sitcoms can be traced to the contradictions of TV paedocracy. At one level, the "appeal to the playful, imaginative, fantasy, irresponsible aspects of adult behavior" becomes a cogent description of the male "eternal teenager" stereotype, or what might be termed an idealized expression of Hip as "paedocratized individuality," exemplified by *The King of Queens*. At another level, sitcoms become a point where the pedagogic and paedocratic regimes converge, whether expressed by cultivating the "inner child" in a kinder, gentler dictatorship on *The Cosby Show*, the loudmouth explosions of infantile tyranny on *According to Jim*, or the Hipper-than-thou authoritarianism on *George Lopez* and *My Wife and Kids*. On many recent sitcoms, the demand is for responsible behavior by adolescents while representing this as a mode of conduct tweens and especially teens are unable or unwilling to engage in without obedience to parental (and, usually, patriarchal) authority. This tendency can also be seen in Disney Channel teen sitcoms like *Hannah Montana* and *Wizards of Waverly Place*; in keeping with recent sitcom logic, on *Wizards of Waverly Place* the mother Theresa Russo served as the strict disciplinarian of the family while father Jerry Russo was a laid-back guy's guy.[11] Indeed, this also entails a contradiction shared by recent teen and adult sitcoms where the requirement for teens to act more "mature" is countered by a glorification of the "childlike" adult male, whereas females are the Square destroyers of fun — with "males" being men and women who act like "guys" and "females" being women and guys who act like "girls."

If paedocracy is defined as "government by rule of children," it is much better represented by *Zoey 101* and Pacific Coast Academy functioning as an effective democratic society through the efforts of the students and the leadership of Zoey Brooks, despite the adult authority of school administration. Nickelodeon consciously constructs brand identity and brand loyalty though programming that, in *both* senses of the word, "appeals" to an imagined audience of adolescents that have the capacity to think and behave like adults, an audience capable of paedocratic responsibility as much as childish irresponsibility. Indeed, Hartley praised the Nickelodeon teen sitcom *Clarissa Explains It All* precisely because the title character was represented as "a mainstream, fully-formed 'adult' character."[12] While teen sitcoms function as a pedagogic regime controlled by adult production that simultaneously contain and legitimize "teen power" for its teenage audience/consumer base, they also often endorse "maturity" as far as personal and social behavior far more than adult sitcoms while they are dismissed as woefully "immature" cultural fare with conformist (read: conservative) messages. In fact, Nickelodeon's programming revolves around neoliberalism and, more specifically, Clintonism as part and parcel of the ideology marketing.

## No Slackers Allowed (or, Bill Clinton Explains It All): Nickelodeon and Neoliberalism

While Nickelodeon's brand identity is constructed around adolescent empowerment, underlying this is an "anti-slacker" ideology as far as "slacker" was defined in the early 1990s with cultural texts ranging from *Beavis and Butthead*, Nirvana's *Nevermind*, or the film *Slacker*. By the 1990s, theories of a "postindustrial capitalism" seemed to emerge in practice with a globalized capitalist economy increasingly driven by consumerism and technology (buying power and computers) rather than production and industry (labor force and factories). In turn, American liberalism shifted away from labor-liberalism and welfare-state capitalism to the business-friendly, centrist, middle-class neoliberalism of New Democrats personified by Bill Clinton. As Eileen R. Meehan noted, "As a 'New Democrat,' Clinton usurped much of the Republicans' neoconservative rhetoric and many of their policy objectives."[13]

The 1992 presidential election was also the first that pitted a candidate representing the World War II-era "Greatest Generation" with the incumbent George H.W. Bush versus a candidate representing the post–World War II "Baby Boom" counterculture generation with the challenger Bill Clinton. As well as the New Democrat move to neoliberalism, an additional factor in Clinton's electoral success was actively courting and mobilizing the 18–29 voting bloc, a constituency often ignored in national campaigns due to their historically high rates of non-voting. Moreover, the Clinton campaign encouraged the active involvement of teens that were not eligible to vote but could contribute time and effort to the campaign. As part of this youth appeal, Clinton consciously projected a Hip image, whether playing saxophone in sunglasses with the house band on *The Arsenio Hall Show* or doing an MTV "town hall meeting" with young people to field pertinent questions about political policy and his underwear preferences. To be sure, Clinton's emphasis on Hipness was campaign strategy. While Clinton might have overdone the efforts to come off like America's cool dad, his campaign was also symbolic acknowledgment that the younger generation mattered in the political process. In turn, the message of Clintonism was that politics should matter to young people as well.

Since 1992, Nickelodeon sponsors Kids Pick the President (KPP) where viewers under the age of 18 can participate in a mock-election, and the Democratic candidates have consistently won KPP (Al Gore won in 2000 and John Kerry in 2004). In 2008, both Barack Obama and John McCain appeared in Nickelodeon spots to encourage kids to "vote" in KPP for their candidate of choice. Nickelodeon also sponsors the Big Help community service initiative in "making a difference" and making the world "a better place." Much of the Big Help centers on fairly non-partisan issues, with Nickelodeon's teen sitcom stars acting as designated spokespeople on specific areas appropriate to their "image" in Big Help public-service announcements. Coinciding with the heavily promoted debut of *Victorious* and the 40th anniversary of Earth Day in the spring of 2010, Victoria Justice appeared in several Big Help spots as spokesperson for recycling, energy conservation, and local clean-up projects.[14] In the summer of 2010 and the annual break in the school year, the members of Big Time Rush promoted physical fitness in the great outdoors. During the fall of 2010, coinciding with the start of a new school year, *iCarly* star Miranda Cosgrove served as the spokesperson for greater teen initiative and involvement in school through fundraising, extracurricular activities, and applying oneself in the classroom. In December 2010, corresponding with the holiday season, *True Jackson, VP* star Keke Palmer was featured in Big Help promos encouraging volunteer efforts to assist the less fortunate (donating time and/or money to food shelves, shelters, toy drives, etc.).[15] Big Help spots in early 2011 featured Cage Golightly (*The Troop*) and Ashley Argota (*True Jackson, VP*) discouraging internet bullying, while Cosgrove and *iCarly* co-star Nathan Kress did likewise with internet piracy. In summer of 2011, it was announced that Michelle Obama would appear on *iCarly* in an episode promoting the "Joining Forces" initiative to encourage support for military families.

Nickelodeon may consciously cultivate the perception that it is not only a socially conscious but progressive and even "anti–Establishment" TV network; however, it is hardly outside the domain of dominant ideology. Indeed, from an Althusserian perspective, Nickelodeon engages in a process of interpellation as far as grooming its adolescent viewers for American citizenship around individual initiative, personal responsibility, and community service. Banet-Wesier noted that "through the framework of the Nickelodeon brand ... consumer citizenship represents part of a larger dynamic of citizenship that constantly moves between *agency and conformity* in media culture."[16] Indeed, "agency versus conformity" is teen culture's highly problematic means of negotiating the individual versus community contradiction that plagues American society as a balancing act between the desire for individual agency and demand for community conformity. Teen culture inherently becomes both a product and producer of the contradiction rather than rectifying it. Nickelodeon's political position and ideology marketing agenda is fundamentally rooted in neoliberalism (i.e., Clintonism), and amounts to the classical liberal model updated for a postindustrial capitalist context where autonomous and self-determining individuals, acting ethically and responsibly in the private and public spheres, can and will construct a viable community. Nonetheless, as Nickelodeon programming and its representation of citizenship "constantly moves between agency and conformity," it offers competing and contradictory lesson plans as far as American politics.

## *Girl Power:* Clarissa Explains It All

> I think it was Karl Marx who said that religion is the opiate of the people. Makes you wonder what Karl would've thought of the Tube. Kind of the potato chips of the people.—*Clarissa Darling, "No TV" (1991)*

*Clarissa Explains It All* (1991–4, henceforth *CEIA*) was an important moment in Nickelodeon programming history. Formally, *CEIA* was an early example of the contemporary sitcom. As the show's creator, Mitchell Kriegman, explained, "I'm not a big fan of the old-fashioned sitcoms, they're so slow. You get one story.... Clarissa tells lots of stories and gives a lot of information. It's a quickening of the pace of the sitcom. You've got a sitcom going on, but she gives a reader's guide on the side."[17] Part of this "reader's guide" was that Clarissa directly addressed the camera as much as she interacted with the other characters on the show. Moreover, the reader's guide entailed the use of video graphics that "visualized" on the TV screen what Clarissa was thinking in terms of a given situation through words, captions, lists, charts, or drawings. In "School Picture" (1991), the situational struggle was between Clarissa and her mother, Janet, over what Clarissa will wear for her annual school photo, and the words "uncool stuff" with an arrow pointing to a pile of rejected items appeared on the screen. *CEIA* also utilized an array of "subjective inserts" of past, present, and future events from Clarissa's perspective which were often done as pop culture parodies (Classical Hollywood cinema, soap operas, 1950s sitcoms, etc.).[18] In "Cool Dad" (1991), one scene depicting Clarissa's view of her father, Marshall, attempting to be Hip was presented as a B-Movie horror film trailer "Dad from Hell" in black and white and enhanced with deteriorating film-stock glitches.

Like many contemporary sitcoms, *CEIA* extensively, and one could also say excessively, referenced popular culture as an essential part of the show. In "Picture Day," Clarissa convinces her friend Jodi to join her in wearing what they want to wear in the school photo by proclaiming, "Our mission: to seek out racy combinations, to boldly wear patterns no one has worn before" as a parody of the opening title narration for *Star Trek* accompanied by a snippet of the *Star Trek* theme music. In the subsequent planning, Clarissa envisions

Jodi as "a cross between Lady Di and Lt. Uluru" and also suggests a cape that is "Tina Turner meets Elvira" whereas Jodi is looking for something more "Winona Ryder." However, Clarissa's first ensemble is more postmodern-political, consisting of what she describes as "Mao collar, Gandhi trousers, Jackie O. pillbox, and Barbara Bush holiday pin" (matched by an on-screen list of each item).

CEIA not only supplied cultural referencing comparable to any adult "smart comedy," but demanded a considerable degree of cultural literacy in order to fully "get it." To this extent, and as far as concurrent sitcoms, CEIA compared as much to the referential comedy of *The Simpsons* while serving as a competing discourse to *Saved by the Bell*. (In the 1990s, a VHS of the CEIA episodes "School Picture" and "Understudy" was released with the title *Clarissa Explains It All: Enslaved by the Bell*.) While Zack Morris's mission was to boldly conquer the hearts and minds of teenage girls and adult authorities while learning supposed moral-ethical lessons in the process, Clarissa was a white, middle-class, teenage girl coping with the daily struggles of family, romance, school, and impending adulthood. CEIA also offered a more positive and non-stereotypical representation of the teenage girl, especially in comparison to *Saved by the Bell*'s trio of the girl-next-door ideal (Kelly), narcissistic consumerist (Lisa), and self-important feminist pseudo-intellectual (Jessie). Clarissa was extremely intelligent, willfully individualistic, and steadfastly rebellious as each situation warranted. She was also the agent through which the situational order was often restored as much as the cause of situational disorder; this was a contrast to previous sitcoms where, if the title character was a tween or teenage girl, she was frequently the source of situational disorder usually resolved by her parents, often the father (e.g., *Gidget, Punky Brewster, Blossom*, and, more recently, *Hannah Montana*).[19]

Nonetheless, CEIA and subsequent "girl power" sitcoms cannot be assessed strictly around the extent they challenge and even dismantle stereotypes. Clarissa was a representation or "role model" for *potential* individual agency. In "Parents Who Say No" (1991), Clarissa wanted to get a temporary job at a carnival, an idea her parents veto on the grounds that she is too young and a traveling carnival is not an appropriate environment for a teenage girl. Clarissa simply wore her parents down until they let her get a job; unfortunately for Clarissa, she was hired to supervise the carnival daycare area and had to dress as Little Bo-Peep for the week. Clarissa succeeded in her struggle to become empowered and make her own decisions about the course of her life. This also meant learning to accept, and adapt to, the potential unwanted consequences of those decisions and actions. Hence, the underlying message of CEIA was not only self-determination but the personal responsibility that came with self-determination, and it was not coincidental CEIA emerged in tandem with Bill Clinton and the New Democrats rebranding traditional American liberalism as a progressive neoliberal alternative to a decade of Reaganism.

Clarissa's parents represented the old of pre–Reagan Revolution American liberalism. However, *CEIA* was a parodic response to *Family Ties* and the political representations of the Keaton family as much as any replication. Steven and Elyse Keaton were former hippies who became middle-class but socially conscious white-collar professionals (Steven was a PBS station manager and Elyse an environmentalist architect).[20] Marshall Darling was also a former hippie who became, as Clarissa sarcastically put it in *CEIA*'s debut episode ("Clarissa's Revenge," 1991), a "modern architect" with Clarissa thankful her family could not afford to live in one of Marshall's kitsch/Pop Art home designs. In the same episode, Janet Darling was described as a health-food fanatic and teacher at the local children's museum, which Clarissa called "a secret indoctrination camp to turn little guys into morons." Indeed, Marshall and Janet had effectively become Squares, as evidenced in "Cool Dad" and the clear cultural-generational gap between parents and kids. Fearing Marshall will embarrass her as a speaker at school career day, Clarissa tries to discourage him from attending. Instead, Marshall decides he needs to become more "Hip ... Now ... Groovy!" When he asks Clarissa if she wants to listen to some Gordon Lightfoot, a baffled Clarissa asks *"What's* Gordon Lightfoot?" In fact, various *CEIA* episodes specified Clarissa was a fan of Echo and the Bunnymen, Pearl Jam, and especially the *outré* punk-pop band They Might Be Giants.[21] Clarissa's taste in music designated her as Hip by being a fan of alternative rock and not a fan of "the oldies" and, as important, "teenybopper music."

The subplot of "Cool Dad" is that Janet Darling had a personal experience where her father embarrassed her badly at her school in front of her peers, so she is more than sympathetic to Clarissa's plight. However, Clarissa's younger brother Ferguson wants to see an R-rated horror film under the pretense of doing a paper for a school assignment in order to, as Ferguson puts it, "Deconstruct the subversive messages in the genre." Janet rejects the idea in favor of *It's a Wonderful Life* and places Ferguson on a crash course of classic novels like *Moby-Dick* and *Crime and Punishment*. As suggested, on *CEIA* Hip was not the high culture of museums and canonical literature, nor was it mainstream "old culture" of Frank Capra or Gordon Lightfoot, let alone Guy Lombardo and Lawrence Welk (both of whom were roundly dismissed by Clarissa in "Picture Day"). Rather, Hip was a pop culture sensibility and literacy — cultural history was perhaps being another matter — informed by current cinema, music, and TV as much as the past; in "A Little Romance" (1993), Clarissa ruminated on the complexities of love and offered a quote, but was unsure if it was Shakespeare or Sting.[22]

As the primary antagonist on *CEIA*, Ferguson Darling was the self-centered, smart-mouthed Young Republican capitalist in the Darling family as opposed to *Family Ties* and Alex P. Keaton serving as the show's popular voice of sharp-witted Hip conservatism. In "Brain Drain" (1991), Ferguson set his plan for "world domination" in motion by becoming a contestant on a kids' game show, winning prize money to invest in stocks, making a fortune on Wall Street, and financing a chain of "Fergus World" shopping malls and conquering the global economy through consumer capitalism (the plan fizzled when he lost badly on the game show). Above all, Clarissa was the antithesis of the unintelligent consumerist Mallory Keaton. While Mallory's goal seemed to be landing a husband and becoming a full-time shopper, *CEIA* ended with Clarissa moving to New York City to pursue a career in journalism out of high school.

Ultimately, while Clarissa Darling was a representation of post–Second Wave Feminism, she also represented the "new and improved" brand of American liberalism heralded by the New Democrats and Bill Clinton. This is not to diminish the feminist concerns of *CEIA*, but suggest the extent Nickelodeon's representation of girl power in the teen sitcoms premiering between 2004 and 2008 are also inseparable from neoliberal ideology, and discussed further through case studies of *Zoey 101, iCarly,* and *True Jackson, VP.* However, and ostensibly anything but a "girl power" sitcom, *Drake and Josh* can be read as one of Nickelodeon's more subversive critiques of gender politics.

## *Who's the Man?* Drake and Josh

A child actor who co-starred on *Head of the Class,* Dan Schneider was involved in the creation, development, production, and writing of Nickelodeon's comedy-variety shows *All That* (1994–2000, 2002–5) and *The Amanda Show* (1999–2002). Since 2004, Schneider created the Nickelodeon teen sitcoms *Drake and Josh, Zoey 101, iCarly,* and *Victorious. Drake and Josh* revolved around two diametrically opposed stepbrothers Drake Parker (Drake Bell) and Josh Nichols (Josh Peck); Bell and Peck were regular cast members on *The Amanda Show,* and *Drake and Josh* was subsequently created around them.[23] Most episodes began with Drake and Josh directly addressing the camera in character, providing some general background to frame the pending situation in the episode (either by crosscutting or a split screen), but they did not engage in direct address over the course of the show. Otherwise, *Drake and Josh* was done in the classical sitcom format using laugh tracks, a multi-camera set-up, and sound-stage locales (the rooms in Drake and Josh's house, the lobby of the movie theater where Josh worked, their high school, and other places as the specific situation entailed). In fact, the positively old-fashioned qualities of *Drake and Josh* became pronounced by the occasional "referencing" of early sitcoms. In the episode "I Love Sushi" (2006), Drake and Josh fell for a con artist who robbed the family home and they got jobs at a sushi-packaging factory to earn some money. The assembly line havoc was lifted directly from the famous candy factory sequence in the *I Love Lucy* episode "Job Switching" (1952).

Emphasizing fast-paced exchanges of dialogue and slapstick physical comedy, *Drake and Josh* was essentially Nickelodeon's teen version of Dean Martin and Jerry Lewis. Drake Parker was suave, lazy, and narcissistic. He coasted through life relying on his charm, good looks, and wits as he pursued his short-term goal of dating as many girls as possible and his long-term goal of becoming a rock star. Josh Nichols was awkward, high-strung, and insecure. He worked equally hard at school and his job and seemed perpetually on the verge of a nervous breakdown. In short, Drake embodied Hip, and Josh personified Square, the distinction established by Drake's effortless exuding of masculine-coded cool and Josh's petulant displays of feminine-coded uncool. Indeed, *Drake and Josh* seemed little more than *Saved by the Bell* with Drake the show's eminently slick Zack Morris, whereas Josh was a pathetic combination of Screech Powers and Jessie Spano. Moreover, like *Saved by the Bell* and most sit-coms (teen or adult), *Drake and Josh* reveled in making nerds and geeks the object of derision and the antithesis to Drake's masculine Hip. Two of *Drake and Josh*'s supporting characters were Josh's friends Eric Blonwitz and Craig Ramirez, two nerds who essentially carried on as gay couple. In "Eric Punches Drake" (2007), Eric accidentally gave Drake a black eye demonstrating a scene he saw in a martial-arts movie and rumors circulated that Eric beat up Drake. While Eric enjoyed a huge surge in popularity, Drake became the high school laughing stock until Craig intervened on Drake's behalf in order in to squash Eric's newfound prestige and restore their "couple" relationship. Nevertheless, it becomes too simplistic to read *Drake and Josh* in the same way as *Saved by the Bell* or *Two and a Half Men* and the latter's clear-cut binary between carous-ing bachelor Charlie Harper (the masculine Hip the viewer laughs *with*) and his milquetoast brother Alan Harper (the effeminate Square the viewer laughs *at*). One of the more crucial episodes in this respect was "Josh is Done" (2007). After becoming the fall guy for Drake's irresponsibility and manipulations one too many times, Josh severed any relationship with Drake beyond the two living in the same house and going to the same school. Josh's life improved immea-surably at every level while Drake's life completely fell apart. In the end, a des-perately contrite Drake realized he needed Josh's will to Square stability more than Josh needs Drake's will to Hip spontaneity.

The continual undercurrent of *Drake and Josh* was the specter haunting male teenagers, the specter of female tween treachery embodied by Megan Parker (Miranda Cosgrove, who subsequently went on to star in *iCarly*, dis-cussed in the following chapter). Megan's seeming *raison d'être* was how much suffering she could inflict on her brothers, and her capacity to do so was only exceeded by her ability to get way with it.[24] A typical episode was "Tree House" (2007). When they are inadvertently trapped in a tree house they are building, Drake and Josh's blind double-date with attractive twin sisters scheduled for that evening is jeopardized. Megan sabotages every effort they make to escape, and, in the ultimate insult, sends Eric and Craig in their place for the blind date. In "My Dinner with Bobo" (2007), Walter Nichols agrees to match the money Drake and Josh have to buy a used car, provided they chauffer Megan as necessary and she has a say in the selection of the car.[25] Drake wants to buy a worn-down Ford Mustang, Josh a reliable Mercury Sable, and Megan prefers a yellow Volkswagen Beetle convertible painted with multi-colored daisies. Devising a get-rich-quick scheme, Drake instead uses the money to buy the used car lot's local celebrity mascot — an orangutan named Bobo — hoping to cash in on personal appearance fees. Drake's plan proves to be a financial bust until a stranger buys the monkey for $10,000. When Megan learns the buyer is an international criminal wanted for eating rare and endangered animals, Drake and Josh attempt to rescue the orangutan but are captured; they are eventually saved by the police courtesy of Megan "on one condition." The scene cuts to Drake and Josh driving the newly purchased, flower-decorated Volkswagen around town, enduring insults from their male peers while Megan sits in the back seat laughing with great satisfaction. In the end, Megan orchestrated another humiliation of her brothers.

While Megan seemed nothing more than a malevolent brat from episode to episode, she was central to *Drake and Josh*, despite being a supporting character. Megan was not necessarily a "positive role model" as far as girl power (i.e., Clarissa Darling), but a representation of girl power nonetheless. On *Drake and Josh*, the recurring message was the tween girl's pivotal role as the determining agent in events where Drake (Hip) and Josh (Square) were set against Megan as the Other in the male-dominated order. As a central force of agency, Megan could often be the cause of situational disorder but just as often reconstituted situational order at the expense of the males. In short, Megan ruled.

## *Students for a Democratic Society:* Zoey 101

Debuting in 2005, *Zoey 101* was something of a departure from *Drake and Josh* and the subsequent *iCarly* and *Victorious*. Falling between the classical and contemporary sitcom formats, *Zoey 101* utilized a single camera and location shooting at Pepperdine University, which served as Pacific Coast Academy (PCA) for the outdoor exterior campus scenes, while studio sound stages served as the PCA dorms and classrooms. However, camerawork and editing was conventional and functional. Rather than the exaggerated "mockumentary" style of *The Office*, *Zoey 101* emphasized pseudo-realism through a non-obtrusive "documentary" style. There was no laugh track and characters did not directly address the camera.

Zoey Brooks was played by Jamie Lynn Spears, best known for being Britney Spears's younger sister. The accusations of nepotism aside, Spears was a regular cast member on *All That* from 2002–4, with *Zoey 101* created as a starring vehicle for Spears. Zoey was an incoming freshman at PCA — and "PC" can also be read as the popular abbreviation for "politically correct" — now a co-educational facility after years of being a boys-only institution. Gender politics were a dominant issue on *Zoey 101*, and the focus of the premiere episode "Welcome to PCA" (2005). Zoey decided to try out for the boys' basketball team, prompting an anti-feminist campaign led by Logan Reese, who was not only PCA's staunchest male chauvinist but an obnoxious "spoiled rich kid" stereotype. The dispute culminated in a "boys vs. girls" basketball game. While the boys barely defeated the girls in the battle, the girls won the war by earning the respect of the boys as well as the coach, who invited Zoey and Dana Cruz to join what would now be a mixed-gender PCA basketball team.

In "Wrestling" (2007) Zoey joins the boys' wrestling team, although she spends practices doing endless calisthenics rather than scrimmaging. Finally allowed to wrestle in an important tournament, Zoey continually wins by forfeit — much to her aggravation — because none of the boys will wrestle a girl with the exception of a testosterone-driven wrestler she is going to meet in the championship match; he warns her that "I hurt everyone just the same!" (Zoey's response: "How ... 'progressive' of you.") When the coach pulls Zoey claiming injury and substitutes his best wrestler, Zoey realizes she has not been a ringer but a dupe, and her role on the team was strictly subterfuge to advance a boy wrestler. Enraged, Zoey tells the referee she is not injured and insists on wrestling, while the PCA students begin chanting "Zoey!" in support. Zoey is not only defeated in record time (the match lasts four seconds) but wakes up in the hospital after being rendered unconscious. As in "Welcome to PCA," Zoey lost the athletic competition but won as far as achieving equal opportunity and, as important, the PCA community rallied around her. Indeed, none other than Logan reprimanded the other wrestler after the match, was promptly beaten up, and is now lying in the bed next to Zoey.

"Wrestling" also offers a comparative reading to the *Saved by the Bell* episode "Hold Me Tight" (1993) as a considerably different treatment of gender politics. Kristi is the new girl in school and the next object of Zack's romantic conquest. When he learns the school forbids Kristi from joining the wrestling team, Zack enlists Jessie in a campaign against school policy: Jessie because she is a liberal-feminist infatuated with causes; Zack because he wants to score with Kristi. After Kristi is allowed on the team, disorder ensues when Jessie becomes jealous of Kristi's friendship with Slater, the team's star wrestler (Jessie and Slater were a couple at this point in the show's run). Additionally, when a wrestler from another school bullies Kristi and Zack on their first date, Zack steps up to defend Kristi's honor, only to have Kristi rescue *him* from a beating. Male ego bruised, Zack dumps Kristi; female fury sparked, Jessie starts a new campaign *against* allowing girls on the school wrestling team. After Kristi quits amid the backlash, Zack and Jessie realize the errors of their behavior. *Zack* convinces Kristi to rejoin the wrestling team, and she defeats her opponent in her debut match: the same wrestler who harassed her and Zack earlier in the episode. While the overt message is female empowerment and Zack learning his requisite ethical lesson — in this case, ostensibly addressing his own sexism — the hidden message is that Kristi is empowered only through the benevolence of the male (Zack) while the feminist (Jessie) reveals herself as the potential, even greater enemy to gender equity. Of course, Zack also achieves his initial goal and gets the girl he was after in the first place.

In this context, the *Zoey 101* episode "Miss PCA" (2007) inevitably invites comparison to the *Saved by the Bell* episode "Miss Bayside" (1990). In order to pad his college résumé, Logan organizes a Miss PCA beauty pageant in which he will be the lone judge. Zoey, Lola Martinez, and Chase Mathews are appalled, informing Logan that beauty contests are "sexist" and "insulting to girls." Logan's response is that beauty pageants are only insulting to "ugly girls." However, Zoey and Lola change their minds and enter the Miss PCA pageant once they learn the winner will have her photo on the cover of a prominent fashion magazine. (The financial backing for the pageant is being provided by Logan's "rich daddy," as Zoey curtly refers to him in the beginning of the episode.) Logan becomes the center of attention of PCA's female "student body," which he exploits to its full advantage as a bevy of potential Miss PCAs slavishly dote on him. Moreover, Logan instigates a bitter feud between Zoey and Lola, and an incredulous Chase points out to Zoey that she, of all people, is now "freaking out, dying to have Logan pick you the prettiest girl at PCA." The transformative action is an almost perverse moment when the personal sniping between Zoey and Lola turns into a public mud wresting match in evening gowns, ending with the mutual realization that their real adversary all along has been Logan and his exploitation of *all* the girls at PCA. Order is restored, with Zoey and Lola dragging Logan into the mud and beating him up while their fellow PCA students cheer in support. The Miss PCA beauty contest is effectively shut down before it can commence.

In "Miss Bayside," Mr. Belding announces plans for a Miss Bayside beauty pageant. Not surprisingly, the lone opponent to the pageant is Jessie. She refuses to enter and convinces Kelly, a probable favorite to win, to boycott as well. Lisa is determined not only to enter but win, and Zack becomes greatly annoyed with Lisa after she rebuffs his offer to wield his considerable clout at Bayside on her behalf. In retaliation, and to make some fast money as well, Zack makes a bet with Slater that he can get "anyone" elected Miss Bayside, only to have Slater pick Screech as the contestant. Fearing that Screech could actually win Miss Bayside, Slater talks Jessie into entering; angered by Jessie's about-face on the pageant issue, Kelly enters as well. Eventually, Slater deploys his secret weapon and *he* enters the Miss Bayside pageant. Eliminating all the girls in the preliminaries, Screech and Slater vie for the Miss Bayside title, with the swimsuit competition remaining and the scrawny Screech having little chance against Slater's beefcake physique; to make matters worse, Screech now sports an unsightly black eye (courtesy of a robot he is building in the episode's subplot). Yet the pageant audience completely shuns Slater while Screech receives a standing ovation and becomes Miss Bayside. As his obligatory ethical lesson, Zack's

The community leader next door: Zoey Brooks (Jamie Lynn Spears), and Chase Matthews (Sean Flynn). Chase appears to have something on his mind (Nickelodeon).

conscience prevents him from accepting Slater's payment on the bet. He admits he planted a rumor (read: lie) that Slater gave Screech the black eye in a fit of competitive pique, which is why the crowd rallied behind Screech. In effect, the bet becomes a moot narrative point. More important than the money, Zack proved yet again he was the puppet master pulling everyone's strings at Bayside.

Beyond the sexism of *Saved by the Bell* versus the feminism of *Zoey 101,* these episodes suggest the considerable differences between Zack Morris and Zoey Brooks as political figures. While *Saved by the Bell* represented individual agency as unadulterated ambition and domination, on *Zoey 101* gender equity and individual agency were necessarily related as the force to build community. The vast majority of episodes took place in and around PCA where the students not only attended classes but lived on campus. In effect, school was "home." However, the students were not so much the cliché of "one big family" but a microcosm of the conflicts and contradictions of liberal society.[26] Parents were generally absent from the show, but occasionally appeared in specific episodes. Instead, adult authority was manifest by the largely incompetent and officious PCA teachers and administrators, while the students were often the ones keeping the school from falling into disarray.[27]

As far as offering a "political education," the ethical form of *Zoey 101* was often a lesson in liberal democratic process through situation (conflicts between individuals) → action (formation of consensus) → situation (sustained community) with Zoey occupying a pivotal role in community leadership. In "Broadcast Views" (2006), Chase and Michael Barrett have a floundering webshow until Zoey and Logan engage in an audible off-camera argument about whether boys or girls have superior taste in movies. When the quarrel provides a considerable boost in viewership, Zoey and Logan are added to the webcast in a "He Said, She Said" segment where Logan insults girls and Zoey responds to his sexist remarks in turn. "He Said, She Said" proves so popular it causes a divisive gender gap at PCA, resulting in Dean Rivers banning the entire webcast. However, a local TV station offers to produce a version of the show, albeit one that exclusively features Zoey and Logan's "He Said, She Said" debates and no Chase and Michael comedy skits. Zoey uses the premiere telecast and her "media visibility" to shift the political focus from gender issues to protesting PCAs censoring of the webcasts, prompting a widespread student demonstration at PCA until Dean Rivers concedes and allows Chase and Michael to resume production of their webshow. Zoey becomes the force by which local political activism is organized to affect change.

A similar yet different process occurred in "Zoey's Balloon" (2007). A psychology class project requires each student write down an embarrassing secret, tie it to a balloon, and release it into the air to free themselves of their secret. PCA's "mean girl" Rebecca finds Zoey's balloon and blackmails her into performing a series of embarrassing stunts lest she reveal Zoey's secret (Zoey was the child model and appeared in a suntan lotion ad where her bikini bottom was being pulled down by a dog).[28] The transformative action occurs when Zoey decides that it is better to have one potentially humiliating secret exposed than continued public mortification, and confronts Rebecca in the PCA courtyard. Before Rebecca can reveal Zoey's secret, and having learned of Rebecca's scheme, Zoey's friends publically disclose an embarrassing fact about themselves. Other students follow suit. Finally, the teacher who initiated the balloon project reveals her secret: that she never passed her teaching certification exams. The students (the public) empower themselves and each other to restore order as the *vox populi* by revealing a secret to their peers whereas an incompetent teacher (institutional authority) and her class project indirectly instigated the disordered situation. With community support gathered and generated around her, Zoey could reveal her secret and negate Rebecca's autocratic power over her.

Specifically in its final two seasons, *Zoey 101* was constructed around a trio of three central female characters and three ancillary male characters rather than *Saved by the Bell*'s three primary male and three secondary female characters.[29] On *Saved by the Bell* there was distinct hierarchy of the characters, stereotypes, and representations that *Zoey 101* did not so much mimic but parodied with distinct political implications.[30]

*Saved by the Bell*

Zack (white male)—cool kid; symbol of *individualism*
Slater (Latino)—jock/sexist
Screech (white male)—brain/geek
Kelly (white female)—girl next door
Lisa (African-American female)—fashionista/consumerist
Jessie (white female)—intellectual/liberal activist; symbol of *community*

*Zoey 101*

Zoey (white female)—cool kid; symbol of *community*
Lola (Latina)—fashionista/ aspiring star
Quinn (white female)—brain/nerd
Chase (white male)—boy next door
Michael (African-American male)—class clown
Logan (white male)—rich kid/sexist; symbol of *individualism*

*Saved by the Bell* revolved around Zack Morris as the scheming individualist learning to be an ethical individualist *ad infinitum*. On *Zoey 101*, Logan was the cause of situational disorder and community friction in many episodes, usually the result of his sexist attitudes, financial privileges, and myopic self-interests. Indeed, Logan's annoying elitism — derived from class, gender, and racial privilege — ran counter to the egalitarian community ideal at PCA (itself a predominately white and middle-upper class environment). Zoey was the figure around whom situational order and community stability was eventually restored.[31] As Banet-Weiser noted:

> The easy dismissal of "girl power" as a media-created now commercial avenue that has no connection with any kind of "real" politics is both inaccurate and misleading about the nature of "reality" in the twenty-first century. The charge by Second Wave feminists regarding the apparent lack of "real politics" of post-feminism may very well indicate, in part, a preoccupation with personal issues and individualism. But this sentiment not only romanticizes the feminist movements of the 1960s and 1970s as concerned only with the social and material spheres. It also caricatures feminist politics of the 1990s as narcissistic and vacuous. The media address of postfeminism and girl power ideology is about tension and contradiction, about the individual pleasures of consumption and the social responsibilities of solidarity.[32]

Girl power ideology can indeed succumb to a valorization of individualism and narcissism, the problem of Madonna's prototype brand of girl power feminism of the 1980s serving as a subsidiary for "Material Girl" and "Blond Ambition" capitalism (an issue returned to in Chapter 9). In contrast, the primary concern of *Zoey 101* was not only personal empowerment but the public sphere of PCA as a metaphor for a functional and self-governing democratic society where gender equality and sustainable community were not only related but inseparable. Like any ideology, girl power is also contradictory as it negotiates between the pleasures of individual agency and the responsibilities of community conformity.

Ultimately, both *Drake and Josh* and *Zoey 101* prove politically problematic, especially within their historical context. On the domestic sitcom front, sexism and outright misogyny reached new levels of "comedy" with the popularity of such shows as *According to Jim* and *Two and a Half Men*, which respectively premiered in 2001 and 2003. In 2003, *School of Rock* represented cultural rebellion around traditions of masculine Hipness and a canon of timeless "authentic rock" at least a generation removed from the teens of the twenty-first century. In the wake of the highly contested 2000 election, shortly followed by 9/11 and the invasion of Iraq in 2003, American conservatism was approved with George W. Bush's reelection in 2004. *Drake and Josh* fell uncomfortably within and outside the politics of its sitcom contemporaries, on the surface perpetuating the ideology of male Hipness while unable to escape its inherent contradictions and offering its own internal criticisms. *Zoey 101* offered a representation of liberal democratic society revolving around the agency of teenagers and especially girls, yet in doing so sustained the ideological "myth" of individuals effortlessly reconciling their differences into an effective, egalitarian community. By 2007, with the political tide decidedly shifting back towards the neoliberalism of the Democratic Party, Dan Schneider created his next and most successful teen sitcom, *iCarly*, and the political problematics manifest in *Drake and Josh* and *Zoey 101* were not ironed out, but exacerbated on almost every level.

# 6

# The Political Dilemmas
# of iCarly

## Transitions: New Democrats, Nickelodeon, and iCarly

Entering 2008, Disney Channel developed a successful line of teen sitcoms with *The Suite Life of Zack and Cody, Hannah Montana,* and *Wizards of Waverly Place.* Moreover, Hannah Montana proved enormously successful as far as cross-marketing into popular music; in 2007, the Jonas Brothers signed to Disney subsidiary Hollywood Records and soon became teen pop superstars. In contrast, Nickelodeon's teen sitcoms that debuted in 2004 — *Drake and Josh, Unfabulous,* and *Ned's Declassified School Survival Guide* — ended their respective runs in 2007, while attempts at cross-marketing into pop music with Drake Bell (*Drake and Josh*) and Emma Roberts (*Unfabulous*) hardly matched the sales of Hannah Montana and the Jonas Brothers. *Zoey 101* was renewed for a fourth season only to have its programming status drastically altered in late 2007, and Nickelodeon part of an unwelcome controversy when 16-year-old Jamie Lynn Spears announced she was pregnant. Debates ensued over the appropriateness of Nickelodeon continuing to even air *Zoey 101* or if the network should take the opportunity to tackle the thorny issue of teen pregnancy. Ultimately, Nickelodeon issued some modestly supportive but non-committal press releases, and quietly aired the already-produced shows along with an unofficial series finale that ended *Zoey 101*'s run in spring of 2008.[1]

Another pressure was a rapidly shifting political climate. In the wake of the badly botched federal response to Hurricane Katrina and the invasion of Iraq becoming a military quagmire, George W. Bush and the Republican Party became highly unpopular political commodities. The Democratic Party took numerical control of both houses of Congress in the 2006 midterm election. Political prognostications in 2007 predicted a 2008 presidential race between centrist, neoliberal Democrat Hillary Rodham Clinton and centrist, neoliberal Republican Rudy Giuliani to be decided by centrist, middle-aged, middle-class voters. While it was expected that the next president would represent a shift towards political moderation after the Bush administration, if Clinton were to win she would be the first woman president. Given that *Zoey 101* ran from fall of 2005 to spring of 2008, which coincided with the growing and widespread unpopularity of George W. Bush while Clinton was a frontrunner in the 2008 presidential race, the subtext of *Zoey 101* can be read as endorsing the role of white, middle-upper class, *female* community leadership while the problems were often caused by the ill-advised endeavors of a none-too-bright white male with a "rich daddy."

Of course, a one-term African-American senator from Illinois named Barack Obama entered the presidential campaign in early 2007.[2] Obama's surprising success owed in no small part to taking a page from the Bill Clinton political campaign playbook and projecting an image as the Hip candidate. As Hillary Clinton's "inevitability" as the Democratic candidate — let alone next president — became less and less inevitable, she made a concerted effort to consolidate support among "Old Democrats," including retirees and middle-aged, blue-collar workers, while Obama mobilized students and younger professionals. Generational politics became ever more pronounced in the 2008 presidential campaign between Obama and John McCain. Obama was in his forties and a product of post-counterculture American liberalism. McCain was in his early seventies and symbolic of a "senior citizen" world-view entrenched in traditional American conservatism.

Within this context of Nickelodeon inaugurating a new line of teen sitcoms and rapidly shifting American politics, *iCarly* debuted in the fall of 2007 and quickly became Nickelodeon's leading teen sitcom; as of 2011, it is one of the highest-rated shows on basic cable, not to mention "teen TV." Created by Dan Schneider specifically around Miranda Cosgrove, who played Megan Parker on *Drake and Josh* and Summer Hathaway in *School of Rock*, Cosgrove portrays Carly Shay, a teenager living in Seattle under the legal guardianship of her older brother, Spencer Shay (played by another *Drake and Josh* alumnus, Jerry Trainor). Rounding out the core cast are Jennette McCurdy as Samantha "Sam" Puckett and Nathan Kress as Fredward "Freddie" Benson, Carly's two best friends; Gibby Gibson (played by Noah Munck) was a frequently recurring character in the first three seasons and officially added as a regular cast member by season four.[3] While the usual teenage tribulations with adults, friendships, romance, and school are ongoing issues on *iCarly*, central to the show is that Carly, Sam, and Freddie self-produce their own comedy webshow "iCarly" and its popularity has made them internet celebrities. (For clarification, *iCarly* refers to the actual sitcom; "iCarly" refers to the fictional webshow.)

Virtually all episodes of *iCarly* have one or more "iCarly" show-within-a-show sketch comedy segments. On some episodes "iCarly" webcasts function strictly as a pre-title cold opening to set up the sitcom situation, while other episodes focus on the complications of doing the live "iCarly" webcast and the show-within-the-show is the bulk of the episode. Often, the situation of the episode and the webshow become entwined. In "iBelieve in Bigfoot" (2010),

The main cast of *iCarly* (left to right): Spencer Shay (Jerry Trainor), Freddie Benson (Nathan Kress), Carly Shay (Miranda Cosgrove), and Sam Puckett (Jennette McCurdy) from the episode "iBelieve in Bigfoot" (Nickelodeon/Photofest).

the "iCarly" webcast segment appeared in the first half of the episode in order to introduce a Bigfoot expert in a "Let's Meet that Nerd" interview segment (said expert later revealed to be dressing as Bigfoot in order to generate publicity for his book); it followed a parody of a cooking show segment where Carly and Sam cover Gibby in tomato sauce and cheese to make "Gibby Parmesan."[4] These "iCarly" segments within *iCarly* are depicted from point-of-view shots of Freddy's video camera with a red "Rec" signal on the upper left and a battery-status sign on the upper right of the screen, clearly differentiating Freddie's camera recording the webshow from the objective camera filming sitcom events as a whole. This also allows the characters to directly address the camera and comment on the show, at least within the confines of "iCarly" webcasts (characters do not engage in direct address otherwise).

Other than the "iCarly" segments, *iCarly* is done very much within the classical sitcom format of multi-camera set-ups, sound stages, and pre-recorded laugh tracks; like *Drake and Josh*, one is stuck by how much *iCarly* has the look and feel of older sitcoms.[5] A fairly limited number of sets contain most of the events in various episodes: the Shay apartment (the living room space downstairs, the "iCarly" webcast studio upstairs, or Carly's bedroom), Ridgeway High School (mostly the main hallway, but also miscellaneous classrooms and offices), the Groovy Smoothie juice-bar hangout, and various other places as plotlines dictate. The reliance on classical sitcom form in *iCarly* and sketch comedy in "iCarly" becomes "the old" juxtaposed with celebrating "the new" of computers and webcasting in terms of cultural production. *iCarly* can be read as an internal debate between twentieth century American ideals and social formations versus the changing perceptions and social conditions of American society in the twenty-first century around gender roles, family structures, the education system, DYI youth culture, the contradictions of community and capitalism and, ultimately, the status of post–Obama American politics.

## Gender Trouble

On the Nickelodeon teen sitcom *Ned's Declassified School Survival Guide* (*NDSSG*) and comedy-action show *The Troop*, a "gendered trio" of primary characters consists of a masculine boy (Ned Bigby on *NDSSG*, Jake Collins on *The Troop*), a highly masculine girl (Jennifer "Moze" Moseby on *NDSSG*, Hailey Steele on *The Troop*), and a less-than-masculine boy (Simon "Cookie" Cook on *NDSSG*, Felix Garcia on *The Troop*); put differently, a trio constructed as a "boy's boy," an "animus-girl," and a "femme."[6] To be sure, the crucial difference with *iCarly* is that a girl rather than a boy is the central character of the show, and the show's similarly gendered trio both reiterates and ruptures the problematic gender politics of Nickelodeon's teen programming.[7] As the heir to Clarissa Darling and Zoey Brooks, Carly Shay represents "normative *girl power*" as opposed to the "normative *masculinity*" of Ned Bigby or Jake Collins in relationship to a masculine girl (Sam) and a less-than-masculine boy (Freddie). Carly is independent, intelligent, and responsible; she can also be insolent, stubborn, and rebellious. As Carly put it in one episode, "I may be bold but I'm not sassy!"

Sam Puckett is a not just a tomboy but the toughest "guy" at Ridgeway High School who is admired by her peers, hated by teachers, and feared by everyone. She spends as much time in detention as in the classroom, and numerous episodes have mentioned arrests, correctional facilities, and her parole officer. Sam's frequent acts of disruptive behavior and outright criminality not only makes Bart Simpson look like the valedictorian of civics class, and also suggests the gendered doubled standard of "rebellion" in American culture. Put differently, boys will be boys on sitcoms; the problem occurs when "*girls* will be boys." Bart Simpson as a *boy* is defiant, individualistic, and irreverent. While largely the same character, and even more "boyish," Sam Puckett as a *girl* is deemed belligerent, incorrigible, and mouthy because her exaggerated male social behavior does not properly conform to cultural constructs of proper or "natural" female behavior.

Sam's "gender trouble" was the focus of "iMake Sam Girlier" (2009). Carly throws a surprise birthday party for Sam; after Freddie reminds everyone not to sing "Happy Birthday," Sam is honored with a rendition of "For She's a Jolly Good Fellow."[8] However, a series of tribute speeches recounting Sam's various assaults, disobedience, and pranks bothers her greatly, especially since she has a crush on a boy who now thinks of her as a "dude." Sam asks Carly to help her learn to act more "soft and girly and weak" although Sam is immediately repulsed when she learns one aspect of her extreme gender makeover will be forsaking boxer shorts in favor of panties. Sam also bristles at another Carly suggestion by stating, "I want to be more girly — not a fruit cocktail!" Sam is willing to compromise and conform by being a girl who acts "soft and girly and weak"; she refuses to become a "fruit cocktail" in terms of making her masculine behavior more feminine or "a fruit cocktail" — a remark indicative of iCarly's tendencies towards heterosexism. Ultimately, Sam's reinvention is thwarted by a female bully terrorizing the school and, after the bully assaults Carly, Sam beats her up. When Sam notices her new beau has witnessed the altercation, she is thrilled he was not offended but highly impressed, and he is looking for a "girl who can kiss good [sic] and snap a bone." The irony is the revelation that what a guy wants is a dude in a girl's body.

At one level, Sam's brand of "two-fisted feminism" is an appropriation of the masculine as personal empowerment. While Sam subverts gender essentialism by demonstrating that gender is performed cultural behavior, Sam sustains the cultural myths of Hip and teen rebellion as the domain of the masculine. Rebellion is still "boy power" albeit performed by a girl. At the same time, Sam reveals the contradictions where the ideology of the Hip and rebel masculinity is taken to comically absurd extremes of civil unrest and he-man violence. The issue becomes how rebellion is framed around masculinity and conformity around femininity. In contrast to Sam, Freddie is a nerd, a tech geek, and a dedicated student. As per stereotype, he is also a wimp whose lack of masculinity owes extensively to being dominated by a highly repressed and repressive mother (an issue to be returned to shortly). Nevel Papperman, one of Carly's frequent antagonists, is also an audio-video expert and computer genius who runs his own "Nevelocity.com" website specializing in snarky commentaries on pop-culture trends. Essentially the evil and more effeminate incarnation of Freddie, Nevel also has an unrequited crush on Carly and his ongoing feud with "iCarly" stems from Carly's refusal to kiss him (and like Freddie, Nevel also has a domineering mother). However, while Nevel is explicitly a heterosexual, the character is played as a mincing homosexual stereotype, and the social performance of gender on iCarly exists within a strictly heterosexual order. Nevel (effeminate boy) and his behavior, usually described on iCarly as "creepy" or "super creepy," becomes decidedly opposed to Sam (masculine girl) as the local troublemaker and Freddie (less-than-masculine boy) as the accomplished nerd.[9]

## Who Are Parents?

> Carly: Some people pay attention to their parents.
> Sam: Losers. — "iQuit iCarly" (2009)

Spencer Shay is the primary adult on *iCarly*, although "adult" is something of a misnomer as Spencer frequently acts *more* immature than Carly, Freddie, and even Sam. A law-school dropout, Spencer produces and sells kitsch Pop-Art sculptures (i.e., "playful" postmodern avant-garde rather than "confrontational" Dada avant-garde). He is also the stereotype of the artist as an eccentric, energetic non-conformist rather than the "artist-as-sissy." In "iMust have Locker 239" (2009), Spencer engaged in a heated debate with a dour woman art teacher over whether the production of art is a process of "spontaneity" (Spencer/the male) or "discipline" (the art teacher/female), although by the end of the episode they reached a compromise by making out.

To be sure, there are definite qualifications on Spencer's masculinity as far as recent sitcom criterion. Spencer is inept in athletics, has no talent as a rock musician, and his forays into industrial arts inevitably result in fires or other household calamities. Like Freddie, Spencer is a science-fiction fanatic. In "iParty with Victorious," Carly and her friends discovered Spencer — *much* to his embarrassment — was in a book club, a pastime which Carly specifically pointed out "isn't the manliest thing in the world." Instead, Spencer's masculinity (as well as his Hipness) is primarily constructed through the "eternal teenager" stereotype. In "iChristmas" (2008), Spencer built an electric Christmas tree that caught fire and destroyed their presents. Enraged, Carly wished Spencer was "born normal," only to have the wish temporarily granted by a Christmas angel. Spencer became a strict, church-going lawyer engaged to Mrs. Benson, Carly and Sam never became friends because Spencer would not let Carly associate with her (hence, "iCarly" does not exist), and Carly's boyfriend was none other than Nevel Papperman. In short, Spencer became a Square adult and Carly's life was much the worse for it.

Given Spencer's immaturity, Carly not only manages her own life but often acts as the head of the Shay household and the parental authority figure for both Sam and Spencer (the two primary "males" of the show). As Jonathan Dees noted, "Carly is living out two fantasies at once; she gets to elude her caregiver's restrictions and do whatever she wants, and she also gets to be the caregiver."[10] In other words, the primary "adult" in the main cast of *iCarly* is Carly. Occasional disputes occur when Spencer exercises his power over Carly as the legal guardian and trumps Carly's "head of household" status. Moreover, higher parental authority is not completely absent in the Shay family and represented in a crucial way. Carly and Spencer's father is a colonel stationed on a submarine. He periodically "appears" on *iCarly* via phone calls but his voice is not heard, while the viewer only hears Spencer and Carly responding to him. What becomes a conspicuous absence is *any* mention of Spencer and Carly's mother on the show; she is non-existent and, in the end, simply negated. To this extent, Carly as the well-adjusted teenage girl is the product of a *male*-dominated family structure (brother, father, grandfather).[11]

The opposite occurs with the gender-maladjusted Sam and Freddie, where the Puckett and Benson families are run, or *ruined*, by "bad mothers." Like Carly's mother, there is virtually no mention of Sam or Freddie's fathers on *iCarly* and all three are living in a single-parent family structure, a situation increasingly common for adolescents over recent decades (although having divorced parents is implied rather than explicitly stated on *iCarly*).[12] Moreover, the maternal parental authority figures are far from the effective parenting ideal. As briefly noted, Mrs. Benson dominates, emasculates, and infantilizes Freddie to the point of Oedipal pathology. In "iMove Out" (2009), Freddie rebelled and got his own place, the elevator room atop the Bushwell Plaza apartment complex where he and Carly live. As irate as Mrs. Benson was with Freddie for moving out, she was equally enraged with Carly for being an object of Freddie's affections and getting his "boy chemistry all out of whack." In "iSaved your Life" (2010), Freddie was injured while saving Carly from being hit by a truck, an incident Mrs. Benson attributed to Carly's "bubbling hormones and all that R&B music [teenage girls] listen to." Carly developed a crush on Freddie and Mrs. Benson caught the two of them kissing. Horrified, she loudly blurted "*What the yuck*?!" After chasing Carly out of the room by beating her with a pair of Freddie's underwear, she doused him with disinfectant spray.

Sam is also the product of a single-mother household, although the parental apathy is antithetical to Mrs. Benson's parental tyranny. Numerous episodes have suggested Sam's mother is "white trash," meaning extremely promiscuous, frequently in legal trouble, and possibly chemically dependent and/or mentally ill. In 2010, Sam's infamous mother was finally featured on-camera ("iSam's Mom"). In an overall rarity for *iCarly* as well as some inspired type-casting, Sam's mom was played by a well-known guest star: Jane Lynch, best known as the tough, malicious cheerleader coach Sue Sylvester on *Glee*. Like Carly, Sam is essentially raising herself; unlike Carly, the absence of *male* parental guidance is producing a "momma's boy" as a tomboy juvenile delinquent.

These gender and parental politics manifest certain contradictions as far as *iCarly*'s status as Nickelodeon's leading "girl power" sitcom, specifically in comparison to the previous sitcoms created by Dan Schneider. While *Drake and Josh*'s overt representation of Hip-Square politics was around the title characters, the male order was internally undermined by the subversive girl power exercised through direct action by Megan Parker. With *Zoey 101*, the show's primary conflict was between Zoey Brooks (community anchor) and Logan Reese (individualist disturbance). On *iCarly*, the ostensible valorization of girl power is undercut by the primacy of the masculine at two levels. One is the representation of Sam's masculine-Hip rebellion versus Freddie's feminine-Square conformity, and especially what amounts to Nevel's "gay" antagonism.[13] Second is though the representation of the *patriarchal stability* of the Shay family versus the *matriarchal dysfunction* of the Benson and the Puckett families. In this framework, reading *iCarly* strictly in terms of feminism or postfeminism proves difficult. The underlying empowerment message of *iCarly* is neoliberalism, with messages of developing and maintaining *individual independence and exercising self-determination* against myriad forces of institutional "repressive powers" ranging from parents, school, corporations, and mass culture.

## Question Authority

As much as parents—at least as far as *mothers*—are satirized on *iCarly*, adult authority in general is treated with derision. On *iCarly*, Ridgeway High School is populated by despotic teachers like Mr. Howard and Ms. Briggs ("brigs" also is a term for military jails). As conservative stereotypes, they are humorless, uptight Squares with authoritarian personalities. Conversely, Mr. Henning functions as the liberal stereotype and is equally Square; he is a woefully out-of-touch hippie whose solution to twenty-first century postindustrial problems is returning to a 19th-century agrarian lifestyle. In "iGo Nuclear" (2009), Spencer recounted that when he went to Ridgeway, Mr. Henning was already "a freaky weirdo who smelled like rotting wood."[14]

The key exception is the school principal Ted Franklin, an African-American who serves as Ridgeway's answer to Barack Obama. ("Ted Franklin" can also be referenced to two of America's more politically progressive presidents, Theodore "Teddy" Roosevelt and Franklin Delano Roosevelt). As the Hip "head of state" of the high school, Mr. Franklin emphasizes restraint, tolerance, and egalitarianism.[15] The disordered situation of "iHave My Principals" (2009) occurs when Mr. Franklin is fired for conduct unbecoming to a school principal after he appears on "iCarly." Mr. Howard and Mr. Briggs are appointed co-principals and promptly turn Ridgeway into an Orwellian totalitarian order. When the Ridgeway students decide to organize in an effort to have Mr. Franklin reinstated, he emphatically informs them that he does not endorse their efforts. Nevertheless, the students engage in a well-planned morning of collective civil disobedience against the new school administration. It ends when an irate Mr. Franklin appears, severely reprimands the students, and promptly restores order. Impressed, the school superintendent reinstates Mr. Franklin; in turn, Mr. Franklin expresses his deep appreciation to Carly, Sam, and Freddie for their efforts.

The episode can be read at two levels. First, Ted Franklin represents the ideal of adult authority that respects the students and, in turn, is respected by them. He understands the difference between providing productive guidance and exercising counterproductive control—a difference that most of the adults on *iCarly* are unwilling or unable to grasp. (As discussed in the following chapter, this same representation of adult authority becomes a recurring message of *True Jackson, VP*). As a political metaphor, Ted Franklin is the neoliberal-democratic leadership ideal who governs minimally and, when he does, governs effectively. A second and related message is the importance of teen power as a force of political action. The Obama campaign learned a valuable lesson in twenty-first century national political campaigning with the abrupt collapse of Howard Dean's presidential run in 2004. While Dean built a successful cyberspace campaign organization to the point of being considered the frontrunner, his disastrous showing at the Iowa caucuses effectively killed his candidacy overnight. His legion of bloggers and on-line fundraisers failed to "show up" as far as the necessary political participation needed to ensure campaign victory by making their presence known at the level of grass-roots politics. The year 2008 represented a crucial change in American politics as political action and information technologies were effectively merged by the Obama campaign. In terms of Nickelodeon's ideology marketing of teen empowerment around individual initiative and community involvement, the focus of *iCarly* is the changing nature of political action within the scope of computer and internet technology, cultural production and consumption, and "consumer citizenship."

## DYI Culture

> We embrace technology, but [*iCarly*] also makes fun of getting too into it.[16] — *Dan Schneider*

Youth culture has always insisted on defining itself as not only separate but *opposed* to the older Establishment. In the 1960s counterculture, the operative term was "underground" with outlets like comic books, films, newspapers, and radio stations providing "oppositional culture." While virtually all the rock bands of the era recorded for major labels, to avoid potential accusations of selling out (not always successfully) bands routinely pushed the envelope as far as content (obscenity, explicitly political lyrics, etc.). Festivals and free concerts were offered as mean to bring the music and the message to the people. In the punk explosion of the 1970s, the operative term was "Do It Yourself" (DYI). The preferred venue was the club rather than the concert hall, and scores of independent labels and fanzines emerged to distribute musical product and critical discourse outside the record and media industries; however, many punk bands signed to major labels and independent labels often had distribution deals with established record companies.[17] By the 1980s, Reaganism and Thatcherism signaled a pronounced right-wing shift in Western politics. The new ethos became "subversion from within," exemplified by Madonna and the New Pop movement embracing consumerism, postmodernism, and "polished product" as forms of cultural opposition.

Nonetheless, all these strategies and tactics were constrained by reliance on radio, TV, cinema, albums, cassettes, and print media (magazines, fanzines). Cable TV and VHS technology that emerged in the 1980s offered forums for

DYI culture with personal video cameras and local public-access programs. The problem was that these shows were rarely able to extend their production and distribution reach *beyond* the local or regional level. By the twenty-first century, unprecedented advances as well as overall affordability of personal computers, audio-visual gear, musical instruments, and recording equipment vastly increased the potentialities for DYI cultural production. As important, computers and the internet made it possible for people to self-distribute as much as self-produce culture to a potential global audience. On *iCarly*, computers and the internet are a means of production and consumption for teen "DYI culture" that can potentially operate "outside" the margins of corporate mass culture; a "democratized" or, to use Gilles Deleuze's terminology, "deterritorialized" teen DYI culture that is crucial to individual empowerment, community formation, and even "nation building."

In *iCarly*'s premiere episode ("iPilot," 2007), Carly takes the blame for a Sam prank and receives detention, a Saturday at school videotaping the school talent-show auditions. She enlists Freddie as cameraman and forces Sam to share her punishment. Most of the auditions are dreadful attempts at popular entertainment (stand-up comedy, rap music) or high culture (Continental theater, classical music, ballet); the lone bright spot is a girl who plays trumpet while jumping on a pogo stick.[18] The auditions are posted on "SplashFace" (*iCarly*'s version of YouTube) as "Talent Show Auditions" for Ms. Briggs to review, and inadvertently includes a recorded break in the auditions when Carly and Sam ridicule Ms. Briggs and her "crazy, pointed boobs." Mistaken for a new on-line comedy show, "Talent Show Auditions" receives scores of positive comments from viewers. Far less complimentary is Ms. Briggs. As Carly puts it, "I just hate it when adults like her get to control what kids can do or see — it ticks me off!" Carly conceives a weekly live webshow starring her and Sam, Freddie acting as cameraman and the technical producer, and, most important, "No adults to say, 'You can do this, you can't do that.' We can do whatever we want. *Say* whatever we want." Calling the show "iCarly," they convert the upper floor of the Shay apartment into a small broadcast studio and feature the kids excluded from the Ridgeway talent show for their premiere webcast, which garners over 30,000 viewers. Teen empowerment is achieved through DYI culture produced by and for teens, and the "iCarly nation" is founded.

Whereas *Hannah Montana*, *True Jackson, VP*, and *Big Time Rush* feature well-known mainstream adult performers as "guest stars," *iCarly* minimizes their presence. The notable exceptions included Jane Lynch in "iSam's Mom," Jack Black as an obsessed science-fiction on-line gamer in the *iCarly* special "iStart a Fan War" (2011), Kenan Thompson playing himself in "iParty with Victorious," and Michelle Obama's *iCarly* appearance could be added as well.[19] *Hannah Montana*, *True Jackson, VP*, and *Big Time Rush* also place a stronger emphasis on a "necessary" role of adult authority in teenager's lives, and the strategy of limiting the adult guest stars is consistent with *iCarly*'s emphasis on representing "autonomous" teenagers and teen culture. One of *iCarly*'s more high-profile guest stars was Lucas Cruikshank, the teenage creator-star of the highly successful, self-produced on-line comedy show *Fred*.[20] In "iMeet Fred" (2009), Freddie's less-than-glowing, on-air assessment of *Fred* was followed by Cruikshank announcing he was discontinuing the show, resulting in an "iCarly" backlash. When Cruikshank finally met with Carly and her friends, he revealed his role in the "feud" was a well-conceived publicity stunt to generate internet buzz and boost the viewership for *both* webshows. Cruikshank then appeared on "iCarly" to announce a peace agreement between the webshows, and premiered a new *Fred* comedy short starring himself in his "Fred Figglehorn" persona with Carly, Sam, Freddie, and Spencer appearing as his co-stars.

Over the course of i*Carly*, the "iCarly" webshow has built up a following of a million viewers and made Carly, Sam and Freddie internet celebrities, even "stars." If "iCarly" is *deterritorialized* teen culture, the ongoing battle is preventing "iCarly" from becoming *reterritorialized* by corporate capitalism and the domain of the Culture Industry. Put differently, the struggle is preventing "iCarly" from becoming mass culture or simply selling out, which served as the basis for "iPromote Tech-Foots" (2008), "iTake on Dingo" (2009), and "iCarly Saves TV" (2008). In "iPromote Tech-Foots," Daka Shoes signs "iCarly" to a $100,000 contract to promote their new Tech-Foot line on their webshow. Tech-Foots also have numerous and considerable defects, such as falling apart when they get wet and bursting into flames if they sustain sudden impact. After Daka refuses to refund their money, dissatisfied "iCarly" fans begin a boycott of the show, with the issue compounded by Daka refusing to release "iCarly" from their contract. In retaliation, Carly and Sam engage in subversion from within and sarcastically "promote" Tech-Foots on "iCarly" in order to reveal their considerable flaws until Daka agreed to not only fully refund the money of Tech-Foot purchasers but buy out the contract with "iCarly" for $30,000. The message is that an internet community of ticked-off teenagers can defeat an unscrupulous multinational corporation.

Considering the rivalry between Nickelodeon and Disney Channel, Disney became the target of satire with "iTake on Dingo." The writers of the "Dingo Channel" teen sitcom "Totally Teri" start blatantly stealing sketches from "iCarly" webcasts. More specifically, Carly and her friends learn of the Dingo Channel's actions from a classmate, who pointed out she only noticed it because her "little brother" watches the Dingo Channel, constructing Hipness around age distinctions within the audience of adolescent culture consumers (i.e., Hip "iCarly" versus Square "Dingo Channel" tweens and teens). A subsequent scene depicts Carly and Sam watching "Totally Teri" with *extremely* pained expressions in order to gauge the extent of Dingo Channel's pilfering of their webshow. For added measure, the Teri character can be heard explaining that she has a plan that involves wearing a wig so no one will recognize her, a sardonic reference to *Hannah Montana*. Carly and her friends travel to Hollywood and ultimately put a stop to the plagiarism by kidnapping the frozen head of dead studio founder Charles Dingo and holding it for ransom in exchange for Dingo Studios' guarantee that they will respect the creative and intellectual property of "iCarly" (recorded on video for insurance) as well as forcing the head writers of "Totally Teri" to appear on "iCarly" in bikinis and throw dog food at each other.

The cold opening of "iCarly Saves TV" shows the programming head of the TVS network noticing his tween daughter watching "iCarly" on-line rather than what she pronounces as his "lame" teen sitcom pilot. TVS offers Carly and her friends their own network show, which proves to be a disaster as "iCarly" is quickly converted into standardized kiddie-show based on executive decisions, creative consultants, and focus groups. Zeebo, a dinosaur character, is added to the cast because "our research shows kids love dinosaurs!" Freddie is demoted to a TVS errand boy. Sam is fired for her "pushy and aggressive" personality and replaced by teenage TV star Amber Tate, who is equally pushy and aggressive off-camera but sweetness and light on-camera. Carly angrily complains that the show "isn't even 'iCarly' anymore" and the TVS executive agrees. The scene cuts to Carly, Sam, Freddie, and Spencer in the Shay living room, freed from their TVS contract and watching the final product that emerged out of the experience: a teen sitcom starring Zeebo and Amber Tate performing the *exact* same scene from the pilot the TVS executive's daughter initially termed "lame." As important, "iCarly Saves TV" concludes with "iCarly" returning to independent on-line broadcasting on its own terms and outside the control of the TV oligopoly.

By championing DYI teen culture that utilizes the potentialities of computer age technology to independently self-produce and self-distribute shows and *their* culture, "iCarly" is presented as oppositional by its very status as a show done by and for teenagers and, above all, teen culture *produced and consumed outside the system*. Yet the glaring contradiction of *iCarly* is its celebration of teen culture produced from "the outside" while it is ultimately a teen sitcom — and a fairly traditional classical sitcom at that — produced within the Culture Industry and the TV oligopoly. This entails another problematic binary *iCarly* constructs between "authentic" teen culture that teens take pleasure in consuming versus the corporate "teen mass culture" that they don't want to consume, and take little if any pleasure in if they do consume it. In "iFix a Pop Star" (2010) Carly, Sam, and Freddie salvage the career of boorish, idiotic, has-been pop star Ginger Fox, clearly meant to represent Britney Spears; they realize her entire career has been the result of record producers, audio-visual technicians, and various other behind-the-scenes handlers because she has no "talent." Overtly, the episode reiterates the standard criticisms of "manufactured" First Wave Teen Pop as inauthentic teen culture.[21] The not-so-hidden message of "iFix a Pop Star" was promoting Miranda Cosgrove's musical career and her rival brand of Second Wave Teen Pop.[22] The world premiere of the music video for Cosgrove's first single "Kissin U" from her debut CD *Sparks Fly* aired during the premiere of "iFix a Pop Star," constructing a contrast between the highly unflattering depiction of Britney Spears (albeit as "Ginger Fox") and Cosgrove as a new and improved brand of teen pop.[23]

As noted, "iTake on Dingo" was a satirical attack on the Disney Channel, and more implicitly, *Hannah Montana*. In "iOMG" (2011), Carly and Gibby's school science project was a chamber in which they could monitor responses to stimuli. Using Spencer as the test subject, they began with stimulus that was "mildly irritating" by playing Radio Dingo and a parody of a Hannah Montana song which Spencer found "horrible" rather than "mildly irritating." The episode "iKiss" (2009) began with Carly and Sam seeing "The First Kiss," a teen chick film with capsule reviews from Sam ("Same as every other stupid teen chick flick") and Carly ("It made me embarrassed to be a teen chick"); the subsequent "iCarly" skit parodying the genre was called "Kelly Cooper: Terrible Movie." The subplot of "iPity the Nevel" (2011) was a satirical "iCarly" sketch of the teen vampire genre which made Freddie the object of attraction for every teenage girl in the neighborhood, provided he stayed in character as the brooding teen vampire he played in the parody.

Considering its status as a preeminent "girl power" sitcom, *iCarly* frequently represents "lame" teen mass culture around the *feminine* and, by extension, utilizes depreciatory stereotypes of the teen culture audience around the *female* cultural consumer (meaning girls and effeminate boys).[24] Carly and her friends were saddled with Mandy Valdez, a fanatical "iCarly" fan who embodied the tween girl-as-teenybopper stereotype, in "iAm Your Biggest Fan" (2008) and "iWant My Website Back" (2009); they were held hostage by crazed teenage "iCarly" fan Nora Dershlin in "iPsycho" (2010). As much as "iStart a Fan War" was a blanket attack on nerds and geeks, the episode included cameos by *Drake and Josh*'s Eric Blonwitz and Craig Ramirez, still a nerd "gay couple," as well as *Zoey 101*'s resident geek Stacey Dillsen as devout fans of the "iCarly" webshow. This subtext of audience representation around "iCarly" becomes the means by which *iCarly* manufactures its own imagined audience ideal of the "iCarly nation" as consumer citizens who are as cool and Hip versus the geeks, nerds, and Squares, pejoratively represented as their fan base "Others."

## Community and Capitalism: "iBeat the Heat" and "iSell Penny-Tees"

> I see nothing wrong with taking advantage of the stupid.— *Sam Puckett, "iEnrage Gibby" (2010)*

The locale of *iCarly* is Seattle, generally perceived as one of America's leading progressive liberal/neoliberal cities. In this setting, Carly Shay represents Pacific Northwest Hip as opposed to California Hip (Drake Parker on *Drake and Josh* or Beck Oliver on *Victorious*), NYC Hip (Alex Russo on *Wizards of Waverly Place* or True Jackson on *True Jackson, VP*), or even Middle America Hip (Miley Stewart on *Hannah Montana* or Kendall Knight on *Big Time Rush*). As important, in the 1990s Seattle was the epicenter of a musical scene that produced Nirvana and the "grunge bands" which became synonymous with the slacker generation.[25] As suggested in the previous chapter, Clintonism and Nickelodeon shared a certain affinity, if not necessarily a direct relationship. The New Democrats, led by Bill Clinton, represented a concerted shift away from traditional American liberalism — and its working class and minority constituencies— to neoliberalism and rebranding the Democratic Party around the younger generation as well as the white middle class. At the same time, Nickelodeon's brand identity as a "kids only" network entails marketing *anti-slacker* empowerment messages as far as the individual and collective agency of teenagers.

In this context, *iCarly* can be read as endorsing teen empowerment, and even teen rebellion when warranted, provided it is channeled into *productive* social change (e.g., "iHave my Principals" or "iPromote Tech-Foots"). The dialectic is constructed between Sam as a Hip delinquent slacker and Freddie as a Square industrious nerd. As the embodiment of the Nickelodeon anti-slacker ethos as well as girl power, Carly serves to effectively synthesize Sam's unfocused rebel élan with Freddie's considerable technological prowess. The end result is a successful enterprise with the "iCarly" webshow as independent, internet-based DYI culture production that can empower teens to subvert and even change the system for both fun and profit.

However, *iCarly* also offers much more ambivalent critiques of American society entering the twenty-first century. In "iBeat the Heat" (2010), Seattle is mired in a record heat wave while Carly is diligently working on a school project for Mr. Henning's class, an elaborate model of a future city that also "promotes good old-fashioned community values" (as noted, Mr. Henning is a befuddled hippie and *iCarly*'s liberal stereotype). Sam has no absolutely interest in the assigned project, and uses Mr. Henning's instruction sheet to dry off her armpits. When a blackout occurs, Spencer fortuitously owns a portable generator which allows them to keep the air conditioner running. Over the course of "iBeat the Heat," many of the recurring characters from past episodes converge in the Shay apartment to take advantage of the air conditioning (one of them, a teenage malcontent named Chuck, wears a "U.S.A." T-shirt). Moreover, as head of the building's safety committee, Mrs. Benson brings all the senior citizens to the apartment; Sam derisively refers to them as "the antique parade." They prove particularly vexing to Carly in that they pose a considerable threat to the safety of her model by aimlessly fiddling with it or setting their drinking glasses on it. Sam simply puts the elderly to work by making them massage her neck for five minutes in exchange for one minute of personal access to the air conditioner. With the apartment unbearably overcrowded, tempers begin to flare, past feuds are rekindled, and new conflicts erupt. Parodying a Frank Capra film, Carly stands on the kitchen counter and gives an impassioned speech, accompanied by generic "stirring" music on the soundtrack:

> You see that big thing on the floor there? That's a model of a utopian society. My teacher wanted me to build it to show in America we can have cities that are modern, but old-fashioned at the same time: the kind of America our grandparents lived in, where people knew their neighbors and cared about them.... Shouldn't we be using this as a chance to make friends, to start really getting to know each other and —

Carly's speech is abruptly curtailed when someone flings the door open and announces the power is back on. The building residents, up to that point visibly moved by Carly's speech, promptly stampede out of the apartment. "Community" is quickly forgotten once individual interests can again be sustained. For added measure, the episode ends with Carly's model utopia accidentally destroyed. Freddie has a potential and, only for lack of a better description, "Amazonian" girlfriend named Sabrina who is meeting him for the first time after video chats. After their neighbors exit the Shay apartment, Sabrina is momentarily blinded by a spray of lemon juice and tramples Carly's model with her high-heeled shoes.

The problematic of "iBeat the Heat" is the target of the satire. On one hand, it can be read as an indictment of the individualization and privatization of (post)modern American life. On the other, it can be read as a commentary on traditional ideals of community that are becoming anachronisms amid the sweep of technological changes. Yet the ideal of community per se is not rejected. Given the overall slant of *iCarly*, the message seems to be that new conceptions of effective community must develop out of changing technological conditions rather than technology adapting to traditional ideals—which perhaps never really existed in the first place beyond ideological myth. Carly's urban-utopian model of the future conforming to "old-fashioned community values" is also founded on "old-fashioned contradictions" between individualism and community which escalate until it ends up as so much rubble. To be sure, "iBeat the Heat" suggests an underlying conservatism in that the failed project of a utopian society is conceived by a liberal hippie, and the teenage girl is ultimately the destroyer of future civilization. However, as the "voice" of the community, Carly is quite serious about the political significance of her utopian model, whereas the Bushwell residents represent the American public as a cross-section of gender, race, and especially generations (i.e., "the antique parade"). They are not only oblivious to the importance of the model, in the end they prove they simply don't care. They "live" the contradiction by taking advantage of the Shays, exhibit the proper emotional response generated by Carly's inspiring plea for community, and then vacate the first moment they can resume their individual lives. Once the ideological rupture is revealed, Sabrina acts as the outside, cataclysmic force of girl power and unintentionally annihilates the model.[26] In the end, a utopian community of tomorrow built on the ideological imaginary of today is inherently doomed.

While "iCarly" generates a wealth of media visibility, it does not generate regular monetary income ("iPromote Tech-Foots" notwithstanding). The Shay apartment in downtown Seattle is more or less a two-floor house with its own freight elevator and one of the rooms on the upper floor converted into what amounts to a small TV studio for "iCarly" broadcasts with all the necessary audio-visual technology. Yet rent and the numerous expenses are never an issue. Like the representation of the family unit where Carly is rarely told what to do as a kid and frequently tells everyone else what to do as the "adult," the economic world of *iCarly* is also one of pure teen fantasy in which any and all consumer wants are fulfilled and money is simply there to spend. While *True Jackson, VP* staunchly valorizes work and work ethics, *iCarly* treats it with surplus derision. Indeed, if neoliberalism is predicated on consumer "buying power," the depiction of work and "earning power" is highly problematic on *iCarly*.

As noted in "iHeart Art," Spencer receives a highly negative appraisal of his sculptures from an artist he admires and briefly quits the art business, finding true unhappiness working as a dental technician. Likewise, in "iOwe You" (2008) Sam's reckless spending and mounting debts to Carly and Freddie forces her to get a job at a local chili restaurant where her work duties largely consist of being getting yelled at by customers and cleaning the restrooms (again, at a chili restaurant). The episode "iGot a Hot Room" (2010) begins with Spencer building a lamp sculpture for Carly's birthday, and inevitably starts a fire that destroys Carly's bedroom. Through a stroke of financial luck, one of the lost items was an antique watch, the insurance settlement for which totals $82,000. Spencer uses the entire sum for a massive makeover of Carly's bedroom while Carly, unaware of the pending remodeling and obviously not enamored with Spencer, gets a job at the Groovy Smoothie. When Spencer asks her how her first day of work was, Carly issued a succinct and curt reply: "*Stupid.*" Of course, Carly and Spencer happily reconcile once the new bedroom is revealed; as important, Carly now has what is effectively her own, eminently Hip loft within the Shay apartment.[27] Gibby provides the episode's ironic lesson with a rhetorical question: "Is there anything money can't do?" The implicit addendum was that while money can indeed do anything, working to earn money is "stupid."

The episode "iSell Penny-Tees" (2010) was *iCarly*'s most overt and concerted critique of capitalism. An "iCarly" segment serves as a cold opening with Carly and Sam auctioning off props seen on previous webcasts as fan memorabilia. The most lucrative item proves to be the "Penny-Tee" which sells for over $300. (To note, "Penny-Tees" are T-shirts with *non-sequitur* expressions printed on them and commonly worn by the main characters on *iCarly*). Aware of a potentially vast profit margin, Carly, Sam, and Freddie decide to start a Penny-Tee business. Initially, Carly and Freddie apply craft labor and happily make each shirt by hand. Sam has apparently skipped work until she arrives with almost 100 completed Penny-Tees, and then proudly shows Carly and Freddie her secret to Penny-Tee mass production: she converted the basement of Bushwell Plaza into a sweatshop employing fourth graders as child labor, paying them five dollars per day, along with a free lunch of dumpster refuse or pet food.

Seeing the extent of Sam's managerial mistreatment and tyranny, Carly and Freddie are aghast and an argument erupts over the exploitation of labor. The work force is divided by half, with Carly and Freddie talking their workers to the Shay apartment where they are provided with extended breaks, ice cream, and receive double their previous wages, pre-paid through the month. Sam's oppressed workforce downstairs eventually revolts and quits en masse, but the situation also deteriorates upstairs because the coddled work force refuses to do any work, prompting Carly to fire them. A negotiation session is held at the Groovy Smoothie, where Sam apologizes for her conduct and Carly and Freddie also apologize for sending the wrong message that work is just about "having fun" (also antithetical to *True Jackson, VP* and the message that work and fun are highly compatible and mutually productive). Ostensibly, there is a validation of the management ideal as a boss who is tough but fair and the worker ideal as someone who merits respect but knows his/her place in the production process. The mixed message is liberal as far as labor maltreatment and conservative as far as the need for no-nonsense workplace management. Nevertheless, the message sustaining traditional labor-management relations is quite sardonically undercut. The fourth graders decline the offer to come back to work, having learned a valuable lesson about capitalism. However, it is not a lesson in the inherent contradictions of capitalism, or even ethical capitalism, but *cutthroat* capitalism. The fourth graders simply stole the idea and are now mass producing and marketing their own line of Penny-Tees, effectively putting the "iCarly" line out of business. In the end, the joke is on Carly, Sam, and Freddie, and the lesson learned is that if you want something done right — let alone not get swindled — "Do It Yourself."

## *"Post-American Society" and Politics as Usual*

While *iCarly* is not a school-centered teen sitcom like *Saved by the Bell*, *Zoey 101*, or *Victorious*, the representation of Ridgeway High School is pivotal as far as framing the show's politics. As noted, Ridgeway is dominated by equally ineffective *liberal* teachers (the hopeless hippie Mr. Henning) and *conservative* teachers (the abrasively authoritarian Mr. Howard and Ms. Briggs). The exception is the school principal Ted Franklin, who calmly runs Ridgeway as the leadership ideal of moderate-to-progressive democratic order (à la Barack Obama).[28] However, American politics have been *anything* but unified since the 2008 election. Instead, the liberal-conservative polarity of American politics had become more and more toxically divisive.

In this context, "iBeat the Heat" and "iSell Penny-Tees" represent Carly as the bleeding-heart liberal and Sam as the hard-hearted conservative. This political binary is also reflected in how Carly and Sam are represented as Hip. At one level, Carly Shea represents the Nickelodeon model teenage consumer citizen, and Sam Puckett the slacker antithesis. Carly is individualistic but not irresponsible, intelligent but not intellectual, metropolitan but not cosmopolitan, economically secure but not rich. Sam is rebellious, streetwise, uncouth, and lower class. Put differently, Carly is white middle-class and Sam is white trash, with Carly represented as liberal "Seattle Hip" and Sam, in effect, as conservative "Southern Hip." This distinction bears directly on the cross-marketing of Miranda Cosgrove and Jennette McCurdy as teen-pop performers. Cosgrove is well within the Second Wave Teen Pop sound highly influenced by 1980s New Wave, while McCurdy is a New Country teen-pop singer.[29] Cosgrove's brand of New Wave teen pop is associated with an assumed audience of white, middle-class, metropolitan, young females; McCurdy's New Country teen pop has an assumed audience of white, rural, lower-class Southerners and Middle Americans. Also *assumed* in this distinction is that Cosgrove's audience tends toward the liberal while McCurdy's audience is conservative.[30] There is a manufacture of "political image" as well as "public image" in the characters of Carly and Sam and the cross-marketed teen pop music product of Cosgrove and McCurdy which becomes inseparable.

Ultimately, *iCarly* can be read as positing a kind of "post-classical liberalism" for the "post–American society" in the twenty-first century (i.e., postindustrial, postmodern, and postfeminist). The struggle is between intrepid individuals (the teenagers) versus an administrated daily life dictated by economic and political institutions (the adults). Yet, if *iCarly* can be seen as an updated valorization of the classical liberal model, *iCarly* is ultimately unable to break from the traditional liberal-conservative binary. Carly Shay is "blue state" whereas Sam Puckett is "red state."

# 7

# *I Have a Dream Job:* True Jackson, VP

## Working Together: The Obama Era and the Teen Sitcom

If art imitates politics, on November 4, 2008 Barack Obama was elected the first African-American president, and on November 8, 2008 *True Jackson, VP* (henceforth *TJVP*) premiered on Nickelodeon, starring Keke Palmer in the title role.[1] One obvious difference between *TJVP* and Nickelodeon's other post-2004 girl-power teen sitcoms (*Zoey 101*, *iCarly*, and *Victorious*) was that True Jackson was African-American. However, *TJVP* was also unlike many teen sitcoms in that the focus was on the workplace, with school second and home/family life a distant third. In this context, *TJVP* can be read as Nickelodeon's immediate response to the Obama-era of American politics as the attainment of, to borrow Oprah Winfrey's term, the "African-American Dream." Nonetheless, *TJVP* was also indicative of the consistently problematic gender, generational, and Hip-Square politics of Nickelodeon's teen programs.

While Dan Schneider and Scott Fellows have been primary developers of teen sitcoms for Nickelodeon since 2004, *TJVP* was created by Andy Gordon (also a *TJVP* writer and executive producer). Gordon previously worked on several primetime shows, notably the workplace sitcom *Just Shoot Me!* (NBC, 1997–2003). Primarily set in the offices of a fashion magazine called *Blush*, conflicts centered on devil-may-care, sexist publisher Jack Gallo and his daughter Mia Gallo, a committed feminist and journalist working at *Blush* out of economic necessity rather than career choice. In effect, *Just Shoot Me!* was built around Jack and Mia's ongoing workplace gender and generational political battles; these areas of friction were reiterated but decidedly reconfigured on *TJVP* as a teen sitcom. Credited as a *TJVP* producer and the director of several *TJVP* episodes, Gary Halvorson directed episodes of sitcoms ranging from *Friends*, *Everybody Loves Raymond*, and *Two and a Half Men* (like *TJVP*, all shows well within classical sitcom conventions).[2] Dan Kopelman was a *TJVP* executive producer and writer who also worked on various network sitcoms, the best known being *Malcolm in the Middle*.[3]

At certain levels, *TJVP* manifested a more traditional sitcom world-view than its Nickelodeon contemporaries, specifically Dan Schneider's teen sitcoms. As discussed in the previous chapter, *iCarly* offers an almost contemptuous representation of adult authority figures and their often counterproductive role in managing kids' lives. On *TJVP*, there was a far more positive representation of adults as productive authority figures; they often provided the useful advice to the teenage characters and, in doing so, relayed a given episode's overt message to the teen audience rather than the teenage main characters. Not unrelated, another difference was *TJVP*'s representation of work. On *iCarly*, work and adherence to the traditional work ethic is a guarantee for daily misery, although entrepreneurialism by any means necessary is a much more problematic issue. On *TJVP*, there was an ideological revision of the traditional work ethic as a synthesis of adolescent irrepressibility and adult decorum into what could be termed "productive fun" that required learning personal responsibility and self-management skills—and here it bears mention that *TJVP*'s assumed audience was adolescents entering or soon to enter the workforce for the first time.

While *TJVP* was conservative in these respects, in other ways it was arguably Nickelodeon's most liberal teen sitcom, especially in terms of identity politics and multiculturalism. As a girl-power sitcom, the main character True Jackson and her best friend, Lulu, were independent, intelligent, and Hip. (How they managed to work full-time corporate executive jobs *and* go to high school at the same time was not explained, but social realism isn't a priority of most teen sitcoms). They were also "Others" as far as race — True an African-American and Lulu an Asian-Pacific American — in an otherwise predominately white cast of characters.[4] Moreover, True's boyfriend, Jimmy Madigan, and Lulu's boyfriend, Mikey J., were both white. In this way, interracial teen romance was, for lack of a better term, "no big deal," at least as far as white males dating non-white females.[5]

Another regular character on *True Jackson, VP* was Oscar, the office receptionist at Mad Style fashions. Oscar was the only African-American adult male in the regular *TJVP* cast and as openly gay as a character could be within the confines of a teen sitcom. In one episode Oscar wore a "Frankie Say Relax" T-shirt for casual day at work, the reference being Frankie Goes to Hollywood and their hit song "Relax," an ode to gay sex. In episodes in which he did not appear, Oscar's absence was usually explained by him being on a "cruise." Max Madigan, the founder and CEO of Mad Style, had a somewhat "flamboyant" comportment that suggested a gay stereotype (one supposes because he was a mogul in the fashion business) although Max was heterosexual and married to the librarian at True's high school. As much as Max and Oscar were the two primary adult males on *TJVP* and both designated as Hip characters, they also fell outside sitcom conventions in having a kind of "non-masculinity" that would cast them as stock objects of mockery (e.g., *Home Improvement, The*

*King of Queens, According to Jim,* or *Two and a Half Men*). They also differed from teen sitcoms that use thinly disguised homosexual stereotypes to represent a "gay" otherness *opposed* to the status quo (Eric and Craig on *Drake and Josh* or Nevel Papperman on *iCarly*). Indeed, Max, Oscar, Jimmy, and True's clueless slacker friend Ryan Laserbeam all served as various counters to the normative masculinity in teen sitcoms represented by the likes of Zack Morris, Drake Parker, Kendall Knight, and even girls like Sam Puckett and Alex Russo.[6]

Overall, *TJVP* lends itself to being read as a New Democrat teen sitcom, especially the episode "Class Election" (to be discussed shortly). The problematic of *TJVP* was that the liberal-identity politics were marginalized by the show's overarching representation of American economic life, where work and fun are two sides of the same coin and social mobility was all but a given if someone exercised enough self-determination. *TJVP* was not a sitcom that preached political tolerance like Norman Lear's 1970s sitcoms; rather, political tolerance was the by-product of "working together" and the Great Melting Pot was not school (*Zoey 101*) or the internet (*iCarly*), but the world of big business.

## True Success

In the *TJVP* premiere episode ("Pilot," 2008), True Jackson is immediately presented as a motivated, entrepreneurial teenager with a summer job selling homemade sandwiches out of a portable cooler in the business district of New York City, as opposed to punching the clock and working the line at a local fast-food chain. She has a fortuitous encounter with Max, who notices True is wearing Mad Style clothing but that it looks different; True unapologetically explains she altered them to her own tastes. Impressed with True's attitude as much as her fashion sense — as well as realizing Mad Style may be out of touch with teenage female consumers — Max promptly offers True a job as vice-president in charge of youth apparel.[7]

The move comes much to the resentment of Mad Style head fashion designer Amanda Cantwell, and True's first day of work quickly becomes contentious when Max asks True for her opinion about Amanda's new line of business wear. With her usual candor, True suggests that the clothes are too dull and need panache as far as colorful accouterments. "*Just because its work doesn't mean it can't be fun,*" True explains (emphasis added) — a cogent summation of *TJVP*'s central ideological message. Max agrees and assigns True the job of modifying Amanda's new clothing line. Needless to say, the move infuriates Amanda, who quickly makes True the office pariah. To compound the pressure, True's redesigned clothes are inadvertently thrown in the garbage and badly soiled.

Overwhelmed, True decides to quit Mad Style when she encounters Jimmy, Max's teenage nephew, who works there delivering the office mail. When True dejectedly comments how terrible her first day is going, Jimmy explains that working at Mad Style and coping with the daily office politics is just like being in high school. Jimmy's observation becomes True's epiphany. Entering the workplace is not one's initiation into the intimidating world of adulthood. Rather, the workplace is simply an adult version of high school and can be treated as such. Put differently, True can choose to act like a mature adult even though she is a teenager, whereas her adult co-workers often act like immature teenagers. True also realizes that she must toughen up to succeed in the workplace. In order to have someone she trusts at Mad Style, True fires her company appointed assistant and replaces her with Lulu. Despite all the obstacles, Max enthusiastically approves True's modifications, and on her first day on the job True successfully establishes herself as a respectable business executive.

On *TJVP*, True represented the "model worker" who took her job seriously and expressed that dedication through hard work, innovative ideas, and pragmatic adaptability to situations while still keeping the job pleasant for herself and her colleagues. In contrast, Amanda represented everything wrong with a workplace where success is not "earned" but gained by ingratiation, intimidation, and office gamesmanship. In "Amanda Hires a Pink" (2009), Amanda hires True's high school nemesis and "mean girl" stereotype Pinky Truso (Jennette McCurdy from *iCarly*) after learning Pinky greatly frustrates and even frightens True. According to plan, Pinky's presence has an extremely detrimental effect on True's work performance to the extent that True is woefully unprepared for a sales meeting with an important client. After Oscar reminds a distraught True that her career success stems from meeting her own standards rather than worrying about the standards of others, True confidently improvises a sales pitch about an "Uncommon Couture" line that convinces the notoriously discriminating buyer to increase his initial purchase from 1,000 to 5,000 dresses. The ethical form is situation (Amanda attempts to sabotage True's work performance) → action (Oscar gives True a pep talk on self-determination) → situation (True achieves success in the workplace). Amanda even concedes to Pinky that True's record of accomplishments is "not luck, it's something else. An open mind, a refusal to be daunted.... It is exhilarating to watch her sometimes, how she manages to turn problems around and create something amazing." Indeed, True Jackson was the teen sitcom personification of the Horatio Alger myth: the pragmatic and plucky rugged individual who makes "Uncommon Couture" out of a botched workplace assignment. The recurring message of *TJVP* was that work is not something to be feared but enjoyed, and that someone can quickly and easily scale the corporate ladder in the process.

## Obama Girls (or, "Colored People")

Barack Obama's election hardly marked an end to racism in America; indeed, race as a political issue has since become much more openly divisive.

Perhaps inevitably, *TJVP* addressed not only the politics of race but Hipness. In the aforementioned pilot episode, Amanda's new line of drab business clothing has the advertising slogan "Black is the new black: black is back!" After True points out the lack of style and the need for some multi-colored accessories, Max agrees that the clothes are "too safe" and coins his own slogan for the line incorporating True's suggestions: "Put some color in your week!"[8] *TJVP* premiered the same week that Obama was elected president, which not only represented a realization of the "African-American Dream," but an African-American getting the ultimate Establishment job. This tension is configured with Amanda (Square) and her "black is back" line of workplace clothes. They are serviceable but signify a serious "strictly business" mentality. In other words, the clothes may be "black" but they still come off as Square. In the context of the 2008 presidential campaign, it was the officious "Square" tendencies of Obama which were frequently criticized as elitist and out of touch with the public. Conversely, True (Hip) thinks the business clothes are fine in black but need "color." What they lack is a sense of exciting Hipness, the quality instrumental in Obama's electoral victory, especially in comparison to GOP candidate John McCain as the stiff personification of Square desperately trying to appear Hip.

In this context, *TJVP*'s most overtly political episode was "Class Election," which first aired in October 2010, approximately two weeks before the midterm elections. Student Council elections are pending at True's high school, and Kyle Sandbox is running unopposed. The blonde-haired, lily-white Kyle kowtows to the teachers, performs his job as hall monitor with authoritarian zeal, and is running on a "stay the course" platform. In short, Kyle is the conservative candidate. After a nasty hallway confrontation, True decides to run against Kyle, motivated more by competitive spite than any commitment to school. After Lulu declines to be her running mate, True selects her friend Shelly; the situation is soon complicated when Lulu inadvertently convinces Mikey J. to run for student council president, and Lulu agrees to be *his* running mate.

While Kyle has a lock on "the jock vote" and True and Mikey J. are splitting the "Brainiac vote," a gender gap has formed within the student body with True the clear favorite among the girls. Pandering for their votes, Kyle selects the rude, self-centered, and vacuous Kelsey as his running mate (read: Sarah Palin). The choice comes much to the displeasure of Kyle's devoted lackey Harvey Mymen, who is livid because he was promised the running-mate slot (read: Tim Pawlenty).[9] In the debates just prior to the elections, Mikey J. bores the students with fact-supported initiatives about healthier school lunches and tackling the school budget. Kyle accuses Mikey J. of hating their high school and labels him "a Communist." True and Shelly opt for style over substance, with their debate responses being sung or rapped slogans that thrill the student body but offer little in the way of specific policy. After Lulu gives an impassioned speech about how the school isn't perfect but they can make it better by working together, True is humbled. True wins the popular vote and Kyle is suspended from student council for trying to rig the election at the last minute, and True's first presidential act is resigning so that Mikey J. and, more specifically, Lulu can run the Student Council. True realizes that work can and should be fun, but politics needs be taken quite seriously.

To be sure, "Class Election" was a cultural discourse for a specific historical moment. On the eve of the 2010 elections, the episode was a thinly disguised reenactment of the 2008 election that offered a highly unflattering representation of the GOP campaign, reminding viewers why McCain lost as much as why Obama won. However, the episode cannot be reduced to a simple "Vote Democrat!" message, and presented as a problematic representation of the Obama campaign, if not Obama himself. As suggested, Obama's success in 2008 owed what might be called his "calm, cool, and collected" balancing act around the Hip-Square binary, despite accusations that his Hipness was limited to stirring but superficial speeches while his intellectualism and perceived elit-ism tagged him as Square. In this way, True's debate performance represented the criticisms directed at Obama's Hipness as exhilarating but empty rhetoric and Mikey J.'s debate presentations the criticisms directed at Obama's Square side as arid and academic. On the eve of the 2010 elections, Lulu delivered the message pertinent to the now in a rational yet passionate way as the "Hope candidate" and the new guiding force for the student body. In reality, the Democrats were trounced and, coincidentally or not, *TJVP* was all but officially canceled by early 2011.[10]

## Having Fun Yet?

At the ostensible level, *TJVP* can be read as representing Hipness within a set of binaries. Ethnic was hipper than white, female was hipper than male, liberal was hipper than conservative, adolescent was hipper than adult, and gay, if not hipper than straight, could be as Hip as straight. However, this becomes a problematic interpretation as far as *TJVP* being a Nickelodeon teen sitcom with the requisite "kid power" and "girl power" agenda versus the show's representation of adult authority and gender difference. In both of these respects, the underlying message of *TJVP* was an ideological representation of *fun*.

To be sure, True Jackson was the main character of the show and in several episodes voiced the overt message. In "Saving Snackleberry" (2010), a dinner party True organizes for Max to impress his upper-crust friends becomes a fiasco when Lulu books Snackleberry, an extremely rundown version of TGIFs. Moreover, the famous cellist True planned for the evening's entertainment is now retired because he is weary of trying to fulfill audience expectations. A snooty socialite incessantly complains about the evening, and True finally loses her temper and tells her to "back off" (in an adult sitcom, one can assume the word "bitch" would have been used at some point). When the cellist makes a surprise appearance and is joined onstage by the Snackleberry staff for an evening of jug-band music, everyone enjoys an evening of unpretentious fun. The cellist explains he decided to perform after True told him that her career success stems from the fact that she does what she does and what people think is "their own dang business" (he exercised self-determination); the socialite admits that the evening was the best dinner party in recent memory (she dropped the pompous bourgeois attitudes). Nevertheless, True apologizes to the socialite for "mouthing off."

Rather than *TJVP*'s overt teen-power message being undercut by a hidden message of "respect for elders," *TJVP* posited the ideal of "bipartisanship" as far as teens and adults getting along, showing mutual respect, and learning from *each other* as far as reaching amicable solutions to situational problems. *TJVP* represented adult authority as potentially productive rather than purely counterproductive, and the positive representations of adult authority can be read as an endorsement of a useful and even necessary role for "paternalistic power." On *TJVP*, it was not so much "power from above" that was inherently objectionable, but power from above when it *dictated* rather than *educated*.

Another issue became gender representation. In "Pajama Party" (2010), True is revealed to have a highly competitive streak to the point that her family and friends let her win at board games for years rather than endure her wrath when she loses. When Amanda crashes True's slumber party and they engage in an extremely heated game of "Llama-Llama-Land," True realizes she and Amanda have something very much in common and, as True puts its, something "ugly." True's mom (guest star Vivica A. Fox) explains that over the years they let True win because "we didn't want you to lose your drive to succeed" but quickly adds a disclaimer that functions as the episode's overt message: "A person isn't measured by how many wins they have; it's how they handle their losses." Yet in keeping with the almost standardized sitcom representation of the mother, True's mom was a hot-tempered, highly intimidating controller and True's underlying character flaws things she gets from her — evidenced in "Pajama Party" when True's mom wonders aloud where True got such a bad temper and then mercilessly berates True's dad over the phone.

The recurring message of *TJVP* was the necessary equilibrium between fun and seriousness as the formula for success in life in work, school, even leisure time. In many domestic sitcoms prior to the 1990s, middle-class men were represented as highly serious in both public life (work) and private life (home); examples include *Father Knows Best, Leave It to Beaver,* or even *The Cosby Show,* where underneath his cloying "inner child" routine Cliff Huxtable (Bill Cosby) was extremely serious when it came to the importance of higher education, economic responsibility, and enforcing his own status as head of household. Since the 1990s and a multitude of sitcoms—*The Simpsons, Home Improvement, The King of Queens, Yes, Dear, Still Standing, According to Jim,*

*George Lopez, Two and a Half Men,* etc.— the ability, desire, even the "need" to have fun is represented as a masculine/adolescent characteristic whereas over-bearing seriousness is represented as a feminine/adult attribute to the point of a predictable essentialism which *TJVP* conformed to as well.[11]

At one level, *TJVP* tended towards representations of "dumb white guys" who lacked the Hipness that True, Lulu, and Oscar "naturally" possessed as the Mad Style "Others." Despite being Hip in the pilot, Jimmy Madigan became considerably less Hip in subsequent episodes. An earnest but hopelessly incompetent drummer (in other words, a white guy with no rhythm), his efforts as a rock musician were abysmal. However, the biggest dent in Jimmy's Hipness— or what made him more of a Square — was taking his low-level job way too seriously. Ryan did not even work at Mad Style but constantly hung around the offices and goofed off for no other reason than that he apparently had nothing else to do with his life. Extraordinarily lazy and quite stupid, Ryan functioned as *TJVP*'s slacker stereotype. Conversely, Amanda epitomized the deadly serious worker, and True had more in common with Amanda's "ugly" side than she'd like to admit in that her competitive drive to *succeed* could veer into a relentless desire to *win*. In these respects, the supporting roles of Max (white male adult) and Lulu (ethnic teenage female) became crucial in framing *TJVP*'s synthesis of fun and work.

In "True Secret" (2010), Max holds "Carnival Day" at Mad Style, replete in ringmaster outfit and a range of sideshow booths and games set up around the offices. When Max sees True and Jimmy kissing, they admit they are dating in violation of company policy prohibiting employee romantic relationships. Max is actually pleased that they are a couple, but one of them has to quit their job by the end of the day. Given his job dedication, Jimmy thinks True should quit, while True, working in her "dream job," thinks Jimmy should quit. The inevitable fight ensues, but True decides to quit her job, only to learn that Jimmy already tendered his resignation. The couple is reunited in the fact that they chose each other over their jobs, and Max admits that "Carnival Day" bombed because he was "trying to raise company morale and making my two happiest employees miserable at the same time." Max announces that *he* is resigning, but quickly agrees with True's suggestion that simply ending the Mad Style no-dating policy is the more feasible solution, and in doing so, succeeds in making the workplace more fun after all.

To be sure, Max was quite eccentric and childlike (as opposed to being childish like Doug Heffernan on *The King of Queens*), and Mad Style was a representation of the workplace as Max's "paedocracy." While he injected a great deal of play into the daily work routine, Max also had enough business acumen to have built an international clothing firm and enough common sense to deliver constructive advice to a distressed teen when they needed a course of action amid a disordered situation, which is to say Mad Style was Max's "pedagogic regime" as well. Max represented the hard-working adult who also understood the place for adolescent/male-coded fun in the workplace, which Ryan always took too far and Jimmy usually didn't apply enough. In turn, True represented the fun-loving adolescent who also understood the necessity of adult/female-coded seriousness in the workplace, which Amanda always overdid and Lulu frequently failed to grasp. In "Mad Rocks" (2010) Ryan offends Lulu when he tells her she has the potential to join him and some unmotivated workers in the secret Mad Style "Do Nothing Club." Aware she can often appear to be a "do nothing" at work, Lulu volunteers to organize the annual Mad Style "Mad Rocks" charity fashion show. After True's clandestine attempts to micromanage Lulu's efforts unintentionally undermine her efforts, Lulu angrily tells True to organize Mad Rocks herself. The episode's transformative action is a talk between Lulu and Max. He is on vacation but monitoring the events at the office via "Max-Cam," a camera helmet and radio worn by Amanda throughout the episode. While Amanda has no interest in Lulu's predicament, she relays Max's advice that Lulu should not be discouraged that True didn't trust her, and instead should work even harder than give up. True also profusely apologizes to Lulu for not trusting her and asks for her help, unaware that Lulu already and single-handedly organized what proves to be a stellar fashion show at the last minute. Lulu learned the value of hard work while True learned the importance of friendship over business.

The recent cultural discourse of work and the workplace has tended towards two representations. One is where work is anything but fun and the employee's best option is to divorce oneself from it as much as possible (e.g., the 1999 film *Office Space* or the sitcom *The Office*); the other is where work is anything but fun and the employees should put forth their best efforts to achieve dominance over their co-workers (e.g., the 2006 film *Employee of the Month* or the TV reality show *Hell's Kitchen*).[12] As a teen sitcom targeting adolescent viewers as the emerging workforce, *TJVP* served as another competing cultural discourse where fun, friendship, and hard work were inherently related and mutually productive within the ethical form of the sitcom and the ethical capitalism of progressive neoliberalism.

# PART THREE

---

# Pop Goes Teen Culture

*It is no accident that tonality was the musical language of the bourgeois era.* The harmony of the universal and the particular correspond to the classical liberal model of society. As in the latter, tonality as the *invisible hand*, took over by means of the individual, spontaneous events, and over their heads. The universal resolution of tension that is effected is intended to make the sum, the balance of credits and debts, come out even. Homeostasis, balance, and the equivalency credits and debts are immediately the same. *This model was never adequate to reality, but was to a large extent ideology.—Theodor W. Adorno, "Difficulties" (1966, emphasis added)*

More than colors and forms, it is sounds and their arrangements that fashion societies. With noise is born disorder and its opposite: the world. With music is born power and its opposite: subversion. In noise can be read the codes of life, the relations among men. Clamor, Melody, Dissonance, Harmony; when it is fashioned by man with specific tools, when it invades man's time, when it becomes sound, noise is the source of purpose and power, of the dream — Music.—*Jacques Attali,* Noise: The Political Economy of Music *(1975)*

# 8

# The Birth of the Pop-Music
# Sitcom: The Monkees, the Archies,
# and the Partridge Family

## Bubblegum: Music and the Masses

In the period from 1966–74, all three of the major networks at the time embarked on TV projects in which a pop band was integral to the show: the Monkees (*The Monkees*; NBC, 1966–8), the Archies (*The Archie Show*; CBS, 1968–9), and the Partridge Family (*The Partridge Family*; ABC, 1970–4). While often critically, and not necessarily incorrectly, assessed as a means by which the TV industry crassly manufactured bands to cross-market into popular music (the limitations of this line of argument to be considered later), these shows and the music associated with them was also engaged in a problematic project of ideology marketing.

During the 1960s, America was in political crisis. Rock music became a primary generational signifier of teens and young adults, serving as the demarcation point between anti–Establishment youth culture and Establishment adult culture. While it is far too common and convenient to romanticize the rock music of the era, specific texts were an effective document of the times, which is *not* to say "timeless music." Jimi Hendrix's version of "The Star-Spangled Banner" at the Woodstock festival still sounds like the aural equivalent of flag burning. Infused with electronic distortion, amplifier feedback, microtonal bends, copious "sour notes," and an absence of rhythmic meter (exacerbated by Mitch Mitchell's free drumming punctuations), Hendrix's rendition of the national anthem achieved disconcerting new meaning in the context of Vietnam.[1] Captured best on their live album *Kick Out the Jams* (1969), the MC5 were a brutal, high-volume collision of garage rock, free jazz, and explosions of feedback. Malcolm Russell suggested that the MC5 "formed a far more apt soundtrack for the urban riots and student unrest of late 1960s America than the drippy flower power of the West Coast."[2]

Bubblegum rock was a competing discourse to the more "confrontational" strains of rock music, originating as a critical and marketing term to describe a specific pop-rock musical genre. Highly popular throughout the 1960s and the early 1970s, bubblegum emphasized cloying three-minute songs, standardized verse-chorus structures, danceable rhythms, cheery harmonic settings, catchy vocal melodies ("the hook"), and lyrics confined to the pleasures and, less often, the pains of romance. Indeed, the sheer sweetness of bubblegum rock was blatantly announced by the product as well as the genre itself. Two famous bubblegum hits were "Yummy, Yummy, Yummy" by the Ohio Express and "Sugar Sugar" by the Archies (both released in 1968); one of more popular bubblegum bands of the era was the 1910 Fruitgum Company.[3] As far as the teen pop of the era, the Jackson Five and the Osmonds were highly popular "bubblegum" bands fronted by Michael Jackson and Donny Osmond, respectively.[4]

It was not coincidental that the Monkees (at least early on), the Archies, and the Partridge Family were considered bubblegum bands. More correctly, they were bubblegum *brands* created by the TV industry to cross-market into pop music. The pandering to commercialism aside, while 1960s bubblegum seemed like so much musical fluff it was ideological in two respects. As Adorno contended, tonality was itself the product and producer of ideology, the signifier of capitalism's "invisible hand" and liberal democracy's system of checks and balances as far as resolving dissonance. Popular music, including rock, operates well within the ideological constraints of Western music: a vertical "class" hierarchy of a dominant melody supported by dissonance-free — which is *not* the same as "noise-free"— harmonic structures and anchored by stable metered rhythm.[5] The overtly syrupy organization of sound into bubblegum pop music signified idyllic social organization, especially in relationship to *The Partridge Family*'s representation of a socially harmonious America at a time where social *disharmony* was rampant.

The second (and not unrelated) issue is bubblegum music and mass culture. In his essay "On Popular Music" (1941), Adorno could very well be writing about bubblegum:

> The music, as well as the lyrics, tends to affect ... a children's language. Some of the principal characteristics are: unabating repetition of some musical formula comparable with a child uttering the same demand.... The limitation of melodies to a very few tones, comparable to the way in which a small child speaks before he has the full alphabet at his disposal; purposely wrong harmonization resembling the way in which small children express themselves in incorrect grammar; also certain over-sweet sound colors, functioning like musical cookies and candies. *Treating adults as children is involved in that representation of fun is aimed at relieving the strain of adult responsibilities.*[6]

As Adorno reiterated throughout this passage, the form and function of popular music as mass culture is *infantilization*, both in terms of musical production and audience consumption, and in this context one can return to John Hartley's problematic assessment of TV as "paedocratic" as opposed to "infantile" (see Chapter 5). In many ways, popular music similarly "paedocratizes" listeners through "a fictional version of everyone's supposed childlike tendencies." Rock music glorifies (male) adolescence as individualistic, anti-authority behavior with examples ranging from the Who's "My Generation," Alice Cooper's "Eighteen," the Clash's "Stay Free," and the Undertones' "Teenage Kicks." It was not coincidental that recent sitcoms featuring adult male main characters as "eternal teenagers" explicitly tied this representation to a passion for rock music (*School of Rock* being another matter in its own right). In a none-too-subtle example, *The King of Queens*' episode "Whine Country" (2000) depicted Doug making a mix tape for an upcoming road trip and adding a classic rock staple, Steppenwolf's "Born to be Wild." Doug's friend Spence, the epitome of the "femme" American male (tech geek, science-fiction fan, etc.), mentioned his favorite song is "Too Shy," a hit in the 1980s by the British New Pop band Kajagoogoo. On *Still Standing*, Bill and Judy Miller both behaved like immature "guys" and were devout fans of classic rock with one of their favorite bands being AC/DC — also a slang term for bisexuality. On *George Lopez*, George was a devotee of hard rock and an amateur guitarist; in his youth, he was a long-haired "metalhead" who dreamed of becoming a rock star: a dream that was largely crushed by his emasculating mother.

The Ramones are considered anything but "bubblegum," at least as far as the term becomes equated with musical product for teenybopper audiences. The Ramones are synonymous with punk rock and teenage rebellion; they are also part of the classic rock canon and received a Lifetime Achievement Grammy Award in 2011 (the contradictions of the Ramones and their centrality to *School of Rock* to be addressed further in Chapter 10). Yet the Ramones were as influenced by bubblegum as much as the proto-punk of the MC5 and the Stooges, and in many ways the Ramones *were* a bubblegum band infused with jackhammer tempos and chainsaw-guitar riffing. *Punk* magazine co-founder Legs McNeil recounted:

> [The Ramones] played the best eighteen minutes of rock & roll that I have ever heard. You could hear Chuck Berry in it ... and the second Beatles album with all the Chuck Berry covers on it. When the Ramones came offstage we interviewed them, and they were just like us. They talked about comic books and sixties bubblegum music and were really deadpan and sarcastic.[7]

When punk exploded on the popular music scene in the mid–1970s, it was hailed as subversive and even revolutionary, and the claim had some validity as far as punk antagonism and minimalism acting as a competing discourse to the stagnation and pretension of rock music during the 1970s. The problem was that punk was highly traditionalist if not retrograde, and offered a great deal of accessibility in its celebration of the old rather than any confrontation of the new (an issue also returned to in Chapter 10). Paul Hegarty recognized the problem with the Ramones specifically: "The incredibly short, loud, repetitive tracks could work as a kind of noise, but ... the formula makes it too easy for an audience."[8] This "formula" was not simply the lineage of 1950s and early 1960s rock music like Chuck Berry, the Beatles, and bubblegum. What inhibited the potentially subversive noise was *tonality* and *meter* in the sing-song melodies and an unwavering backbeat, while an eight-note barrage filled in for harmony within conventional song structures.

Nonetheless, bubblegum is frequently dismissed (if not disparaged) in rock's critical discourses precisely because it is deemed an "immature" and "innocuous" musical product appealing to the trivial concerns and bad taste of an assumed audience of *female adolescents*. The convenient loophole for the male rock consumer and critic is that bubblegum can be appreciated as "well-crafted" as opposed to "manufactured" pop music; it can also be consumed as a kitsch "guilty pleasure" by acknowledging its alleged inferiority but salvaging it through a camp or cheese aesthetic. In this way, the term "bubblegum" becomes far more nebulous in describing a specific genre through *musical classification* of cultural producers and much more explicit about describing an imagined audience of cultural consumers through *audience differentiation*. More specifically, bubblegum becomes a rhetorical term used to designate and distinguish disparate brands that constitute "authentic rock" appreciated by equally authentic fans (the Beatles, Led Zeppelin, the Ramones, Nirvana) versus divergent brands of "inauthentic pop" bought by equally inauthentic consumers (Britney Spears, Hannah Montana, the Jonas Brothers, Justin Bieber).

As discussed with *iCarly,* the cross-marketing of Miranda Cosgrove and Jennette McCurdy into the pop-music market constructs an imagined audience as a certain demographic for musical as well as ideological marketing signified by the respective characters they play on the show. Carly Shay (Cosgrove) is downtown, middle-class white whereas Sam Puckett (McCurdy) is rundown, lower-class white trash. Cosgrove's brand of Second Wave Teen Pop — highly influenced by 1980s New Wave and power pop — is equated with an imagined audience stereotype of white, middle-class teenage girls ("teenyboppers"). As a New Country teen pop performer, McCurdy's brand of teen pop brings with it stereotypical presuppositions in its imagined audience being predominately white, Middle American conservatives ("hicks").[9] At the same time, and even though they are stylistically different, both Cosgrove and McCurdy can be dismissed as the "bubblegum" musical product by teenage girls for teenage girls. Miley Cyrus's demands for self-determination in the quasi-industrial stomp of "Can't Be Tamed" or the pulverizing Eurodisco-meets-grunge of "Robot" are a far cry from Justin Bieber pining away for his girlfriend in the smooth, white soul-teen pop setting of "Baby." Yet because they are both teen pop performers with a predominately female tween/teen fan base, both can be consigned to bubblegum status. But as far as maintaining one's Hipness, it is probably safer to admit to liking Justin Bieber more than Miley Cyrus.

# The Pre-Fab Four: The Monkees

The Beatles were the most popular rock band in the world during the 1960s and branched off into feature films with *A Hard Day's Night* (1964) and *Help!* (1965). Both films were directed by Richard Lester, who employed unorthodox camera work and editing more akin to French New Wave cinema than classical Hollywood musicals. In 1966, Bob Rafelson and Bert Schneider sold NBC a sitcom project very much derived from the Beatles-Lester films, a show about four young men in a rock band and their weekly misadventures with the added incentive that a pop band could also be manufactured and marketed in conjunction with the TV show.

The first step was hiring the principal cast. The legend around the Monkees is that the group was assembled through a cattle-call audition of hundreds of aspiring actors and musicians. In fact, the Monkees were not newcomers to the entertainment industry. An experienced actor-singer from England, Davy Jones appeared on Broadway in 1964 as the Artful Dodger in the musical *Oliver!* (Jones was nominated for a Tony). Jones was also among the cast members that performed selections from *Oliver!* on *The Ed Sullivan Show* the same night the Beatles made their legendary American TV debut, which Jones pinpointed as the moment he decided to make a career move from musical theater to popular music. Micky Dolenz was also a singer and TV actor who played the title role on *Circus Boy* (NBC, 1956–7, ABC, 1958; billed as "Mickey Braddock"). The two other Monkees were not actors but musicians working the L.A. folk-rock circuit. Guitarist-singer Michael Nesmith, whose song "Different Drum" became Linda Ronstadt's first hit single in 1967, had little interest in acting but auditioned for the show; he reportedly impressed Rafelson because of his highly indifferent attitude. Multi-instrumentalist Peter Tork was recruited for the show after being recommended to the producers by Stephen Stills.[10]

Not only did the Monkees mimic the Beatles as far as pop-music product and the visual style of their films for the sitcom, they essentially adopted the same public images generated around the Beatles. Jones was the cute one (Paul McCartney), Dolenz was the funny one (Ringo Starr), Nesmith was the defiant one (John Lennon), and Tork was the quiet one (George Harrison). Jones was also the designated teen idol and Dolenz the comic relief, and they tended to dominate the TV show (Dolenz's manic style and constant mugging could make Jerry Lewis appear to be a master of restraint in comparison). However, Nesmith and Tork did not function as the balance as far as musical product. The Monkees' production team of musical director Don Kirshner and songwriters Tommy Boyce and Bobby Hart exercised creative control over the musical production, and Dolenz was assigned the bulk of lead vocal duties, save for some singles reserved for Jones. Moreover, and what became a point of considerable controversy, most of the backing tracks were done by studio musicians. The Monkees' involvement on the early record releases largely amounted to vocals, sporadic musical contributions, an occasional Nesmith or Tork composition, and their faces on the album cover. In fact, use of studio musicians on rock records was a fairly common practice at the time. The Beach Boys albums of the era, specifically the canonical *Pet Sounds* (1966), were recorded by a team of session musicians under the direction of the Beach Boys' leader Brian Wilson while the rest of the Beach Boys were on concert tours, who then added vocals to completed musical tracks. Nevertheless, the Monkees were widely and often virulently singled out for criticism and deemed "inauthentic" by the rock press.

Nesmith particularly resented the lack of musical involvement, and the situation reached a head in 1967. After two chart-topping albums, Nesmith led a Monkees mutiny and they demanded creative control over the future albums, which meant playing their own instruments, final song selection, and production oversight. A highly acrimonious battle ensued between the band, Kirshner, and the Monkees' label, Colgems Records.[11] Kirshner ultimately resolved the impasse for everyone when he authorized the release of a Monkees single with a B-side not approved by the band, a direct violation of their contract with Colgems; facing possible legal action by the band, Kirshner was fired. The Monkees made a resolute effort to move away from their bubblegum origins and towards a more contemporary West Coast psychedelic rock sound with decided country-western, folk, and R&B influences (e.g., the Byrds, Country Joe and the Fish), although they certainly did not move into avant-garde musical territories (e.g., the Mothers of Invention or the Velvet Underground). The sitcom and especially *Head*, their infamous foray into cinema, were another matter.

Hailed for its (then) innovative and unorthodox approach, *The Monkees* won the Emmy for outstanding comedy series for its first season. *The Monkees* also pioneered the contemporary sitcom format by utilizing fast-paced non-continuity editing, disorientating camera zooms, optical effects, non-diagetic inserts, and fast-motion filming. The weekly musical performances, usually intended to showcase a current or pending single release, might be inserted into the show at any point: a staged band performance, live concert footage, or the song used as a soundtrack for a madcap chase sequence during the show. There was on-camera improvisation, self-reflexive commentary, direct address to the camera, and flubbed takes. One of the more inspired moments came in the penultimate *Monkees'* episode "The Monkees Blow Their Minds" (1968). It began with Mike Nesmith dressed to resemble Frank Zappa and guest star Frank Zappa dressed to resemble Mike Nesmith. "Zappa" (Nesmith) railed against the triteness of the Monkees' music while "Nesmith" (Zappa) issued feeble justifications. Nesmith's fake nose repeatedly fell off during the mostly improvised exchange.

*The Monkees* quickly earned the kudos of the counterculture elite. John Lennon hailed the show as the counterculture answer to the Marx Brothers. Dr. Timothy Leary, the "high priest" of the Psychedelic Revolution, was effusive in his praise:

Oh, you thought it was silly teenage entertainment? Don't be fooled.... At early evening kiddie-time on Monday the Monkees would rush through a parody drama, burlesquing the very shows that glued Mom and Dad to the set during prime time.... And woven into the fast-moving psychedelic streams of action were the prophetic, holy words. Mickey [*sic*] was rapping quickly, dropping literary names, makings scholarly references; then the sudden switch to the reality channel. He looked straight at the camera, right into your living room, and up-leveled the comedy by saying: "Pretty good talking for a long-haired weirdo, huh, Mr. and Mrs. America?"[12]

While Leary's hyperbolic review needs to be taken with a grain of salt (or something more pharmaceutical), the points are worth noting. *The Monkees* was the first TV show to feature counterculture young people as the stars, rather than the stock "bohemian" or "hippie" stereotypes on mainstream sitcoms that served as the butt of jokes for the viewing pleasure of Establishment adults. As four young adults living on their own yet acting like teenagers, *The Monkees* made the adult Establishment the target of the jokes. Yet in saying that the Monkees acted like teenagers, this was a vastly different representation than the eternal teenager stereotype that currently dominates American popular culture. Defining the generation gap on primetime TV in the 1960s, the Monkees were irreverent, intelligent, and Hip whereas older adults were humorless, moronic, and Square. As important, the anti-adult and anti–Establishment politics were manifest in the willful violation of classical sitcom conventions and parody of the standard TV shows and genres.

What the TV series hinted at, and the final few episodes began to deliver, was achieved with considerable overkill in the Monkees' feature film *Head* (1968). The film was directed by Bob Rafelson, who co-wrote the screenplay with Jack Nicholson (allegedly in a marijuana-fueled weekend writing marathon), and had as much affinity to Jean-Luc Godard as the Lester-Beatles films. A concerted effort to demolish the Monkees project and self-criticize their Culture Industry creation, *Head* as a deliberate act of "career suicide" was manifest in the opening minutes of the film with the Monkees jumping off the Golden Gate Bridge followed by a psychedelic underwater sequence modified with intense color threshold effects. To bring the film full circle, *Head* ends with a reprise of the underwater sequence which dissolves into the Monkees trapped in a large aquarium on a flatbed truck being driven onto the Columbia Studios lot. In between the opening and closing of *Head*, there is no narrative. Instead, the film is a collection of disconnected, fragmentary sketches that do not begin or end, but abruptly start and stop. Along with the caustic internal attack of the Monkees phenomenon, *Head* took a highly pronounced and strident stance against the war in Vietnam. One memorable montage sequence consisted of the infamous film footage of a South Vietnamese Army officer shooting a suspected Viet Cong member in the head intercut with screaming teenage girls at Monkees concerts.

*Head* was a colossal commercial and critical disaster, the accompanying soundtrack album also sold poorly, and the failure of *Head* marked an irreversible and fairly rapid downward slide. NBC canceled *The Monkees* in 1968, if for no other reason than no one seemed interested in continuing the show. The Monkees wanted to be a rock band and Rafelson wanted to make films. Within the confines of the traditional comedy-variety show, *The Smothers Brothers Comedy Hour* (CBS, 1967–9) became the highly controversial battleground of youth culture and left-wing politics. Meanwhile, NBC struck "counterculture comedy" gold with the debut of *Rowan and Martin's Laugh-In* in early 1968, in which the traditional comedy-variety show format, mildly risqué burlesque jokes, and moderate political commentary was filtered through the unorthodox formalism of rapid jump-cuts and zooms popularized by *The Monkees*. At the end of 1968, Tork left the band and Nesmith departed in 1969. The Monkees disbanded in 1970.

# Would You Like Some Sugar on That Bubblegum? The Archies

> The importance is the image of Archie, which everybody knows is good, clean, wholesome stuff.[13] — *Archie Comics CEO Michael I. Silberkleit, 2005*

In the early 1940s, MLJ Comics began publishing *Archie* (originally titled *Archie Comics*), the tepid stories of white, middle-class teenagers and their problems revolving around school and romance. As a tranquil domestic-front antidote to the WWII-themed superhero comic books, Archie Andrews and his friends proved enormously popular and, in 1946, MLJ Comics officially changed the company name to Archie Comics. An *Archie* radio show aired during the 1950s, and in the cultural and political unrest of 1968, TV beckoned.

As noted, by 1968 the Monkees franchise was well into self-destruct mode, and *The Smothers Brothers Comedy Hour* ignited a firestorm of controversy by overtly bringing counterculture music, performers, and especially *politics* to primetime TV.[14] *The Archie Show* was a half-hour animated show that began airing on Saturday mornings in the fall of 1968 (retooled versions of *Archie* shows were part of the CBS weekend morning line-up throughout the first half of the 1970s).[15] In the wake of *The Monkees* and *The Smothers Brothers Comedy Hour* becoming primetime TV counterculture forums, it was not surprising that CBS opted for Saturday mornings and the decidedly conventional form and conservative content of *Archie* to build a pop music-TV franchise with a younger target audience.[16] Indeed, *The Archie Show* offered a highly anachronistic and ideologically affirmative representation of white, middle-class American teens. Save for Betty and Veronica's medallions and miniskirts, watching

*The Archie Show* it seemed America had yet to enter the 1960s, let alone being immersed in the political crises of 1968.

Each *Archie Show* was divided into two short segments that featured Archie and his friends in various predicaments. While cartoons, they were constructed and presented along the lines of the classical sitcom style, and even incorporated a laugh track. Produced by Filmation Studios, the animation of *The Archie Show* largely replicated the visual style of the *Archie* comic books. Moreover, Filmation reused animated sequences with infuriating frequency (which is to say the imagined audience of kids was assumed to be too stupid to notice). This was especially evident in the musical performances by the Archies in the midpoint of *The Archie Show*, where the same limited number of shots depicting various individuals and the band were continually recycled throughout the song with (sometimes) changing backgrounds. Of course, the Archies' musical product was actually the work of studio musicians and singers. Fresh off his rancorous divorce from the Monkees, Don Kirshner was enlisted as the musical director of *The Archie Show* (Kirshner reportedly commented that the best thing about working in animation was that the characters couldn't talk back). One of the first songs Kirshner used for the Archies was the aptly titled "Sugar Sugar," a turgid piece of bubblegum that Kirshner originally brought to the Monkees: they rejected it. To pardon the expression, "Sugar Sugar" was sweet revenge for Kirshner, as it topped the charts for a month. In tandem with *The Archie Show*'s representation of a younger generation who were seemingly impervious (or oblivious) to the dangerous blight of the counterculture, the Archies' bubblegum music affirmed the illusion of social harmony through saccharine musical harmony.

## Get Happy: The Partridge Family

In 1970, ABC entered the pop-music sitcom market with *The Partridge Family*. Singer-actress Shirley Jones starred as Shirley Partridge, a single mom (widowed, *not* divorced) raising five children in suburban California, seeking to maintain their middle-class lifestyle amid counterculture turbulence while playing in a successful pop-rock band with her kids.[17] Like *The Monkees*, *The Partridge Family* was produced by Screen Gems, and the company was presumably in no mood for another round of production controversies, disputes, and problems that surrounded the Monkees. The initial plan was that non-musician actors would appear on the show while session musicians would serve as "the band" for the musical product. Circumstances changed when David Cassidy got the role of eldest son Keith Partridge.[18] Cassidy had aspirations of being a rock musician as well an actor, and lobbied for the job of lead singer on the Partridge Family recordings. As well as possessing highly marketable teen idol good looks, Cassidy proved to be a strong singer with a distinctive voice, and the producers agreed.

*The Partridge Family* was, and continues to be, largely reviled by critics; the music, even more so. However, it is difficult to distinguish the Partridge Family musical product as being substantially different — meaning *worse*— than much of the bubblegum and pop-rock of the era (e.g., the Monkees, the Archies, or even bands like the Turtles or the Lovin' Spoonful). A requisite song performance was written into almost every *Partridge Family* episode and done as a straight musical performance: rehearsing in the garage, recording in the studio, playing at a posh nightclub or some other mainstream venue like a city park or county fair. These numbers also served as a weekly, promotional "music video" of the Partridge Family. While some appeared in the middle of the episode, the usual tactic was to include them at the end as a musical coda and concluding statement to the episode after the sitcom had completed its ethical form trajectory, or simply forcing viewers to sit through the entire show if they wanted to see "the band" perform a song.

"Whatever Happened to Moby Dick?" (1971) begins with Shirley and Keith awakening at 5 a.m. by loud noises and what Keith suspects is a burglar. The noise of a "home intruder" is actually Danny listening to Laurie's record (at extremely loud volume) of whales in the garage. Danny explains that the "sounds" are "songs." In terms of Jacques Attali, the whales are designated as making an inherently natural "music" rather than strange disruptive "noise" outside the social order of humans. Danny, who throughout *The Partridge Family* was much more concerned with the money rather than the music the band and various side projects could produce, envisions a Partridge Family record with the band accompanied by whales as "a million dollar idea ... to cash in on the ecology movement." The rest of the family abhors the idea of exploiting whales and their "music" and unanimously rejects the plan. However, the owner of a large aquatic park is thrilled with the concept, hoping such a project could raise awareness of the plight of whales as an endangered species. Shirley agrees on the condition that all the profits go to charitable organizations saving whales, much to the disappointment Danny and band manager Reuben Kinkaid (Dave Madden).

The disorder occurs when Mr. Flicker, an unscrupulous pier owner on whose property the beached whale was rescued, claims co-ownership of the whale and demands half of the record profits under threat of a frivolous but time-consuming lawsuit (for added measure, Mr. Flicker is an uncouth Southerner). Danny is particularly bothered by the turn of events and has the epiphany of ethical as well as ecological awareness, telling his mother that meeting Mr. Flicker was like encountering himself and it felt "rotten." In turn, Shirley Partridge enlists ABC sports announcer Howard Cosell (playing himself) to conduct an ambush interview with Mr. Flicker live on national TV, effectively forcing him to sign a release on-camera guaranteeing his 50 percent of the profits will go to whale preservation.

The sitcom situation resolved, the episode concludes with a performance

Partridge Family entertainment (from left to right): Shirley Partridge (Shirley Jones), Tracy Partridge (Suzanne Crough), Keith Partridge (David Cassidy), Chris Partridge (Brian Forster), Danny Partridge (Danny Bonaduce), Laurie Partridge (Susan Dey) (ABC/Photofest).

of "Whale Song," at the marina, intercut with footage of the Partridge Family sitting on shoreline cliffs staring pensively and stock footage of whales. Shirley Jones sings lead, providing a mainstream adult credibility to the song's "hippie" environmentalist political message. Indeed, "Whale Song" is a maudlin ballad that inevitably compares to the pro-environment, MOR-folk-pop music popularized by John Denver during the 1970s. Recordings of whale sounds are mixed well into the background in "Whale Song" and, as noted, these sounds are specifically termed "whale *songs*" and a form of *music* in nature rather than communicative sounds per se (while birds are described as "singing" the sounds of cows mooing are not usually termed "cow songs"). It is through the rhetorical tactic of defining the whales as producers of music rather than noise alien to human society that their "music" and the popular music produced by humans can be synthesized into a whole rather than placed in a dialectic tension. The same domination of nature by humans the sitcom episode so stridently attack is ultimately captured in and through the music. In short, the whale sounds are not integrated into the blandness of "Whale Song" but *colonized* by it.

Unlike *The Monkees'* unorthodox form, *The Partridge Family* was done well within the conventions of the classical sitcom format, and the formal traditionalism paralleled the conservatism in the content. *The Monkees* featured a group of young men with no career goals except to be musicians. They had little, if any, guidance from adult authority figures, and those that did appear were often ridiculed rather than respected. *The Partridge Family* depicted an American family that was not severely divided along generational lines and their marked cultural tastes, but quite the opposite. Their mutual love of popular music and the economic success attained by performing together in a band as a "family business" was precisely what held them together. "Where Do Mermaids Go?" (1971) involved the Partridge Family's encounter with Jenny, a nomadic hippie.[19] Accepting an offer to stay the night at the Partridge home, Jenny compliments Keith on his family and how they are "all so together" but also feels sorry for them because they don't have real "freedom" and have to "work." Keith responds that they could have much worse jobs than being professional musicians, and the only reason his mom sanctioned the band was is in order for them to earn money to eventually put them through college. The next morning, they find a note from Jenny explaining she inherited millions of dollars when her parents died; in effect, she dropped out of Square society to live a life devoid of work and responsibility. To this end, she also left a bank book and gave the Partridges a million dollars in the hope they can attain "freedom." The money brings anything but freedom but instead initiates a flood of pushy salespeople and unappreciative friends. Shirley insists that the family give the money back, and the messages of the episode are made perfectly clear:

> SHIRLEY: There's nothing wrong with money if you work for it. It's a symbol of your labor so you can respect it, appreciate it. But if it's given to you it really isn't the same, it really isn't yours.
> KEITH: Money isn't freedom. If it were, you wouldn't be living the way you do.
> JENNY: I guess you're right — I hardly spend any money at all.
> KEITH: That's why you feel free: you do it yourself.

One message, especially in the context of the early 1970s, is a strong anti-welfare position and that money only "belongs" to someone if they work for it as opposed to having it given to them (i.e., "handouts" to "welfare bums"). The second message is that it is not Jenny's wealth that provides independence; it is her thrift and self-reliance that makes her free. When Keith states that the overt message that "money isn't freedom" the hidden message is that *work is freedom*. The conversation cuts to the Partridge Family at work and exercising their freedom as a band, performing a song at a nightclub. Jenny is happily in the audience, wearing a dress rather than jeans and a T-shirt, having learned her lesson and rejoined bourgeois society thanks to example set by the Partridge Family.

*The Partridge Family*'s recurring theme was that adults and kids could get along, as much as that had *not* happened in America in the years prior to the show's debut, nor necessarily happening across America when the show began its run. In "Dr. Jekyll and Mr. Partridge" (1971), Keith decides to assume a more active leadership role as "the eldest male" in the family, and as a better "role model" becomes more of a "father-figure." The problem is that Keith quickly becomes a Square. He forcibly exposes Danny, Chris, and Tracy to what Chris unenthusiastically terms "intellectual stuff" like classical music, modern art, and evenings at home reading the encyclopedia. He intrudes on Laurie's personal life and insists a new suitor take her to a PG movie — and *no* drive-ins. Danny devises their revenge and they give Keith more parental responsibility than he can handle. Chris and Tracy go to Keith for "career counseling" on how to become "Negros" when they grow up; Laurie inundates Keith with a fake friend's highly intimate romantic problems; and Danny makes Keith give him "the facts of life" in all of their messy details. (Danny: "Why do people go through all that trouble if they *don't* want babies?") Keith realizes that the parenting is best left to his mom, but the problem is exacerbated when Shirley and Keith catch the rest of the family bragging about the subterfuge. Humiliated, Keith retreats to the garage. After being roundly reprimanded by Shirley, the kids individually apologize. All is forgiven and things returned to normal with Keith again the Hip older brother and not the Square father-figure. This cuts to a concluding nightclub performance where pop music, *working* as a band, and Shirley's parental presence are the stuff that hold the Partridge Family together.[20]

In this way, a rather uncomfortable trajectory runs from *The Partridge Family* to both *School of Rock* and *Hannah Montana*. In all three cases, the production of music by teens is under the control of the adult, both in terms of adult authority and the adult's world-view. To be sure, the particulars were different. Shirley Partridge was a suburban mom representing the stabilizing effect of middle-class mores when she joins her kids' band. On *Hannah Montana*, Robby Stewart represented traditional Middle American values and strict parental control over his daughter, Miley Stewart, as well as being the manager and songwriter for her pop star alter-ego Hannah Montana. In *School of Rock*, Dewey Finn was the Hip teacher who represented the mythic spirit of authentic rock insurrection on a quest to enlighten a new generation of teens lest they hopelessly succumb to the inauthentic of current trends pop music and the life of Squares. What all three shared was a view that the music of the kids is best produced under the supervision (and even domination) of the adult authority figure. Moreover, rock ideology's primary tenet of individuality was the valorization of self-determination and social mobility rather than self-will and social rebellion.

While Shirley Partridge was the main character, and Shirley Jones a well-known mainstream performer, Keith Partridge and David Cassidy quickly became the show's focus and star. In "Fellini, Bergman, and Partridge" (1972), Keith and Laurie argue over some "underground" films they saw, films Laurie loved while Keith considered them amateurish and pretentious slop that in no way matched the "art" of Federico Fellini or Ingmar Bergman. He bets Laurie that he can make a better film than so-called experimental "geniuses," but his artistic vision is stymied by the prohibitive production costs which he estimates will be a whopping $15 (it was the early 1970s). Danny has the available money and agrees to produce the film, which amounts to a home movie. After a successful test screening with the family, Danny is convinced the film could be a hit and arranges a premiere in the garage, which attracts zero paying customers. Danny is greatly bothered by the financial failure, but for Keith the problem is different: "I'm not interested in the money, I'm interested in aesthetics. I want to be judged by my peers."

As far as the target audience market of "teenyboppers," David Cassidy was undeniably an early 1970s phenomenon and he soon realized that "Keith Partridge" was going to be his career albatross. What Keith Partridge asked for, David Cassidy soon after received, and the aesthetic judgment by his peers was far from supportive. Cassidy was featured in a 1972 *Rolling Stone* article written by Robin Green, "Naked Lunchbox: The David Cassidy Story," along with a cover shot where Cassidy posed in the nude (the bottom of the photo was cut off just above his groin). The accompanying interview was peppered with Cassidy's negative comments about the entire Partridge Family project, as well as Cassidy discussing his active sex life and recreational use of illegal drugs. Indeed, Cassidy's intended message was that he was all about the sex and drugs, but his involvement with the Partridge Family was constraining the rock and roll. In retrospect, it is not surprising the interview completely backfired. As Norma Coates noted, the article's intent was not assisting Cassidy in reinventing his image but ridiculing him as well as

> his teenybopper fans, and the entire television establishment and what it represents. Television, as characterized in this article, is populated and perpetuated by middle-aged producers who realize the medium is inauthentic by design, and do not care to change it. Moreover, they could not care less about rock music. Their, and Cassidy's, aesthetic malaise is implicitly contrasted to the other "authentic" artist profiled on the pages of *Rolling Stone*.[21]

Any attempt to manufacture counterculture credibility by Cassidy was dismissed as a blatant and even calculated effort to put distance between him and his teen-idol image. Rather than cultivate a new fan base of rock fans, Cassidy alienated much of his existing audience. With no one particularly enamored with the new David Cassidy public image, and Cassidy obviously less than enthused about the show that made him a star, *The Partridge Family*'s ratings eroded, ending its run in 1974.

## The Great Divide: Rock and TV

The end of the pop-music sitcom era ca. 1974 coincided with primetime comedy-variety shows becoming the domain of mainstream pop music acts like Donny and Marie Osmond, Sonny and Cher, Tony Orlando and Dawn, and Captain and Tennille. Rock music underwent a kind of "voluntary marginalization" to late-night programming, ranging from concert shows such as *The Midnight Special* (NBC, 1973–81) and *Don Kirschner's Rock Concert* (syndicated, 1973–82) and comedy-variety shows like *Saturday Night Live* (NBC, 1975- ) and *Fridays* (ABC, 1980–2).[22] In other words, "real" rock and roll happened on TV after both the tweens and middle-aged adults went to bed.

Popular music's relationship with TV was drastically and permanently altered when MTV was launched as an all-music, all-day-and-all-night cable TV channel in 1981. MTV soon became the dominant means of marketing popular music to a mass audience. While previous TV-pop music nexus were generally treated with suspicion (if not derision) by the rock community (i.e., the pop music sitcoms or shows like *American Bandstand* and *Shindig!*), MTV was idealistically greeted as potentially "revolutionary" as far as increasing the exposure of myriad bands with varying degrees of name recognition to wider audiences through innovative music videos. Instead, MTV quickly became an outlet for standardized music videos that were little more than big-budget commercials for new songs by current stars in what soon amounted to a Top 40 rotation.[23] By the mid–1980s, Hollywood jumped on the music video craze and routinely included rock bands on the soundtracks in order to produce "music videos" that served as movie trailers inserted into MTV rotation (e.g., Kenny Loggins's "Danger Zone" music video/trailer for *Top Gun*). TV again assumed its perceived role as the killer of rock and roll. As Dewey Finn lamented to his students in *School of Rock*, "There used to be a way to stick to the Man. It was called rock and roll.... The Man ruined that too, with a little thing called MTV!"[24]

MTV directly bears on the critical revisionism surrounding the Monkees, something the Partridge Family have not experienced, and this has as much to do with the sitcom as any assessments of qualitative differences in the musical product. The ideology of rock music codes oppositional culture around masculinity, whereas conformist mass culture manifest in pop music is coded around femininity. On *The Partridge Family*, the space of rock music was colonized by the adult, and adherence to traditional adult-parental authority became central in band operations. Given the counterculture penchant for male chauvinism as much as the credo of not trusting anyone over 30, the very idea of playing in a rock band with mom was about as lame as it could possibly get in the early 1970s.[25] Put differently, Jim Morrison probably would have gotten his fire lit less often had his mom been the Doors' keyboardist.

In contrast, *The Monkees* personified "free, white, and 21" as a representation of young adult males doing their own thing with anarchistic flair in the face of the Establishment. After its cancellation by NBC, CBS purchased the rights to *The Monkees* and aired it as a Saturday afternoon show from 1969–73; ABC then purchased the show and did likewise from 1973–4. However, the definitive redemption of the Monkees occurred in the mid–1980s when MTV added reruns of *The Monkees* to its programming schedule, even if MTV was less motivated by cultural history and more by the necessity to provide some variety around a steady steam of the same music videos. *The Monkees* attained even greater status as ground-breaking TV for a new generation of viewers introduced to the show. To be sure, *The Monkees* was a prototype contemporary sitcom and included early examples of music videos. What became as crucial was that the music of the Monkees, previously disparaged as bubblegum pandering to teenyboppers, was critically and historically revised. The Monkees were now deemed well-produced and well-performed pop music that withstood the test of time and was, therefore, "authentic" after all.

This critical change of mind was as much politically as aesthetically motivated. As discussed in Chapter 2, in the early 1980s a second "British Invasion" hit America with New Pop bands ranging from ABC, Culture Club, Duran Duran, Frankie Goes to Hollywood, the Human League, Tears for Fears, and Wham! Their anemic mergers of American black music (disco, funk, soul) and white pop (bubblegum, MOR, lounge), often foregrounding synthesizers and a highly affected crooning style, was heinous enough for American critics bound by the rock authenticity line. Moreover, because music video was quickly becoming integral in establishing a foothold in the popular music market, New Pop bands consciously emphasized highly stylized image as much as highly stylized music. Several New Pop bands became stars primarily through MTV exposure, and the network became a highly contentious battleground over national musical territory. More correctly, MTV was now perceived as part of the problem and not part of the solution. The Monkees—both in terms of their now "classic pop" music and as the "inventors" of music video—became the evidence for the MTV generation that Americans not only did it first, but did it better *a generation ago* in the 1960s. The fact that the Monkees were routinely castigated in their own time was now beside the point.

The upshot of the pop-sitcom era was the construction of an inherently antagonistic relationship where TV assumed the role of the corruptor of rock music, a view expressed by Darrell Y. Hamamoto:

> What was once the popular music of marginal people which *lyrically* told of their quotidian struggles became converted into the leisure time diversion of a highly coveted market segment with large disposable incomes. As a "commoditized dream," rock music became completely absorbed by the system of capitalist production. As in the sitcom, expressions of dissent from ideological orthodoxy were permitted in rock music only so long as they remained purely aesthetic, not political oppositions.[26]

There are considerable problems with this assessment, not the least of which is that it relies on the romantic counterculture myths of rock and roll as inherently oppositional music by and for the "marginal people," whereas TV is inherently mass culture for the mainstream herd. Rock music was not "completely absorbed by the system of capitalist production." Rock music has *always* been part of a capitalist system of production that reflected the dominant ideology of liberalism from the outset. It has always been a "commoditized dream" as far back as when Chuck Berry simultaneously sang the praises of rock and roll and the Horatio Alger myth in his hit song "Johnny B. Goode" (1958).

When Hamamoto claimed "expressions of dissent from ideological orthodoxy were permitted in rock music only so long as they remained purely aesthetic, not political oppositions," this reduces the politics of rock music to overt content, specifically the *lyrics*. "Aesthetic expressions" can effectively manifest dissent in rock music beyond or even devoid of lyrics, as powerfully expressed by Jimi Hendrix's version of "The Star-Spangled Banner." Conversely, housing oppositional lyrics in conventional and standardized form can be politically counterproductive.[27] As former Henry Cow member Tim Hodgkinson cogently put it, "You can't play reactionary rubbish, and say 'I'm a socialist' with the lyrics. You can't play the same music as used by the system to oppress people."[28] This problem was demonstrated by Bruce Springsteen's *Born in the U.S.A.* (1984) and specifically the title track, which became a hit song. After attending a Bruce Springsteen concert, conservative pundit George Will wrote a laudatory column about Springsteen as the embodiment of the promise of the America Dream, even though Springsteen's songs are frequently about the *failed* promises of the American Dream. When Ronald Reagan soon after name-dropped Springsteen during the 1984 presidential election campaign, a highly displeased Springsteen issued a pointed response that he and his songs were not to be associated with the Republican Party or Ronald Reagan (Springsteen has since officially aligned himself with the Democratic Party). Longtime Springsteen booster Dave Marsh unconditionally defended Springsteen and denounced Will's assessment as

> such a perversion of what Springsteen was trying to communicate that it bordered on obscenity. Yet the column was well received. Released at a time of chauvinism masquerading as patriotism, it was inevitable that "Born in the U.S.A." would be misinterpreted, that the album would be heard as a celebration of "basic values," no matter how hard Springsteen pushed his side of the tale.... Certainly, any popular song that honored the Vietnam War veteran in the age of Reagan and *Rambo* was going to be misconstrued as celebrating the war.[29]

Marsh's defense hinges on the criteria of artistic intent and that the message of Springsteen's song and his stance was, and should have been, self-evident to the listener. Moreover, Marsh also provided a highly convenient loophole in asserting that no matter how much effort was exerted by Springsteen, the song was doomed to be manipulated by the Right.[30] On one hand, the question raised is why Springsteen even bothered to write a song like "Born in the U.S.A." if it was bound to be co-opted and misinterpreted. More importantly, the issue is *why* George Will and Ronald Reagan were able to use "Born in the U.S.A." in a completely disingenuous way when songs like the willfully inaccessible avant-garde rock of Henry Cow's "War" or even the malevolent metal murk of Black Sabbath's "War Pigs" offer far greater resistance to being politically misused. Ultimately, "Born in the U.S.A" was subverted by its own form as well as right-wing misappropriations. Amid the continually repeated, keyboard-driven melody and the thunderous backbeat and drum fills, Springsteen's hoarse bellow all but rendered the scathing lyrics in the verses unintelligible, focusing even more attention to its fist pumping, rock anthem chorus repeating the song's title to the point that vehement protest was replaced by patriotic fervor.[31]

    This is not to single out Bruce Springsteen for criticism, but rather to situate the discussion of the problematics of popular music and, especially, rock music. "Born in the U.S.A." was very much intended as a protest song, but the lyrical protest was ultimately constrained, if not negated, by the musical form. The following chapter examines Britney Spears, the seeming epitome of inauthentic mass culture, and how her music and career — intentionally or not — can be read as a radical critique of American society.

# 9

# Teen Pop in Opposition: Britney Spears versus Madonna

> The role is a consumption of power. It locates one in the *representational* hierarchy, and hence in the spectacle: at the top, on the bottom, in the middle — but never *outside* the hierarchy.... No matter how much or how little limelight a given role attains in the public eye, however, its prime function is always that of social adaptation, of integrating people into the well-policed order of things.[1]—*Raoul Vaneigem*

## Showing Some Class: Madonna, "the Material Girl"

If Britney Spears can be read as the antithesis of Madonna, it is first necessary to discuss Madonna as the thesis. Raised in Michigan, Madonna Louise Ciccone was in her late teens when she moved to New York City in 1977. She worked persistently to establish herself in the music industry, ranging from stints with modern-dance troupes, rock bands, and recording dance demos for nightclub DJs. In 1983, Madonna signed with Sire Records (a TimeWarner subsidiary), and soon after became one of the more important figures in pop music.

Realizing marketing image was as important as marketing the song itself, Madonna's stardom directly owed to MTV and music videos as much as radio and hit singles. Indeed, Madonna was arguably the first pop superstar star produced by and for MTV consumers. Postmodernism was and remains a key to Madonna's artistic and commercial strategy, especially the early and extensive quotation of iconic star images like Marlene Dietrich, Greta Garbo, and especially Marilyn Monroe. Madonna's "Material Girl" video (from 1984's *Like a Virgin*) was a direct parody of Monroe's musical number "Diamonds Are a Girl's Best Friend" from *Gentlemen Prefer Blondes*. Mildly shocking imagery was also referenced from Catholicism, canonical artwork, fashion magazines, pin-up photography, and softcore pornography — the juxtapositions of which generated considerable controversy in the dominantly conservative mindset of the 1980s. Madonna's rendition of "Like a Virgin" at the 1984 MTV Video Music Awards (VMAs) became pop-culture legend. Dressed in a tattered wedding gown with an oversized, stainless steel crucifix around her neck, Madonna punctuated the performance by simulating masturbation and orgasm.

Musically, Madonna's musical output in the 1980s (her eponymous debut, *Like a Virgin, True Blue*) tended towards traditionally structured verse-chorus pop songs merging propulsive disco and funk dance rhythms with melodic and harmonic elements drawn from 1960s bubblegum as well as 1980s synthpop: the essential ingredients of First Wave Teen Pop.[2] Sexually themed lyrics became the hallmark of Madonna's songs. On her early hits, Madonna celebrated unrequited lust ("Burning Up"), one-night stands ("Lucky Star"), well-endowed men ("Like a Virgin"), the thrill of teen pregnancy ("Papa Don't Preach"), and, above all, the erotic correlation between sex and wealth ("Material Girl"). As hip-hop, rap, techno, and electronica became more dominant genres in pop music, Madonna's later albums, ranging from *Erotica* (1992), *Music* (2000), *American Life* (2003), and *Hard Candy* (2007), emphasized beat-driven, studio-produced songs geared towards club dancing and the soundtrack for visual staging (music videos, concert spectaculars) as much as listening.

Entering the 1990s, Madonna also reinvented her early "boy toy" image. Pivotal in this transition was Madonna dropping the squeaky, sing-song style on the early recordings in favor of a sultry, mature vocal approach. Madonna also shelved the mallrat eclecticism in favor of sophisticated glamour images combined with sexually charged fashion accessories (corsets, high heels, latex, leather, lingerie, metal bras, etc.). Rather than simply singing about sex, Madonna openly addressed fetishism, masochism, interracial sex, and same-sex relationships. In 1990, Madonna's video for "Justify My Love" was banned by MTV for its sexual content; it was subsequently released as a VHS "video single" and, fueled by the controversy, sold in droves. Appearing on ABC's *Nightline* to offer artistic free speech and sexual liberation defenses over "Justify My Love," Madonna was also indignant — or simply had the temerity to complain — that her fans had to buy her VHS single rather than watch it on MTV for free.

The controversy over "Justify My Love" prompted a defense of Madonna by Camille Paglia in a 1990 *New York Times* opinion piece, "Madonna — Finally, a Real Feminist." Beyond hailing the ostensive breaking of sexual taboos by the video, Paglia championed Madonna as a cultural icon and "role model":

> Madonna grew, flourished, metamorphosed and became an international star of staggering dimensions. She is also a shrewd business tycoon, a modern woman of all-around talent. Madonna is the true feminist.... Madonna has taught young women around the world to be fully female and sexual while also exercising total control over their lives. She shows girls how to be attractive, sensual, energetic, ambitious, aggressive, and funny — all at the same time.... Feminism says "No more masks." Madonna says we are nothing but masks.[3]

The issue is not Madonna's status as a positive feminist role model, but the extent to which Paglia positioned Madonna as a positive *capitalist* role model. As a merger of free enterprise and free love, Madonna's ideology was consistent with *Playboy* magazine which, as Gay Talese defined it, associated "romantic adventure with upward mobility and economic prosperity."[4] The year 1992 saw the simultaneous release of the *Erotica* CD and *Sex*, a coffee table book of softcore pornographic photos.[5] Inevitably overshadowing *Erotica*, *Sex* amounted to a kind of R-rated version of Robert Mapplethorpe. Put less charitably, photos of Madonna and Vanilla Ice making out in their underwear may not have been what Georges Bataille had in mind when he proclaimed that "the sexual act is to time what the tiger is to space." Nonetheless, all of the hoopla surrounding *Sex* made Madonna synonymous with "decadent chic." It was guaranteed to infuriate conservative America, but stayed well within the ideology of the Sexual Revolution and the myth of the "Repressive Hypothesis."[6] Madonna took on the self-appointed role of the great liberator of sex against a tide of repressed and repressive Puritanical forces in American society. As important as *Erotica* and especially *Sex* were in terms of defining Madonna's image around "bedroom adventure and upward mobility," underlying the project was indeed "economic prosperity." In 1992, Madonna co-founded Maverick, an entertainment company in partnership with Time Warner. *Erotica* and *Sex* were Maverick's intentionally controversial inaugural products.[7]

Over the course of her career, the veneer for Madonna's ideological project is increasingly provided by *cosmopolitanism* and steadily distancing her cultural iconography away from her "Blond Ambition" and "Material Girl" ethos of the 1980s, seeking to dispel any residue of Reaganism in the process. Regardless of whatever reinvented version it manifests, Madonna consciously constructs her brand identity — or, more correctly, *identities* — around ideals of diversity, empowerment, equality, individuality, irony, multiculturalism, postmodernism, progressivism, sexual liberation, spirituality, tolerance, urbanity, and world citizenship. In 2003, Madonna reinvented herself politically with *American Life*, shifting from decadent chic to revolutionary chic. The liberal and occasionally self-critical lyrical sentiments were matched by a CD cover shot of Madonna referencing the iconic photo of Che Guevara (so much for Marilyn Monroe). In 2004, she publically endorsed Wesley Clark during the Democratic presidential primary campaign and used concerts as a forum to publically and often profanely castigate George W. Bush throughout much of his second term as president. In 2008, Madonna vociferously supported Barack Obama, and was particularly vitriolic in her criticism of Sarah Palin whenever a microphone was provided.

## Pop Tart: Britney Spears, "the White Trash Madonna"

In contrast to Madonna's tenacious rags-to-riches climb to the top of the music business and the liberal bourgeoisie, Britney Spears was in "pre-production" by the Culture Industry for almost a decade. Born and raised in Louisiana, Spears was eight years old when she auditioned for Disney Channel's revival of *The Mickey Mouse Club* (*MMC*) in 1989. Considered too young for the show, Spears nonetheless impressed Disney producers who assisted her family in securing career management. Spears attended the School of Performing Arts in New York City and made her national television debut performing on the syndicated talent show *Star Search* in 1991. The following year, Spears re-auditioned for *MMC* and was hired, appearing on the show from 1993–4.[8] Later signed to Jive Records (a subsidiary of Sony Music), Spears released her debut, chart-topping single "Baby One More Time" in 1998. By 17, Britney Spears was "always-already" a manufactured pop star.

While highly influenced by Michael Jackson and especially the more robotic pop-funk of Janet Jackson, Britney Spears's brand of First Wave Teen Pop was based on the early Madonna "dance rhythm-bubblegum melody-sex sells" triumvirate. Spears also quickly demonstrated a capacity to generate controversy that surpassed even Madonna. "Baby One More Time" pushed Madonna's pop-music realm of sexual liberation between consenting adults to the far less comfortable domain of consenting teenage girls. As tangibly sleazy as it was slickly produced, "Baby One More Time" was a half-time grind of funk rhythm topped with saccharine melodies over which Spears provided a compendium of breathy, cooing, and groaning vocals. The inevitable comparison was porn film soundtrack. What the song aurally suggested, the video for "Baby One More Time" delivered short of possible federal prosecution under the Mann Act. Clad in pigtails and a disheveled schoolgirl's outfit for the first verse, Spears prowled about a high school hallway mixing stiff dance choreography, strip tease posturing, and alternations between come-hither looks and post-coitus expressions.

In this context, the respective marketing of sex by Madonna and Britney Spears can be read around the nebulous cultural constructs that distinguish between "sophisticated" and "sordid." Madonna's mysterious netherworld of sexual kink was ultimately less disturbing than Britney Spears's mainstream parade of teenybopper softcore, and inhibiting the rupture Spears provoked proved far less convenient than Madonna championing "alternative lifestyles."[9] While the marketing of Spears as the Lolita next door offended almost everybody, it also usurped Madonna as popular music's queen of controversy, and, above all, drove sales of the Britney Spears brand of pop music.

This distinction between "sophisticated" and "sordid" can also be applied to how Madonna and Britney Spears represent *class* in both senses of the word. As suggested, Madonna's attainment of upper-class status was matched by adopting upper-class etiquette through conscious performances of personal refinement and *noblesse-oblige* social conscience. Britney Spears's approach to stardom came off as a real-life version of *The Beverly Hillbillies*. One of the defining images of Britney Spears was a paparazzi photo of her in late pregnancy wearing cut-offs, a midriff-revealing tank top, oversized sunglasses, and lighting a cigarette. While Madonna emphatically aligned herself with the liberal-left opposition on *American Life*, in 2003 Spears did a CNN interview with conservative pundit Tucker Carlson in which she proclaimed, "We should just support the President in everything he does" (with the assumed answer to the unissued follow-up question being, "I was only following orders"). While Madonna fervently supported Obama, Spears was dragged into the 2008 campaign — not by choice — due to a John McCain campaign ad labeling Obama "the celebrity candidate" with unflattering comparisons to Spears and Paris Hilton: the respective embodiments of ignorant, white trash *nouveau-riche* and vacuous, bourgeois idle-rich in American pop culture consciousness. Obama issued a succinct riposte in the rhetorical question, "Couldn't they have done better?" Indeed, neither Democrats nor Republicans wanted to be associated with Britney Spears or Paris Hilton, who became BFFs on the A-list of political undesirables.

In the "representational hierarchy," Madonna and Britney Spears not only assumed antithetical roles of stardom and class, but the American Dream. Madonna personified the ambitious, rugged individual whose upward mobility was matched by a well-cultivated image of cosmopolitan, upper-class liberalism. Britney Spears signified Culture Industry product and a manufactured star commodity that was still "lower class" no matter how much money was added to the checking account. In this way, Madonna and Britney Spears ultimately became antithetical representations of bourgeois ideology. While Madonna affirmed it, with Britney Spears it turned on itself.

## *Look Back in Anger:* Blackout *and* Circus

The 2003 VMAs opened with Madonna, Britney Spears, and Christina Aguilera performing a medley of Madonna's "Like a Virgin" and "Hollywood" (the then-current single from *American Life*). Madonna wore a "butch" black outfit while Spears and Aguilera donned white wedding-themed fetish lingerie as a further reference point to Madonna's famous 1984 VMAs performance. During "Like a Virgin" Madonna shared an open-mouth kiss with Spears and then Aguilera. While the immediate controversy was over the sexualized aspects of the performance (i.e., androgyny and homosexuality), the kisses were interpreted as a symbolic gesture of Madonna handing down her "Queen of Pop" crown to the next generation of female pop stars. In actuality, it was the "kiss of death," signifying the end of the First Wave Teen Pop era.

Indeed, by 2003 First Wave Teen Pop was an exhausted genre. The Spice Girls broke up in 2000 amid plummeting popularity. Boy bands became the object of almost unanimous critical derision; by 2002 Backstreet Boys, 'N Sync and 98 Degrees officially or unofficially disbanded. An immense critical and commercial success in 2003, *School of Rock* served as the rallying cry for rock tradition and ideology against current pop-music trends. By 2006, First Wave Teen Pop was all but extinct. Christina Aguilera graduated to the adult pop market with the aptly titled *Back to Basics*, a CD of dance-pop highly informed by blues, soul, and jazz which showcased her considerable vocal skills.[10] The same year, the debut of *Hannah Montana* was instrumental in launching a Second Wave Teen Pop sound largely influenced by rock subgenres, in particular 1980s New Wave and stadium rock, rather than 1980s dance-pop.

From 2005–8, Britney Spears's life was a *well*-publicized series of personal and professional crises and debacles that only need be briefly summarized here: an array of bizarre late-night escapades, reported drug addiction and mental illness, stints in rehab, involuntary commitment in a psychiatric ward, an acrimonious divorce, losing custody of her two children, and, eventually, legal action that placed her personal and professional affairs in a conservatorship run by her father. As Spears's unraveling became a national obsession, she also became a commodity-fetish exploited to its fullest by the media industries. Rather than tragedy, it was presented as farce. Becoming the butt of a national joke, Spears served as a conduit for the sadism of mass culture where resentments towards America's wealthy, undeserving stars and contempt for its poor white trash could be conveniently channeled into the same target.[11]

In the midst of the downward spiral and media scrutiny, Spears's CD *Blackout* was released in 2007, her first CD of new material since 2003's *In the Zone*.[12] It was largely eclipsed by the ongoing media furor and a disastrous "comeback" performance at the 2007 VMAs; Spears lip-synched a rendition of "Gimmie More" (the first single from *Blackout*) which could be charitably described as resembling someone's audition as an extra in a zombie movie.[13] The controversies aside, on *Blackout* Spears's brand of First Wave Teen Pop did not "mature" into mainstream adult pop like Christina Aguilera or undergo a Madonna-style postmodern "reinvention."[14] Instead, it entered the Second Wave Teen Pop era by undergoing a drastic deconstruction, if not outright disembowelment. Dance rhythms were reduced to metronomic, mechanistic, electronically processed beats. Samples and synthesizers produced various noises as much as supplying any stable musical foundations of melody and harmony. Within the conventional verse-chorus structures, songs were not so much recorded and mixed but assembled though digital effects and editing to the point that they bordered on cut-up methods.

The second single from *Blackout*, "Piece of Me" was an explicit lyrical attack on the media industries.[15] Musically, it serves as an even harsher attack on capitalism. The mid-tempo rhythm of "Piece of Me" is a constant backbeat but not drums or even a drum machine. Rather, it is a studio-generated noise that can be variously described as sounding like ratcheting machinery, jingling coins, and shackled, shuffling feet. These sounds as aural signifiers — industry, money, and slavery — become inseparable as the rhythmic drive of the song.[16]

The kiss heard around the world: Britney Spears (left) and Madonna (center) hook up at the 2003 VMAs (at right, Christina Aguilera) (MTV/Photofest).

The verses are structured around a menacing eight-bar configuration with distorted synthesizer eight-note thumps on the one of each bar (omitting the sixth bar): C#-E-B-B-C#-rest-C#-G#. Synthesizers also produce an array of electronic *noises* at various points throughout the song. Sluggish, churning sound waves underscore the chorus. Sudden surges punctuate the endings of the eight-bar verses while sporadic, ricocheting blurts and pings dominate the bridge and outro of the song. Especially disconcerting are the song's opening and transitional points between verse, chorus, and bridge. Falling on the three between the backbeat are alternations of what sound like, for lack of better descriptions, a clucking chicken having its neck wrung and a woman gasping in orgasm. The sounds of animal slaughter and sexual arousal construct an unsettling aural montage in relationship to the backbeat sound of cash, chains, and machinery.

Spears's half-sung/half-spoken vocals contain all the overdetermined "sexiness" that characterizes her vocal style and songs. The vocals are also monotone, largely devoid of any melodic variation, save for the final verse where melodic changes are produced by studio-generated pitch modification as much as the singing itself. Hence, the vocals throughout "Piece of Me" are overly sexualized to foreground the female voice as "sex object" but also saturated with studio effects that render the human voice "inhuman." Indeed, *every* sound in "Piece of Me" is manipulated into something sounding electronic, mechanical, and synthetic; the vocals become another cog in the song-apparatus. While serving as the chorus hook, the title of the song also acts as a recurring rhetorical question, offering both a defiant challenge and pathetic inquiry as to who wants the next piece or "cut" of Britney Spears.

Jacques Attali evocatively suggested, "The hypotheses of noise as murder and music as sacrifice are not easy to accept. They imply that music *functions* like sacrifice ... listening to noise is a little like being killed ... listening to music is to attend a ritual murder."[17] "Piece of Me" converted teen pop into an "industrialized" grind of commerce and dismemberment where the myriad *noises* produce disruptive violence in the song, with the listener becoming a participant in the "sacrifice" of Britney Spears as commodity-fetish on the altar of consumer capitalism.[18] In this respect, Attali's conception of "noise" also offers the starting point as far as reading Britney Spears as a potentially "oppositional music." More specifically, Attali hypothesized a possible convergence of "mass music" (pop music) and "theoretical music" (avant-garde and experimental music):

> The linkup of these two productions may seem a priori artificial: one uses the most traditional of harmonies to avoid startling anyone, while the other ... refuses to accept the dominant trends and cultural codes. One addresses itself to a mass audience with the aim of inciting to buy, the other has no market or financial base.... Yet both belong to the same reality, that of hyperindustrialized Western society in crisis. They are thus necessarily linked to one another, if only by virtue of being radical opposites.[19]

This "linkup" can take many forms, and Attali was ambivalent as to whether this would result in a revolutionary infusion of noise into the constraints of popular music or the final colonization of noise within the confines of popular music. Possible examples (and by no means the only ones) could range from Frank Zappa, Captain Beefheart, Can, Henry Cow, Kraftwerk, the Residents, Throbbing Gristle, the Pop Group, Public Enemy, or Sonic Youth.[20] While more unlikely, even unintentionally, Britney Spears also suggests a possible "linkup" of the "radical opposites" of mass music (teen pop, bubblegum, dance-pop, jingles, porn film soundtrack) and theoretical music (*musique concrète*, electronic music).[21]

Admittedly, from an orthodox position of Adorno, arguing Britney Spears is a potentially oppositional music amounts to patent absurdity. Indeed, one could take Adorno's essay "On Popular Music" (discussed in the previous chapter) and simply insert the comment "(e.g., Britney Spears)" after any number of Adorno's assessments of the infantilism and innocuousness of popular music. Moreover, Adorno and Attali's critical theories of music diverge considerably, especially concerning the subversive potential of popular music, which Adorno dismissed and Attali idealized. Nonetheless, both Attali and Adorno share a similar premise. The ideological function of music is the signifier of "social harmony" through the organization of sound into the confines of melody, harmony, and metered rhythm while banishing disconcerting and displeasing sounds—"noise" for Attali and "atonality" for Adorno.[22]

Adorno championed the 12-tone music of Arnold Schoenberg in which the role of atonality (a.k.a. "wrong notes") had a revolutionary aspect, both formally and politically. The inherent and inevitable moments of tonal dissonance that occurred in Schoenberg's 12-tone system became an "immanent critique" of the ideological role of music: "To a degree, it resembles the monad of Leibniz; it 'represents,' to be sure, not a pre-established harmony, but certainly a historically produced dissonance, namely social antinomies."[23] In what Adorno described as "music of alienation," Schoenberg's music was a rejection of tonality as the cultural signifier of social harmony (capitalism's invisible hand, liberal democracy's checks and balances) in favor of atonality as a signifier of social disharmony and the inherent contradictions of capitalism and liberal democracy.

As much as Adorno hailed the music of Schoenberg, he hated the work of Igor Stravinsky, which he termed "objectivist music," which is to say an objectification of musical forms rather than any formal objective critique, and what Adorno dismissed as "music about music."[24] There was also an ideological consequence for Adorno: "In every objectivist music the attempt is made to correct the alienation from within ... without any clear view of social reality. *This explains the inclination of all objectivism to dance forms and to rhythms originating in the dance*; they are thought to be elevated above historical change and accessible to every age."[25]

In Madonna's song "Music" (the lead-off track and first single from her 2000 CD *Music*), the dominant instrument is the drum program.[26] Mixed to the forefront of the song, it provides a stable and stabilizing dance beat while undergoing an array of subtle rhythmic variances (syncopated fills, brief starts and stops, momentary accelerations and pauses, minor alterations in the program). As the beat percolates, the other sounds spaciously intermingle within its dominant pulse — not as "monads" but "pre-established harmonies" as far as being recognizable musical reference points. The vocoder strongly recalls the disco hit "Funky Town," the squiggling guitar riff as well as the squealing synthesizer line that punctuates the outro mimics the signature funk style of Parliament-Funkadelic, and the languid strings echo synthpop. When Camille Paglia suggested, "Madonna says we are nothing but masks," Adorno made a similar comparison in his assessment of Schoenberg's music of alienation versus Stravinsky's objectivist music as the difference between Schoenberg's "absence of illusion" as opposed to Stravinsky's "seductively arbitrary change of masks, whose wearers are consequently identical but empty."[27]

As previously suggested, the dance beat in "Piece of Me" serves as a disconcerting signifier of capitalism by manifesting interrelated sounds of industry, money, and slave labor in which noises collide within the framework of a pop song. In "Music," the invisible hand of capitalism and checks and balances of liberal democracy are also represented by the dance beat rather than tonality (i.e., Adorno). Nevertheless, it serves the same function as the corrective for the musical elements integrating as "social atoms" (points of *cultural pastiche*) rather than colliding as "social antinomies" (points of *political conflict*). Indeed, music as a means of achieving unitary culture is precisely the message of "Music."[28] Lyrically, the dance floor is described as a space of gyrating bodies becoming a *classless* society through the collective libidinal release of dance floor bump and grind: one might say "the invisible hand-job."[29] As a metaphor of liberal society, the dance floor becomes the Great Melting Pot. While the lyrical message is that music forms a community of free and equal individuals, the musical message of "Music" is that *music creates order*. Containing and rectifying disparate musical parts via pastiche and negating any potential conflict through the dance beat, "Music" also becomes objectivist music where "the attempt is made to correct the alienation from within."

In contrast, alienation, competition, and exploitation are the recurring themes of Spears's *Circus*. The title track, which was also the second single, specifically addressed the media "circus" of the previous years, but musically also provides a far different critique of liberal society.[30] In the first verse of "Circus," Spears lyrically describes the world as being composed of people who act and people who watch, and here "acting" can be used both in the terms of agency and performance. More implicitly, the world is also divided into those who act and those who are acted upon. Musically, the verse sections of "Circus" are built on a two-bar 4/4 rhythm track. A thudding bass drum sound and distorted bass synthesizer emphasize the one; handclap sounds provide the back beat, but omit the four in the first bar. This does not provide a relaxing pause or rest in the rhythmic drive, but exacerbates tension through silence and the absence of a sound that "should" be there in the logic of dance music. This omission becomes crucial in that if, as suggested, the flow of the dance beat rather than the resolutions of tonality is now the (post)modern musical representation of capitalism's invisible hand, in the verse sections of "Circus" the dance beat is still in the process of gathering its momentum or "forming its grip."

Between each verse and the chorus, there is a brief transitional segment in which the drumbeat drops out entirely, replaced by eight-note electric guitar riffing and quarter-note samples sounding somewhere between a string section and an electric sander. The vocals are more conventionally sung rather than the half-speaking/half-singing style used in the rest of the song; however, they are multi-tracked and effects treated to an extent they become part of the musical "machinery" as well. At the same time, the sudden prominence of the vocal melody — and equally sudden absence of the drumbeat — shifts the focus to Spears's voice as the individual amid the crowd. This becomes crucial as the lyrics describe the exhilaration of being the primary object of attention on a dance floor.

Reaching the chorus, a drum machine abruptly enters with a clattering backbeat with the invisible hand of capitalism now locked in its rhythmic groove, and all things now secured "in its grasp." The fuzz bass synthesizer produces what amounts to syncopated, marginally melodic pulses of electronic static. Sporadic sounds resembling turntable "scratching" are also inserted into chorus and bridge sections. Lyrically, the delineation of human agency in the verses, followed by the description of starring in the spectacle in the sections after the verse, becomes a declaration of establishing dominance over others in the chorus. Fragmented, effects-altered samples of male voices mechanistically and repetitively grunt sounds of submission in rhythmic response to Spears's multi-tracked vocal pronouncements, reiterating her status as center of attention as well as the ringmaster of the circus with whip in hand orchestrating what is occurring on the dance floor. During the 2009 concert tour, officially billed as "The Circus Starring Britney Spears," Spears performed "Circus" dressed as a ringmaster and brandishing a whip; the visual effect might be described as somewhere between drum majorette and dominatrix.[31]

Following the bridge and Spears's additional spoken declarations emphasizing she is in charge of the proceedings, "Circus" ends with the chorus repeated twice. A disorientating density of noise develops amid a crush of clanking backbeat, the belches of the bass synthesizer static, the abrasive scratching sounds, and the disembodied vocal interjections of compliance. Moreover, there is another signature dance music sound, the funk synthesizer "squeal" (as noted, also utilized in "Music"). Heard sporadically throughout "Circus," in the final restatements of the chorus they become louder and more frequent; through the increased and pronounced use of modulation they border on disconcerting electronic whines and shrieks, suggesting both retching screams and whirling saws. As "Circus" builds to its conclusion, the effect verges on industrial music. Specifically, Simon Reynolds described the final Throbbing Gristle single "Discipline" (1981) as "the beat sounds like a jackboot ... while gruesome shearing sounds conjure up an abattoir atmosphere."[32] The same could be said for "Circus" in the incongruous context of dance-pop rather than Throbbing Gristle's predilection for avant-garde noise assault.

Attali proclaimed, "With noise is born disorder and its opposite: the world. With music is born power and its opposite: subversion."[33] This becomes the difference between "Music" and "Circus." "Music" ends with a fade-out as the various parts effectively integrating into a musical whole around the beat to signify that "Music" accomplishes popular music's ideological purpose even after the song ends. "Music" represents the dance floor as the ideal of liberal democratic society, popular music idealizing itself as its vehicle for a unitary culture, and the formation of order in and through the power of *music*. In contrast, the increasing inner frenzy of *noise* in "Circus" only abates when the song pounds to an abrupt stop. The dance floor is not a great melting pot but a disorganized mass of agitated bodies while Spears demands both complete attention and complete submission amid the escalating din. At its most ominous, "Circus" suggests the final solution belongs with the individual who hogs the spotlight, wields the whip, assigns the herd their roles, and ultimately brings order out of the cacophony and chaos of the musical and social circus. Britney *über alles.*

## The Comeback Kid

By 2008, the critical and cultural discourse around Britney Spears shifted beyond uniform ridicule. In a February 2008 *Rolling Stone* cover story "The Tragedy of Britney Spears," Vanessa Gringanolis cast Spears as the symbol of what had gone from bad to worse in American society entering the twenty-first century: "She's the canary in the coal mine of American culture, the most vivid representation of the excess of the past decade.... We want her to survive and thrive, to evolve into someone who can make us proud again. Or maybe, we just don't want the show to end."[34] A far more chilling and oddly sympathetic study was the *South Park* episode "Britney's New Look" which first aired in March 2008. A despondent Britney Spears literally blew her head off with a shotgun, leaving only a jawbone and waggling tongue spouting gurgling gibberish. Nonetheless, the headless Spears still recorded, performed live, and remained hounded by the media until Spears was ritually killed — or finally put out of her misery — by a horde of people using cameras with flash bulbs as mass culture's weapon of sacrificial murder.

At the 2008 VMAs, the pervious year's "Gimmie More" fiasco was apparently forgiven. Spears's music video for "Piece of Me" was the surprise winner of three awards, including Video of the Year. Whether this amounted to promotion for *Circus* can be left open to debate. Critical response to *Circus* was far from universal acclaim, but there was a general sense that everyone was trying to be "supportive." *Circus* and the subsequent 2009 concert tour also proved Spears was still a highly marketable cultural commodity. *Circus* sold over eight million copies (as of 2011), produced three Top 20 singles, and the tour grossed over $100 million. At the 2009 Teen Choice Awards, Spears was presented with the Lifetime Achievement Award at age 28; it seemed proof positive that in teen culture life indeed ends at 30. The presenter was Miley Cyrus, who proclaimed Britney Spears "my hero."

In 2010, *Glee* did a Britney Spears tribute episode "Britney/Brittany" which can be compared to the *Glee* Madonna tribute episode "The Power of Madonna" (2010). In "The Power of Madonna," the contradictions of Madonna are ironed out through the construction of a binary. Ruthless cheerleader coach Sue Sylvester admires Madonna as a symbol of personal empowerment by any means necessary ("I'm strong, confident, and independent ... and if that makes me a bitch, so what?"). Conversely, the progressive glee club advisor Will Schuster

**Saving Britney Spears (and her career): Spears receives the Lifetime Achievement Award at the 2009 Teen Choice Awards (Ray Mickshaw/FOX).**

understands and greatly respects Madonna as a cultural symbol of empowerment promoting "equality." In the context of *Glee* and Will serving as the show's hero and Sue the villain, Sue's reverence of Madonna is "politically incorrect" whereas Will's respect for Madonna is "politically correct." In 2000, Madonna proclaimed music has the power to forge egalitarian community in her song "Music." A decade later, *Glee* decreed the same about the power of Madonna.

In "Britney/Brittany," the glee club wants to perform a Britney Spears showcase for the school homecoming rally (leading the charge is the openly gay male on the show). Will adamantly vetoes the idea because he doesn't "think she is a very good role model." The subplot is that Will is in the early stages of a midlife crisis, compounded by repeated accusations he is "uptight" (read: Square). He begins to act irresponsibly, and realizes the only other person at the high school who despises Britney Spears as much as he does is Sue Sylvester, and largely for the same reasons. Repulsed that he might actually have something in common with Sue, Will not only lets the glee club perform Britney Spears songs for homecoming, but *he* will join them onstage. The inevitable disaster occurs when Will performs a highly risqué version of Spears's "Toxic" and incites, at Sue terms it, a "Britney Spears sex riot" in the gymnasium. In the end, Will concedes he better appreciates the musical and cultural significance of Britney Spears. The more important lesson learned by a sadder but wiser Will is the necessity of self-restraint and personal responsibility. Indeed, it is through Madonna that Will understands liberal society as embracing ideals of freedom and equality; through Britney Spears he grudgingly accepts the need for some "conservatism" in daily life.

F. Scott Fitzgerald famously remarked, "There are no second acts in American lives." The curtain did not so much fall but the entire stage collapsed in the first act of Britney Spears's life as the American Dream. The comeback and redemption of Britney Spears is not so much the charity of a second chance bestowed by the American public, but the necessity for a second act to conciliate them. Where *Rolling Stone* got it wrong is that "the show" was not only the downward spiral but Spears satisfying the demand that she "evolve into someone who can make us proud again." In this second act, Spears's role "in the representational hierarchy, and hence the spectacle" is playing the redemption of the American Dream itself. As of 2011, the saga of Britney Spears appears to have a happy ending — or at least an ideologically affirmative one.

# 10

# *My Generation:* School of Rock and the Revival of Rock Ideology

"Rock and roll star" is probably the purest manifestation of the American Dream.—*Tom Petty, induction speech, Rock and Roll Hall of Fame (2002)*

## Rock and Roll Is Here to Stay

Rock is the dominant popular musical genre in America. Over the last 50 to 60 years, it has undergone numerous permutations and developed a multiplicity of subgenres along the way. Nonetheless, rock and roll is now entering "retirement age" in all senses of the term. Generational politics become increasingly problematic for a musical genre whose ideological basis has been teen rebellion, Hipness, and anti–Establishment. The drive to sustain rock music's "subversive nature" is increasingly contradicted by rock music becoming more and more part of mainstream American popular culture with each successive generation. Radio stations are specialized to occupy specific consumer niches, with "classic rock" stations the nostalgic bastion for a middle-aged adult rock fan to escape from the horrors of contemporary genres. In rock journalism, *Rolling Stone* doggedly perpetuates the alleged tradition of rock music's inherent "authenticity" and progressive "opposition" born out of the 1960s counterculture. On television, staples of PBS programming—especially during pledge drives—are documentaries on the heyday of "the Woodstock Generation," profiles of early rock and pop-music icons, and celebrations of 1960s rock and pop music for an imagined audience of middle-class liberals (more specifically, ex-hippies). Cinema actively sustains the myths of rock rebellion with *Almost Famous* (2000), *Rock Star* (2001), *Taking Woodstock* (2009), *Pirate Radio* (2009), and focus of this chapter, *School of Rock* (2003). Indeed, as *School of Rock* made abundantly clear, rock and roll refuses to grow up, let alone age gracefully.

To contextualize *School of Rock*, popular music—and teen culture along with it—was in a state of flux throughout the 1980s and 1990s. While the generational signifiers of the 1970s were Led Zeppelin and the Ramones (more correctly, bands constructed as the decade's generational signifiers after the fact), the generational signifiers of the 1980s were Michael Jackson and Madonna. Jackson's *Thriller* (1982) remains the best-selling album in pop-music history. Madonna's postmodern formula for superstardom was pastiches of black music rhythms, white pop melodies, and a self-conscious manipulation of public image and star iconography. During the 1980s, New Wave became the more commercial form of punk. Rap emerged as a dominant popular musical genre, with the Beastie Boys, Public Enemy and Run-D.M.C., achieving commercial and critical success. New Kids on the Block achieved stardom as the prototype "boy band" seemingly and exclusively loved by a legion of teenage girls.

In 1991, the direction of rock music was drastically altered with the release of Nirvana's *Nevermind*, a record that quickly became a generational signifier of the 1990s as the slacker decade and a teen rebellion of individual alienation, apathy, and listlessness (on TV the generational signifier of "slackerism" was the MTV cartoon series *Beavis and Butt-Head*). While rooted in 1980s hardcore punk, *Nevermind* drew from 1970s heavy metal as well as bubblegum pop; as Kurt Cobain put it, "We sound like ... the Bay City Rollers being molested by Black Flag and Black Sabbath."[1] Nirvana's breakthrough hit single, "Smells like Teen Spirit," was a continually repeated F-A#-G#-C# riff altered only by dynamics (relatively quiet in the verses, extremely loud in the chorus). Cobain's mostly intelligible vocals veered between moans and screams as a primal expression of the "teen spirit" of male-adolescent angst, but delivered with a deliberate dose of irony. The title, which does not appear in the lyrics, was taken from the advertising slogan for the Teen Spirit brand of underarm deodorant whose target consumer demographic was teenage girls.[2]

Cobain's suicide in 1994 served as the cryptic accompaniment to "alternative rock" (lower-case a) evolving into "Alternative rock" (upper-case A) during the 1990s, becoming its own standardized genre defined by a varying mix of punk, metal, pop, psychedelic, and black music influences (funk, rap, reggae, ska, etc.). The latter half of the 1990s was dominated by First Wave Teen Pop, which effectively ran its course by 2003. Gayle Wald argued the collapse of this teen pop market owed to several interrelated factors, and not the least of which was the critical and consumer consensus that the various brands of teen pop were "corporate" as well as "effeminate" mass culture produced for a "teenybopper" audience.[3] The crucial difference was that the rupture and resultant void in popular music was not filled by a dominant artist, band, or musical movement, such as punk exploding out of the ennui of mid–1970s rock. Rather, what emerged was a cinematic celebration of "authentic rock" with all of its surplus ideology: *School of Rock*.

## Rebellion 101

*School of Rock* (henceforth *SoR*) was directed by Richard Linklater, previously known for his films about anti-authority individuals and outsiders such as *Slacker* (1991) and *Dazed and Confused* (1993), the latter revolving extensively around the rock music and teen culture of the 1970s. *SoR* also catapulted Jack Black to stardom. Black's comedic career was long connected to rock music, and specifically the development of Black's comedic persona around the "eternal teenager" stereotype of adolescent frenzy trapped in the body of an adult driven by the metaphysical power of rock. In 1994, Black teamed with Kyle Glas to form the comedy/music duo Tenacious D., a simultaneous homage and profane satire of the mythos of hard rock. From 1997–2000, Tenacious D. had a show on HBO, and released their debut album in 2001. The songs were not done as an acoustic/electric guitar duo but full band renditions drawing from a pool of Alternative, metal, and punk musicians (notably former Nirvana drummer Dave Grohl).

Black's growing popularity lead to *SoR*, a film project specifically designed as a vehicle for Black within a more mainstream and marketable context. Keeping objectionable content in check, *SoR* was rated PG-13, which insured unrestricted access to an under-17 audience. However, the target audience of the film was not necessarily teens but middle-aged adults who could bask in the nostalgic valorization of the past over the present.[4] In *SoR*, Black plays Dewey Finn, a down-and-out rock musician. Through what amounts to identity theft, Dewey poses as his best friend, retired rock musician-turned-substitute-school-teacher Ned Schneebly, and takes a temporary job at a private prep school in order to generate some much-needed income. Disgusted by the fact that his students listen to Puff Daddy (black music) and Christina Aguilera (female teen pop), and incredulous they have never heard of Led Zeppelin (white male hard rock), Dewey embarks on a class project by forming a rock and roll band.

Part of Dewey's project entails educating the Square prep school kids on the mythology—*not* history—of rock; more specifically, *SoR* establishes a "canon" of rock drawn primarily (if not exclusively) from hard rock, heavy metal, punk, and Alternative. While 1970s classic rock and heavy metal is in the foreground, the concerted inclusion and referencing of the Ramones throughout *SoR* bears particular mention. Besides their cultural status as the embodiment of punk rock and anti-authority teen rebellion, the Ramones co-starred in *Rock and Roll High School* (1979), a musical-comedy that depicts school as a quasi-fascist system that represses any and all expressions of teen power, especially through rock music.[5] A student revolt takes place against the educational apparatus and the film has a literally explosive climax: the high school is blown up with a bomb while the Ramones perform a concert for the liberated student body.

*SoR* initially constructs a similar representation of school as a repressive institution designed to instill social conformity while rock music, as Dewey proclaims, is the means to "stick it to the Man." This also becomes the point of contradiction. While Dewey espouses the traditional rock ideology tenets of freedom and rebellion, he runs his class in a fairly authoritarian manner, utilizing his always-already established power as the adult and the teacher. In effect, he acts like "the Man" to instill his self-defined subversive rock and roll order on his students. Informing them he will be the lead singer in their rock band "student project," the class questions why Dewey should even be part of it, let alone its focus. In response, Dewey makes the class recite a parody of the "Pledge of Allegiance" (to the *band*) in which the students swear never to question any of his decisions or creative control. Another contradiction of *SoR* is that the Square Establishment is *not* represented by "the Man" but "the *Woman*" ranging from the class factotum Summer Hathaway, school principal Ms. Mullins, and especially Ned's odious girlfriend Patty Di Marco (the gender politics of *SoR* to be returned to shortly). As discussed in Chapter 2, rock ideology entailed constructing the "feminine Other" versus the "masculine authentic" of rock. In *SoR*, Hipness and anti–Establishment is represented by the *adult male* as "the Man."

Dewey's rock canon is situated as both timeless and inherently oppositional music, and the choice is *either* embracing it and a future of being forever Hip *or* rejecting it and damnation to being eternally Square. Equally important is what is not only consciously *included* but *excluded* as well. In other words, the *SoR* canon is comprised of omitting what is *not* within the "spirit of rock" in order to define what *is*. Noticeably marginalized in the *SoR* curriculum are African-Americans and women in popular music. While Jimi Hendrix as classic rock is prominent, the black presence in popular music as far as genres like blues, Motown, disco, rap, and hip-hop are conspicuously absent; jazz is primarily represented by white drummer Buddy Rich while Puff Daddy is explicitly singled out as not rock and roll. In the context of the culturally coded relationship between masculinity and oppositional culture rebellion versus femininity and mass culture conformity, the presence of women in rock and roll is also minimized, expect for Blondie and Stevie Nicks (Blondie's lead singer Deborah Harry and Stevie Nicks also being 1970s rock icons). Teen pop, with the specific mention of Christina Aguilera, is deemed right out. When Tomika — a shy, overweight African-American girl — asks for a singing role in the band, she impresses Dewey with several seconds of Aretha Franklin's "Chain of Fools." He lets her in the band as a background singer and assigns her homework by studying the background soul singers on Pink Floyd's *Dark Side of the Moon*.

In fairness, *SoR* offering a comprehensive history of rock and roll would have resulted in a film that lasted an entire academic semester instead of 109 minutes. Much of rock and roll history is condensed to a montage sequence. Dewey is shown explaining the genealogy of popular music genres through an elaborate flow chart on the blackboard, along with photos slides and video clips as part of his lectures. Classic rock heroes presented are Pete Townshend and Keith Moon (the Who), Jimi Hendrix, and Angus Young (AC/DC). Punk is represented by Iggy Pop, the Ramones, and the Clash. Also included is the patron saint of alternative rock, Kurt Cobain. Equally important is the song used to accompany this sequence, the Ramones' "My Brain Is Hanging Upside Down (Bonzo Goes to Bitburg)," released in 1985. Again, the Ramones and punk rock serve as the musical accompaniment for a seamless history of rock and roll represented as unbridled rebellion. Moreover, "My Brain Is Hanging Upside Down" was the Ramones *only* attempt at an overtly left-liberal "political song." Co-written by lead singer Joey Ramone (who was Jewish) and bassist Dee Dee Ramone in response to Ronald Reagan giving a controversial commemorative speech at a cemetery in Germany where Nazi SS soldiers were buried, the song's title was "Bonzo Goes to Bitburg" when it was first released in Europe as a single; the less-politicized title was used for the song's American release. Nor did it reflect a unified stance by the Ramones, in that guitarist Johnny Ramone was an outspoken ultra-conservative and staunch Reagan Republican. (When the Ramones were inducted into the Rock and Roll Hall of Fame in 2002, Johnny Ramone ended his acceptance speech with "God bless President Bush and God bless America.") The Ramones were already politically suspect amid the glut of anti–Reagan hardcore bands that dominated the early 1980s, at the forefront being the Dead Kennedys and the yodeled diatribes of Jello Biafra. "My Brain Is Hanging Upside Down (Bonzo Goes to Bitburg)" seemed more a concerted attempt to reestablish diminishing punk "credibility," as sincere as the intent may have been.

When the punk rock movement began in the mid–1970s, it generated a great deal of controversy for its radical politics being seen as far right rather than far left, especially given the references to Nazism and use of Nazi imagery by some punk bands, including the Ramones.[6] As J. Hoberman and Jonathan Rosenbaum noted, "New York punk was *initially* characterized by a combination of *reactionary politics and extreme formalism*; London punk was equally *form conscious* but more generally left-wing.... What was radical in both New York and London was an attempt to create a new youth culture from the ashes of the old."[7] Moreover, the ethos between the NYC and the London punk scene concerning the sanctity of rock music was vastly different. Joey Ramone recounted that "[the Ramones] wanted to kind of save rock and roll, keep it exciting and fun and the whole bit."[8] The Sex Pistols' mission was not to save rock music, but to bury it. In one of his more hyperbolic moments, Greil Marcus argued, "The Sex Pistols happened upon the impulse of destruction coded in the form, turned that impulse back on form, and blew it up."[9] To be sure, the Sex Pistols introduced a strain of unprecedented virulence to the form, but the form itself was hardly "blown up," let alone radicalized. Chuck Berry and the early Who could easily be heard as primary Sex Pistols influences. Subtracting the venomous vocals and provocative lyrics, it is difficult to distinguish "Anarchy in the U.K." and "God Save the Queen" from most other 1970s hard rock anthems. Rather, as Paul Hegarty observed, "The noise of the music did shock

... (*whether it would have without the non-musical elements is more debatable*)....
Their noise is the social disruption pointed out by Attali (without reference to
punk), where social and political authorities reject a troublesome, popular
entertainment."[10]

Indeed, the impact of the Sex Pistols largely owed to a "situationist use of
music" and executing what manager Malcolm McLaren envisioned, and feebly
attempted, with his brief stint managing the New York Dolls ca. 1974.[11] Simon
Frith noted, "McLaren's ambition was to turn spectacle — the passively lived
structure of reality that we, as consumers live with — into situation, the structure blown up, its rules made clear, [and] the possibilities for action and desire
exposed."[12] In this sense, the Sex Pistols became a grotesque "serious-parody"
or *détournement* of the rock and roll band. Rock and rock has always been
defined and *self*-defined as crude, defiant, flippant, irreverent, and loud. The
Sex Pistols exaggerated and exacerbated rock's imaginary self-image into a
repellant real. As Andrew Hussey suggested, "A perfect series of negative rever-
sals had replaced politics with art, made the audiences artists, and abolished
the prevailing cultural consensus all in one single move ... the spectacle dis-
rupted and faced with its own negative reflection."[13]

The problematic "radicalism" of punk was its complete repudiation of the
current state of mid–1970s rock and roll excess (concept albums, elaborate concert spectacles, technology-driven music) through a return to 1950s and early
1960s traditionalism. Late 1960s hippie music (and, more so, the "peace and
love" vibe), progressive rock and "art rock," disco and black music in general,
and hard rock/heavy metal were *all* deemed "dinosaurs" by punk. By the end
of the 1970s, post-punk bands began exploring assemblages of punk, black
music genres, and avant-garde/experimental music; the more notable examples
included the Talking Heads' *Fear of Music*, the Gang of Four's *Entertainment!*,
and the Pop Group's *Y* (all released in 1979).[14] Metal and punk continued their
musical and subcultural animosity into the mid–1980s, finally reaching an
accord when hard rock and heavy metal influenced hardcore bands (Bad Brains,
Black Flag, Die Kreuzen, Soundgarden) found common ground with punk
and hardcore influenced speed metal bands (Anthrax, Metallica, Megadeth,
Slayer).[15]

In summary, this educational montage sequence in *SoR* does not present
rock's contradictory and contentious history of competing internal discourses,
but instead establishes a hegemonic rock mythology in order to construct "a
new youth culture from the ashes of the old" around what is now *adult culture*,
manufactured between the 1960s through the 1990s. Like the Ramones, the mission of *SoR* is the *saving* rock in all of its mythic "anti–Establishment" glory.
In passing down the great tradition of "rock rebellion" as a canon of white male
hard rock (a.k.a. "cock rock"), the "authentic masculine" of rock culture and
rock ideology is further produced by *SoR* as much as the film is a product of
that culture and ideology.

## The Boys in the Band (or, Rock and Role)

Dewey's "learn by doing" approach to rock music converts the classroom into a microcosm of rock culture, encompassing a band, stage technicians, roadies, security, set designers, groupies, and management. At the surface level, *SoR* goes to great lengths to present the class project of becoming a rock and roll band as an egalitarian, multicultural, and gender-mixed community. As briefly touched on, the problem is how this is undercut in the film and, rather than inclusiveness, there is a *marginalization* of diversity. In other words, in *SoR* some are more equal than others in the rock and roll classroom order.

The band is eventually named "School of Rock" (henceforth referred to as "SOR band") with Dewey the lead singer, rhythm guitarist, and exuberant front man. The rest of the band is comprised of four kids. Two are white males; Zack is an introverted guitarist and Freddie a rebellious drummer.[16] The third is Lawrence, a nerdy Asian-American boy who studies classical piano. Fourth is Katie, a nondescript white female who plays cello and becomes the bass player by default. However, the inclusion of a female in the core band is not necessarily a nod to the increased role of women in rock music, but a play on the rock in-joke that bass is the easiest job and therefore done by the least competent musician in the band: the only girl.[17]

Three other girls (two African-American, one white) assume the role of the back-up singers and their job is indeed "backing up" Dewey and the band (in that order) with some onstage choreography and vocal punctuations largely repeating and supporting Dewey's vocals (their occasional vocal solo bits notwithstanding). Billy, a rather effeminate boy, asks for and is given the job of the SOR band "stylist," doing hair and wardrobe. The rest of the class are given jobs as stage sound and lights, roadies, security, and for the girls for whom Dewey can't find jobs, "groupies." Summer Hathaway, the smartest and snottiest girl in class, fails her audition for back-up singer and is eventually consigned to the groupies. Greatly offended at her lowly status in the class project — "I researched groupies on the internet: they're *sluts!*" — Summer threatens to tell her *mom* on Dewey and thereby reveal his entire fraud. Again, "the *Woman*" becomes the potential force to kill both the fun and rebellion inscribed in rock music around the masculine. While ostensibly presented as a show of respect, Dewey makes her the SOR band manager. Dewey realizes that Summer may not have what it takes to be in the band, but her penchant for (female) ruthless manipulation has all the hallmarks of what every band needs most: a cold-blooded, cut-throat manager. Summer retains her will to stereotypical female vindictiveness, but it is through Dewey that any human side actually emerges. To frame it in Jungian terminology, Dewey represents the masculine-Sol that allows the light to emit from the feminine-Luna of Summer. Indeed, Dewey's epiphany that he must be the kid's guiding light towards rock Hipness occurs when he sees them going through the motions of a rudimentary neo-classical

Dewey Finn (Jack Black) explains the history of rock. Note he is pointing out "Hard Rock" (Paramount Pictures/Photofest).

composition in their music class. The moment is matched by Cream's "Sunshine of Your Love" on the soundtrack.

The authority and authoritarian figures in *SoR* are represented by women (despite Dewey's own tendencies towards autocratic rule in the classroom). The tightly wound school principal, Ms. Mullins, develops a close but platonic relationship with Dewey, who rekindles her own "inner teenager" and her forgotten love for rock music through Stevie Nicks and the song "Edge of Seventeen." However, at the end of the film Ms. Mullins is clearly attracted to one of the rival band members at the battle of the bands and assumes the more "natural" role of the woman in the rock culture: groupie. By far the most hateful character in *SoR* is Patty Di Marco, Ned's humorless, obnoxious, emasculating girlfriend. Patty despises Dewey and browbeats Ned. When Ned discovers Dewey's fraud, it is at Patty's insistence that he exposes Dewey to the school administration. Patty is the personification of Square Establishment and "the Man" in the form of the stereotypical "animus-woman" who has an inherent drive or "natural instinct" to kill every semblance of rebellious fun in the male psyche, especially when expressed by rock music.

In *SoR*, the theory and practice of rock "empowering" young people to be unrepentant individuals is underscored by the message that said individualism will ensure greater personal success in life and, in turn, a better liberal-democratic society. *SoR* presents rock rebellion as *productive not destructive* (so much for punk anarchy). Indeed, rock is not just carefree non-conformity and the directionless rebellion of being a slacker. Rock is about dedication and perseverance to make one's dreams a reality, which Dewey makes clear when he sternly lectures Freddie after he becomes enamored with a group of musicians smoking cigarettes and drinking beer in their van at the battle of the bands auditions. In the film's battle of the bands finale, Dewey is dejected that the SOR band lost to the band that fired him early in the film. However, the kids quickly point out to Dewey they are the real "winners" and Dewey's lessons have been well learned. Individualism is self-determination, doing things one's own way, building personal self-esteem, and sculpting the singular character necessary to achieve one's highest goals and become a success in life.[18]

Moreover, the SOR band fulfills rock music's mission of forming community. While Dewey's deception is discovered, he is quickly forgiven by the incensed faculty and parents when they are unanimously wowed with the SOR band's performance at the battle of the bands; Dewey is hired as the full-time music teacher.[19] The generation gap — a central demarcation point of teen culture politics — is bridged rather than exacerbated. The kids are alright because they have embraced the rock tradition of their parents, and the parents can take pride in the fact that their cultural legacy is still relevant. The rock ideology of yesterday is imposed on the youth of today and is translated into good citizenship rather than anti–Establishment opposition. In doing so, the contradiction is inhibited by Dewey Finn as the cultural "archetype" of wise elder as well as eternal teenager. He converts rock history and rock ideology into timeless rock myth, while rock music organizes society rather than rock noise disrupting it.

In *SoR*, teen rebellion is ultimately represented as a process of explicitly learning the musical-cultural language of the adult and replicating it under the guidance of the adult to actualize a productive "pseudo-non-conformity." In the film's closing segment, Summer is on her cell phone in hardball negotiations with promoters who want to book the SOR band while they diligently practice in the classroom but revel in the joy of rock music at the same time, performing a cover of AC/DC's "It's a Long Way to the Top (If You Wanna Rock and Roll)." In effect, *SoR* ends with the same "have fun + hard work = social mobility" messages of *True Jackson, VP* (discussed in Chapter 7). However, the AC/DC song is not so much a celebration of living the rock and roll dream but an account of the arduous labor of being in a rock band (the grind of touring, playing piecemeal gigs, living on minimal income, etc.). In *SoR*, the drudgery of rock and roll expressed by AC/DC is converted into a celebration of individual initiative and team effort that pays off as far as achieving personal and social success.

Moreover, the Ramones are again referenced as Zack is wearing a Ramones T-shirt. While the Ramones' punk mythos of teenage rebellion becomes the visual signifier, the end message of *SoR* is antithetical to the end of *Rock and Roll High School*. School and rock are no longer inherent enemies and the struggle ended with rock destroying school; instead, school and rock can very much work together. While punk becomes a visual signifier (posters of the Ramones and the Sex Pistols can also be seen in the classroom), classic rock remains the aural signifier. The Ramones juxtaposed with AC/DC becomes another moment of historical revision in *SoR* to suggest punk and hard rock were always-already at one with each other as far as cultural "opposition." The finale also betrays the film's adherence to the masculine domination in rock ideology. Dewey calls for each *male* member of the SOR band (guitar, drums, and keyboards) to do a brief solo and showcase their individual talents. Katie, the bass player and the only girl who plays an instrument in the band, is *not* called on to do a solo. In fact, this marginalization of Katie occurs twice in the film. Dewey assigns homework to the members of the band, a CD by a 1960s or 1970s band to study. The white girl back-up singer is assigned Blondie, the African-American girl back-up singer Pink Floyd's *Dark Side of the Moon*, the male drummer Rush's *2112*, the male keyboardist Yes's *Fragile*, and the male guitarist Jimi Hendrix's *Axis: Bold as Love*. Katie is *not* assigned a CD for homework, in that the bass and the girl playing it are seemingly irrelevant in the SOR band. While the three-girl back-up singers are allowed brief moments to showcase their vocal abilities, it is only after Dewey cues them and explicitly tells them to "repeat what I say" before he launches into some enthusiastic rock vocal gibberish and the girls repeat it accordingly. The order in *SoR* is established — and thoroughly Establishment — as far as the leader and the followers. The adult rules over the teen, the male rules over the female, the educational apparatus rules over the students, and the self-proclaimed Hip rules over those they pronounce as Square.

As stressed, *SoR* represents a conversion of rock history and rock ideology into rock mythology. History, especially as far as generational politics and teen culture is concerned, is a two-way street. To be sure, there is certain legitimacy in addressing the loss of rock history over successive generations. However, it is not enough to nostalgically pine for the glory days of classic rock and its always-already assumed authenticity and oppositional status. Black Sabbath's *Paranoid* (1970) may or may not "stand the test of time" but what is important is that *Paranoid* was both a disconcerting product and profound commentary on the times. Dense, ominous rock with Ozzy Osbourne's plaintive nasal wail almost desperately trying to cut through the din, *Paranoid* emerged while the counterculture political concerns were raging (Vietnam on "War Pigs" and the threat of World War III on "Electric Funeral") while the counterculture dream was self-destructing (drug addiction on "Hand of Doom" and personal alienation on "Paranoid"). Three decades later, when Dewey teaches Zack the riff to "Iron Man," the best-known song from *Paranoid*, Black Sabbath becomes a signifier of "classic rock" and nothing more. In discussing Adorno's criticism of Stravinsky, Richard Leppert's analysis expressed the problem:

> Stravinsky ... recognizes the historicity of style but ignores the consequences of this history; hence he employs style not as an integral demarcator of music *in*

history, but as decorative resonance; as it were, "history" as in Disneyland. Stravinsky borrows style like a tourist who passes pleasurably from Frontierland to Tomorrowland, one ersatz façade to another. To the extent that history is reduced to mere quotation (not the least regressive feature of postmodernism, though that's a different matter) history is fact forgotten.[20]

Not so much the tourist but the tour guide, Dewey Finn leads his students through the selective canon of rock and roll and the great *men* of rock history presented as the role models of youth rebellion and where the style inherently entails the opposition no matter how much it becomes Establishment culture over time.

## Competing Discourse: What a Girl Wants

*What a Girl Wants* (2003, henceforth *WaGW*) can be read as the riposte to the gender and generational politics of Hipness manifest in *School of Rock*. *WaGW* stars Amanda Bynes, who was one of Nickelodeon's early teen stars, achieving initial recognition on the comedy-variety show *All That*, on which Bynes was a regular from 1996–2000. In 1999, she was promoted to her own comedy-variety program, *The Amanda Show*, which ran until 2002; Bynes then moved to primetime with the sitcom *What I Like About You* (the WB, 2002–6).[21]

*WaGW* featured Bynes as Daphne Reynolds, the impetuous, intelligent, and independent figure of girl power. Daphne has lived a bohemian lifestyle, growing up in the Chinatown district of New York City with a single mom, Libby Reynolds—her first name a pun on "liberation"—who ekes out a living happily singing in a mediocre wedding band. The void in Daphne's life is that she has never met her father, Lord Henry Dashwood, a powerful British aristocrat and politician who married Libby in Morocco during his younger, wilder days. Due to the intervention of ruthless family advisor Alistair Payne, Libby's pregnancy was concealed from Henry and she was forced back to America, ending the marriage. Payne is now on the verge of consolidating his position and power as the Dashwood patriarch with Henry's forthcoming marriage to his snobbish daughter Gynnis and Henry's election into Parliament, with Payne his chief advisor and campaign manager. Daphne decides to go to England and meet her long-lost father, and in the process meets her true love, Ian, a working-class commoner who is also an aspiring rock musician (his ensemble somehow seems to be the house band for every social gathering in London).

Without question, *WaGW* can be criticized as contrived, sentimental, and predictable — although the terms are vague enough they also could be applied to *SoR*. The issue is the film's gender and generational politics versus *SoR*, as well as the class and nationalist subtext of *WaGW*. As discussed in Chapter 2, the cultural conflict between Europe and America, and the superiority of the latter over the former, is a long-standing issue in American cultural discourses. Daphne represents the unrefined Americanism of adaptability, adventure, individualism, pragmatism, and spontaneity: she is a Hip "social atom." As Daphne makes clear in an argument with her teen antagonist Clarissa Payne, "If you'd take your nose out of the air for one second, you'd see that you're designer; I'm vintage. You have a mansion; I have a five-floor walk-up. You're snotty little 'Miss Cranky Pants' and I go with the flow." However, these are traits she gets from her free-spirited mother, Libby, whose compact van is painted with the stars-and-stripes pattern of the American flag. In contrast, the aristocratic English are generally pompous, snobbish, and uptight Squares. The immediate exception is Henry's mother, Lady Jocelyn Dashwood, who quickly takes a liking to Daphne in that Lady Dashwood has come to detest the hypocrisy of upper-class society and the Payne family in particular (and the obvious pun on "Payne" and "pain"). Indeed, Lady Dashwood's fondness for afternoon clay-pigeon shooting on the grounds of the Dashwood estate amounts to an excuse to use the ornate statutes in the gardens for target practice.

Daphne's love of the good time over good manners becomes embarrassingly irritating to some (namely the Payne family) and refreshingly infectious to others (particularly the older women and teenage girls in high society). At a deadly dull debutante ball, Daphne and Ian get the party started with some James Brown and disco dance moves; a full-scale musical revue number ensues until they "bring the roof down" and an expensive chandelier crashes to the floor. To be sure, black music is used in order to signify the white teenage girl Daphne as the Hip American disturbance amid a stuffy world of English Squares. Yet it becomes a marked difference to *SoR* and the use of classic rock to signify the white, male adult as the messenger of the Hip to teens well on their way to becoming Squares.

Indeed, Daphne's arrival rekindles Henry's own long-suppressed wild side that was effectively squashed when his marriage to Libby was sabotaged and his father died, which abruptly forced him into adult life with all of its obligations and responsibilities. When Henry's increasingly less-than-sophisticated public behavior begins to jeopardize his political career, Daphne decides to conform to the ways of the English upper-class and, as Ian points out when he breaks up with her, the new Daphne is not the "real you." As the seamy foundations of upper-class society becomes clear, Daphne realizes that she indeed has to be the "real Daphne" and rejects the Dashwood heritage in favor of her former life in America. In turn, Lady Dashwood tells Henry that, after 20 years of fitting in with the plans and ambitions of others, he has long lost touch with the "real Henry." After withdrawing his candidacy, ending his engagement with Gynnis, and terminating Alistair's employment (punctuated by punching him in the face), Henry and Ian travel to America where Henry and Libby, Ian and Daphne, and Henry and Daphne are all reunited.

Now living in the Dashwood estate and going to Oxford, Daphne gets "what a girl wants" in a fairy-tale reality that far surpasses her wildest dreams, and achieved precisely because she decided to be herself. Much like *SoR*, Hip individualism trumps Square conformity and becomes the ticket for social mobility as well as societal rebellion. The difference is that *SoR* represents the Hip as the domain of the adult male (Dewey Finn) and the Square as the domain of women (school administrators, controlling girlfriends), the teenager (stodgy prep school students), and especially the teenage girl (the problematic status of Summer Hathaway). *WaGW* reverses this by representing Square as the domain of the adult male (the "out-of-touch" side of Henry and, especially, Alistair Payne) while Hip as the domain of women (Libby, Lady Dashwood), the teenager (Ian), and, above all, the teenage girl (Daphne).

# 11

# *Keeping It Real and Imaginary: The Ideological Contradictions of* Hannah Montana

> In ideology [people] do indeed express, not in the relationship between them and their conditions of existence, but *the way* they live the relationship between them and their conditions of existence.... Ideology, then, is the expression of the relation between [people] and their "world," that is the (overdetermined) unity of the real relation and the imaginary relation between them and their conditions of existence. In ideology the real relation is inevitably invested in the imaginary relation, a relation that expresses a will (conservative, conformist, reformist, or revolutionary), a hope or nostalgia, rather than describing a reality.[1]—*Louis Althusser*

## *Second Wave Teen Pop*

The pop-music sitcom, a genre largely defunct after the cancellation of *The Partridge Family* in 1974, was resurrected with the debut of the Disney teen sitcom *Hannah Montana* (2006–11).[2] Well within the formal traditions of the classical sitcom of multi-camera set-up, sound stage sets, and a laugh track to the point of anachronism, *Hannah Montana* could easily be mistaken for a lower-budget 1980s sitcom (so much for Disney production values), and this highly "retro" aspect of *Hannah Montana* was more than appropriate as far as cross-marketing Hannah Montana into pop music.

Like First Wave Teen Pop, Second Wave Teen Pop is rooted in 1980s popular music. However, First Wave Teen Pop was highly influenced by the dance-pop sound of Michael Jackson's *Thriller* and Madonna's *Like a Virgin*. Second Wave Teen Pop's primary sources are New Wave and stadium rock. Alternative music is also prevalent in Second Wave Teen Pop's punk-metal components, specifically the emphasis on guitar riffs and backbeat drumming over synthesizers and funky drum machines or samples. The requisite dance-beat factor in Second Wave Teen Pop tends towards the steady thump of 1970s disco and Eurodisco as well as incorporating contemporary rap, hip-hop, and techno influences and production techniques. To be sure, there are also "bubblegum" aspects as far as Second Wave Teen Pop's emphasis on sing-along vocal melodies and an often sugary harmonic coating. Ultimately, if Michael Jackson and Madonna were the godparents of First Wave Teen Pop, women in rock music ranging from Deborah Harry, Stevie Nicks, Joan Jett, Cyndi Lauper, the Go-Gos, Bananarama, Gwen Stefani, Liz Phair, and even Britney Spears became the musical sources and role models for Second Wave Teen Pop performers.[3]

As suggested in Chapter 1, one contradiction of Hannah Montana is the music product championing teen empowerment and self-determination (agency and freedom) versus *Hannah Montana* as a sitcom product containing the requisite messages of teens acting within the norm (conformity and obedience). "We Got the Party" is the opening track from *Hannah Montana 2*.[4] Structurally, the song is fast, basic rock to the point of punk minimalism largely constructed around one, two, or four-bar alternations between B and A while driven by a snare backbeat and, for the most part, a pounding floor tom. The lyrics express the teenage will to freedom, where power is assembled within mobile and exclusive communities of teens which can be actualized in any place and at any time, provided it is outside the institutional confines of school and home. The shift from verse to chorus is both drastic and jarring, but executed *rhythmically* rather than *melodically* (the varying B-A chord alternations make up both the verse and chorus). Drawing from ska music (or, more likely, an effort to mimic No Doubt's popular brand of punk-ska-Alternative), the drums maintain the thumping backbeat while the guitars play staccato on every upbeat. However, the chorus of "We Got the Party" does not manifest the fluid bounce of ska but instead produces a clunky, mechanistic jumpiness that veers perilously close to falling apart musically. At one level, the aural signification suggests images of a carousel and its bobbing horses, where being a teenager is the experience of "life is a carnival." Another, less innocuous way to interpret the aural imagery is a combustion engine and its churning pistons, where assembled teen power set in motion is a volatile "war machine."[5]

To be sure, the struggle between teen autonomy and adult authority represented in "We Got the Party" is the exception to the rule of Hannah Montana songs. Rather than "negative" messages of teenage defiance, most Hannah Montana lyrics contain "positive" messages of self-determination, self-confidence, and good self-esteem. "Life's What You Make It" (*Hannah Montana 2*) exemplifies the Hannah Montana brand of teen pop. The title is self-explanatory as far as message, and the lyrics are a corny series of self-help affirmations; the catchy melody and sing-along chorus provide bubblegum qualities. As far as the musical framework, the song is a stadium-rock anthem with a New Wave robotic dance beat and keyboard lines that resemble the synthpop of Devo, while the start-stop distorted guitar riffs oddly recall the punk-metal band Helmet.

It was not coincidental that Second Wave Teen Pop largely emerged in the aftermath of *School of Rock*'s critical and commercial success as far as reiterating and revitalizing rock traditionalism.[6] At one level, Second Wave Teen Pop exhibits much more pronounced rock influences than First Wave Teen Pop to manifest a greater sense of "authenticity" as far as pop music marketed for an assumed "teenybopper" audience. Second Wave Teen Pop also shares the problematic aspect of *School of Rock* as far as being primarily informed by white pop and rock genres—bubblegum, classic rock, punk, New Wave, stadium rock, Alternative, even country and New Country—and what could be called an overall "whiteness" in Second Wave Teen Pop (the utilization of disco, funk, rap, etc. notwithstanding).[7] Above all, Second Wave Teen Pop echoed *School of Rock*'s subtle but crucial shift in the emphasis of rock ideology from social rebellion to individual self-determination. Once the surface messages and the quality arguments are put aside, there is little, if any, ideological difference between *Hannah Montana: The Movie* and *School of Rock* except that Hannah Montana's "conservatism" can be read through its contradictions as a political position that ruptures and falls apart under the weight of its ideology, whereas *School of Rock*'s "opposition" can be read through its contradictions as an affirmation of Establishment ideology which inhibits rebellion rather than endorsing it.

## The Best of Both Worlds

On *Hannah Montana*, Miley Stewart (Miley Cyrus) was an unsophisticated and sometimes impertinent Southern teenage girl living in Malibu leading a double life as Hannah Montana, a brash and occasionally obnoxious teen pop-music superstar. (For clarification, "Miley" refers to Miley Stewart unless specifically stated as Miley Cyrus). As far as back story, the Hannah Montana persona was largely the creation of Miley's old-fashioned, pragmatic, and strict father Robby Stewart (played by Miley Cyrus's father, singer and actor Billy Ray Cyrus).[8] Robby Stewart was a former country-pop star known as "Robby Ray" who left the music business to raise his children, Jackson and Miley, after his wife died. He allowed Miley to pursue a career in the music business, but only through the guise of Hannah Montana as a "public" star identity to separate show business and wealth from Miley's "private" identity as an ordinary teenage girl; Miley transformed into Hannah Montana with a blonde wig and trendy clothing. Under his own public persona, "Robby Ray Montana," and wearing a fake moustache in public to conceal *his* private identity, Robby Stewart not only acted as Hannah Montana's business manager but wrote the songs Hannah Montana converted into hit singles.

In "Ready, Set, Don't Drive" (2008), Miley failed her driver's test but wanted to drive to a big party. Going back to the DMV as Hannah Montana, she bribed the clerk with Hannah Montana backstage passes and immediately got a driver's license. Unfortunately, the license was issued to Hannah Montana and Miley was arrested for driving with a fake license. If the punishment fits the crime, the episode ended with her father driving her to the party and using a bullhorn to announce to all her friends that Miley failed her driver's test. "Ready, Set, Don't Drive" was typical of *Hannah Montana*'s ethical form as situation (Miley Stewart deciding to use the advantages of being Hannah Montana to fulfill her immediate wants) → action (the plan backfired) → situation (Miley learned the importance of doing things the right way, even if she didn't get what she wanted in the end). In effect, this was largely the same ethical form as Disney's concurrent teen sitcom *Wizards of Waverly Place*, except Miley learned not to abuse her hidden star power while Alex Russo learned not to exploit her magical abilities and what amounted to the hidden power of God. As briefly alluded to in Chapter 5, compared to the recent representations of self-responsible girl power on Nickelodeon (*Zoey 101, iCarly,* and *True Jackson, VP*), the Disney brand of girl-power sitcoms like *Hannah Montana* and *Wizards of Waverly Place* represented the teenage girl as more incorrigible and, therefore, more in need of strict parental authority to rein in her rebellious nature in direct proportion to power she can potentially actualize.

As a pop-music sitcom, *Hannah Montana* seemed little more than a patriarchal version of *The Partridge Family*. However, the Partridge Family was a group of normal suburban kids with normal lives, responsibilities and problems and also happened to have successful careers as pop musicians. In the context of the early 1970s, "flower power" had given way to Altamont, Charles Manson, and the Weather Underground. The message of *The Partridge Family* was that white, middle-class teens could still be good kids and good citizens even if they enjoy rock and roll, (or a watered-down version of it) as family entertainment, up to including their mom as a member of the band, along with the mutual understanding that the band is a family business designed to earn money. *Hannah Montana* began its run in 2006, and public displeasure with American conservatism was evident. The Republican Party was, as George W. Bush put it, "thumped" in the 2006 midterm election, leading to the triumph of New Democrat neoliberalism in 2008, a shift especially popular with younger people. At the same time, *Hannah Montana* operated within the overall conservative tendencies of the sitcom genre; moreover, as a Disney product, it was expected to contain overt messages affirming traditional American values, usually manifest in *highly* conservative political positions. In terms of being a girl-power teen sitcom with an assumed audience of tween/teen girls, *Hannah Montana* needed to offer some sense of an empowered main character that wasn't just acting as a mass culture drone thoroughly controlled by her father (hence, the Nickelodeon response with *iCarly* in which Carly Shay is both a successful independent DYI culture producer as well as a teenager effectively living on her own with minimal adult supervision). As noted, cross-marketing both Hannah Montana and Miley Cyrus into pop music involved a concerted effort to avoid being tagged pure teenybopper product through conscious attempts at manifesting rock authenticity and rock ideology via the Second Wave Teen Pop genre. In short, *Hannah Montana*'s problematic was presenting itself as Hip within industrial and ideological constraints that could easily render the whole project Square beginning with the representation of a white, Southern, teenage girl as Hip.

Within these tensions, two issues *Hannah Montana* tackled were *class* and *mass culture*. While the genre format suggested *The Partridge Family*, *Hannah Montana* was more comparable to *The Beverly Hillbillies* (CBS, 1962–71) in its representation of a political struggle between Southern-lower class and West Coast-upper class, which is not to say class politics of "haves versus have-nots" (rich versus poor). Like the Clampetts on *The Beverly Hillbillies*, the Stewarts were simple Southerners—and proud of it—who attained considerable wealth but refused to conform to upper-class and West Coast lifestyle. Unlike the Clampetts, the Stewarts "earned" their fortune through years of hard work in the music industry. The Clampetts became miraculously rich when they accidentally discovered they lived in rural squalor over an oil deposit, sold the property for millions of dollars, moved to Beverly Hills, and were simply unable (and unwilling) to adapt to bourgeois conventions. As the Clampett family stood out as the "white trash" sore thumbs of their posh surroundings, family patriarch Jed Clampett was the bastion of pragmatism and common sense amid the unremitting smarminess and snobbery of Beverly Hills, and in particular the pathetic attempts by his nephew Jethro, and daughter Elly May to ingratiate their way into the socioeconomic elite.[9] On *Hannah Montana*, Robby Stewart performed an almost identical function, allowing Miley to pursue her dream of pop stardom, but *only* as Hannah Montana and *not* as Miley Stewart, and in doing so having "the best of both worlds," with Hannah Montana leading the glamorous life of wealth and fame while Miley retained a separate and simple life adhering to traditional American values.[10]

On *Hannah Montana* Miley and Jackson's chief nemesis was Rico Suave, a thoroughly obnoxious and profit-motivated "rich kid." Miley and her friend Lilly Truscott's primary high-school antagonists were a clique of condescending rich girls, whereas Hannah Montana's closest friend was Traci Van Horn, a pretentious and shallow teen socialite. Robby had an ongoing feud with neighbor Albert Dontzig, an abrasive snob (who also came off as an "old queen" gay stereotype); Dontzig despised the Stewarts and often referred to them as "hillbillies." In "The Test of My Love" (2008), Miley and a rich boy, Trey Harris, begin a romantic relationship complicated by Trey's insufferably snobbish parents (played as parodies of Thurston and Lovey Howell from *Gilligan's Island*). Constantly belittling Miley's "hillbilly" roots and demeanor, Miley invites the Harris family to the Stewart home and her family tries to act sophisticated to no avail. Finally losing her temper, Miley orders Mr. and Mrs. Harris out of the Stewart home, effectively breaking up with Trey, who asks Miley if he can stay. When Mr. Harris curtly informs Trey that he is "disappointed" with him, Trey responds that the feeling is mutual, and the episode ends with the Stewarts teaching Trey how to eat Bar-B-Q ribs with his hands.

As far as mass culture, *iCarly* is the teen sitcom that most directly seeks to inhibit the contradiction of teen culture being adult-produced mass culture through Carly and her friends being DYI culture producers with their "iCarly" webshow. Moreover, *iCarly* constructs a clear difference between the teen-culture kids take pleasure in versus the products of the teen-culture industry that teens consume but rarely if ever enjoy. Specific targets on *iCarly* included the untalented "Ginger Fox" (a parody of Britney Spears) and the unscrupulous "Dingo Channel" (the parody of the Disney Channel) as the more egregious examples of "inauthentic" teen culture foisted on teenagers. On *Hannah Montana*, the critique was more subtle. As noted, Miley's father, Robby, invented and controlled the Hannah Montana enterprise, managing her career and even writing her hit songs. Even if inadvertently, *Hannah Montana* revealed the contradiction of teen culture as *produced and controlled by adults for teen consumption*. Hannah Montana represented mass culture in the form of the teenage girl/pop star that was, quite literally, "inauthentic" as a consciously manufactured pop-star image and commodity. With apologies to Henri Bergson, Hannah Montana was "more than image" and "less than reality" whose artificiality is made abundantly clear and yet assumes a life in its own as far as the cultural marketplace and the society of the spectacle.

In this regard, Hannah Montana songs like "Best of Both Worlds," "Rock Star," and "Supergirl" are self-referential and even self-parodic songs about stardom (at what point the self-parody is intentional versus unintentional is another matter). "Best of Both Worlds," the lead-off track from the *Hannah Montana* debut CD as well as the sitcom title theme, contrasts the benefits of stardom (media attention, the red carpet, celebrity soirees) with the advantages of leading the mundane normal life (anonymity, going to school, slumber parties). "Rock Star" (*Hannah Montana 2*) is about a girl having a crush on boy who doesn't notice her when she could be many things he would be impressed with, including the pop star that may well be the object of his adoration. As much as typifying the Hannah Montana brand of bubblegum-New Wave-stadium-rock hybrid, "Rock Star" makes a crucial appearance in *Hannah Montana: The Movie*. "Supergirl" (*Hannah Montana 3*) is a song constructed around dialectical tension. The verses describes pop-star life as work that can be far from rewarding labor, and housed in the style of mechanistic synthpop. The chorus describes what the public thinks the life of a pop superstar is like, and done as overblown hard rock rave-up. The irony is that the reality of the music industry is expressed through "inauthentic pop" (the synthpop verses) whereas the imaginary of stardom is expressed through "authentic rock" (hard rock) in what sounds like two entirely different songs spliced together in the studio and abruptly colliding in musical montage.[11]

Hannah Montana (Miley Cyrus) rocks out in *Hannah Montana: The Movie* (Walt Disney Pictures/Photofest).

As discussed in Chapter 9, stardom is itself a "role" played *offstage* as much as *onstage*, and performed antithetically by Madonna and Britney Spears. *Hannah Montana*'s first two seasons coincided with the daily media saga of Britney Spears and the parallels were unmistakable as far as a Southern "white trash" girl attempting to cope with the pressures of fame and show business while playing the role of (manufactured) pop star for public consumption. In "Yet Another Side of Me" (2008), Hannah Montana meets her idol "Isis, the Queen of Pop," an obvious and rather unflattering parody of Madonna, whose hits include "Immaterial Girl" and "Impress Yourself." In a highly affected upper-class voice, Isis lectures Hannah on the importance of planning the "next next" thing to stay ahead of the audience, which is to say being a star who consciously "reinvents" oneself in a series of products to be consumed by the public (Madonna) versus the star simply being consumed by the public (Britney Spears).[12] Miley seriously contemplates a radical change until she has a nightmare about a new Hannah Montana punk/metal image causing a riot at a Sunshine Girls troop luncheon, and realizes that a key aspect of "playing the role" of Hannah Montana is being a "good role model" to her fans and giving the fans what they expect from her: a dependable and safe cultural product.[13]

Nevertheless, Hannah Montana did *not* represent "the imaginary" and Miley Stewart "the real" as the sitcom scenario would dictate. Rather, Hannah Montana and Miley Stewart were *both* ideological representations. The Hannah Montana song "Just Like You" appears on the *Hannah Montana* debut CD and is also featured in the second episode ("Miley Get Your Gum," 2006). As the title makes clear, the message is that Hannah Montana achieved her dreams and made them "reality," but underneath the pop star image she is no different from the assumed audience of ordinary tween/teen girls who can achieve their dreams as well. Hannah Montana represents the end result of the American Dream attained (fame, riches, superstardom); Miley Stewart represents how the American Dream is attained in the first place (family values, hard work, humility, etc.). In the best of both worlds, Hannah Montana allows Miley Stewart to live the American Dream as pop stardom while not succumbing to it, and effectively manages American society's separation of the public sphere (community life, work, citizenship) and private sphere (individual life, home, family). The problematic was how *Hannah Montana* posited public and private life existing independently, which required the same person to play different and conflicting roles in society. For Hannah Montana to exist, Miley Stewart had to cease to exist, and vice versa. Likewise, Robby Stewart adopted the identity of "Robby Ray Montana" and Miley Stewart's best friend, Lilly, appeared in public with Hannah Montana as the ditzy "Lola Luftnagle" in a variety of gaudy wigs and outfits (with Lola serving as the stereotype of the teenybopper fan to Hannah Montana's stereotype of teen-pop star). Indeed, different personas were required for admission into the imaginary order of Hannah Montana so the reality of Miley Stewart could survive and, as important, the imaginary of Hannah Montana could survive as well.[14] As Guy Debord termed the society of the spectacle:

> What ideology already was, society has now become. A blocked practice and its corollary, an antidialectical false consciousness are imposed at every waking moment on an everyday life in the thrall of the spectacle — an everyday life that should be understood as the systematic breakdown of encounter, and the replacement of that faculty by a *social hallucination*: a false consciousness of encounter, or an "illusion of encounter." *In a society where no one is any longer recognizable by anyone else, each individual is necessarily unable to recognize [their] own reality. Here ideology is at home; here separation has built its world.*[15]

## *When Worlds Collide:* Hannah Montana: The Movie

The ideological tensions of Hannah Montana became the crux of *Hannah Montana: The Movie* (2009, henceforth *HMTM*). The initial situation of *HMTM* is that the Hannah Montana phenomenon is becoming unsustainable.[16] Miley Stewart is not only spending an inordinate amount of time as Hannah Montana fulfilling career duties, but wants to play the role of pop star Hannah Montana much more than live the humdrum private life of Miley Stewart. Robby Stewart, much to his chagrin as well as his growing impatience, is becoming acutely aware that the Hannah Montana alter-ego he originally created to shield his daughter is now taking over. To complicate matters, Hannah Montana's ambitious publicist, Vita, seems more interested in the "imaginary life" of Hannah Montana than the "real life" of Miley Stewart, and a seamy British tabloid reporter, Oswald Granger, is intent on discovering the "real story" behind Hannah Montana. Putting Hannah Montana on indefinite hiatus, Robby takes Miley back to her Tennessee hometown of Crowley Corners for her grandmother Ruby's birthday, hoping Miley rediscovers her "real self" as an old-fashioned country girl. Miley initially does not so much have trouble fitting in; she wants no part of fitting into life in Crowley Corners. Nonetheless, she begins to readjust to her old life (i.e., pre–Hannah Montana life), the change owing considerably to Miley developing a romantic relationship with a local boy, Travis Brody, as the unpretentious personification of Middle-American values such as common sense, hard work, humility, and straight talk.

The underlying crisis is that the continued existence of Crowley Corners is threatened by a ruthless real estate developer Mr. Bradley, who is intent on buying the nearby land known as "Crowley Meadows" in order to build a shopping mall. The citizens of Crowley Corners hold a fundraising concert in a desperate attempt to raise the money to outbid Mr. Bradley; the fundraiser also provides a means to include musical performances by Billy Ray Cyrus, Taylor Swift, and Miley Cyrus, albeit as characters within *HMTM*.[17] When Miley Stewart is encouraged to perform a song, she responds with "Hoedown Throwdown." She announces, "I'm gonna add a little hip-hop to this hoedown," which is to say Miley is going to add some Hip in the form of urban black music to the Square of rural white music. The strained pastiches of hip-hop rhythms, country/bluegrass music, and a vocal combining pop, rap, and square-dance calls all merge together as "objectivist music" (discussed in Chapter 9). The disparate musical styles and the cultures they signify (black/white, urban/rural, young/old, Coastal America/Middle America, etc.) do not collide in musical friction but blend into musical and social harmony. Indeed, "Hoedown Throwdown" turns into a full-scale revue number where Miley and the citizens of Crowley Corners—young and old, African-Americans and white, men and women—join together on the dance floor and bust their moves to the stiff choreography of the "Hoedown Throwdown." Whether one is critically discussing the high culture of Aaron Copland's "Hoedown" or the mass culture of Miley Cyrus's "Hoedown Throwdown," in the end *both* fall within the domain of "objectivist music" and both serve as musical and ideological representations of America as a harmonious space of unitary culture and the myth of the Great Melting Pot: the former by merging classical and operatic form with American rural dance and folk-music idioms; the latter by merging pop, country, and hip-hop.[18]

After "Hoedown Throwdown" concludes, the sense of community is quickly and toxically negated when the townspeople notice Mr. Bradley at the fundraiser. His presence prompts a livid reaction:

RUBY: You got a lot of nerve comin' in here!
MR. BRADLEY: Oh, I'm sorry. I thought this was a community event.
RUBY: *Community?* You wouldn't even know what that word means!
MR. BRADLEY: Well, I know your idea of it is a thing of the past.

As discussed in Chapter 6 and the *iCarly* episode "iBeat the Heat," it is unclear whether the increased individualization and privatization of American life is being satirized, or if the object of mockery is the long-standing ideal of traditional community that may now indeed be "a thing of the past" as America enters the neoliberal and postindustrial era. In contrast, the underlying drive of *HMTM* is preserving the ideological tenets of traditional community (not altogether surprising given it is a cultural product of Disney). While this reflects an essential conservatism in *Hannah Montana*, this ideology ultimately ruptures and collapses at the end of *HMTM* as much as the film desperately attempts to inhibit and rectify it. Travis reveals that Miley told him she is a friend of Hannah Montana and the townspeople ask Miley to convince Hannah Montana to perform a benefit concert in order to raise the money needed to save the town. The role of Miley Stewart as the simple country girl forging egalitarian community leading "Hoedown Throwdown" is negated by the intrusion of corporate capitalism (Mr. Bradley), and the only "person" who can ultimately save the town and the ideal of community is Hannah Montana, the manufactured pop star.

Community order: Miley Stewart (Miley Cyrus) leading the "Hoedown Throwdown" in *Hannah Montana: The Movie* (Photofest: Walt Disney Pictures/Photofest).

Indeed, the contradiction is that Miley Stewart was forced to return to Crowley Corners by her father in order to escape being overwhelmed by Hannah Montana and relearn the traditional values that formed Miley Stewart. Now this very community and the traditions it represents faces extinction unless Hannah Montana saves it precisely at the point when Miley is rediscovering her roots and reconsidering if she wants to continue being Hannah Montana.

Miley agrees to enlist Hannah Montana in the cause, and the attempt to be both Hannah Montana and Miley Stewart in Crowley Corners fails abysmally. Hannah Montana's presence brings disarray to the town, effectively ruins the relationship between Miley and Travis, and sabotages Robby's own tentative forays into a romance with his old friend Lorelai. Nonetheless, the show must go on. The benefit concert opens with Hannah Montana performing "Rock Star." Midway through, she suddenly stops the song and announces: "I can't do this ... I've loved being Hannah but I just don't think I can do it anymore. At least not here.... This is home.... The last time I stood on this stage.... I was just Miley. And I still am." She takes off her blonde wig and reveals the truth to the shocked community, and then asks to sing the next song as Miley, which is titled "The Climb." As a nexus of New Country and stadium-rock "power ballad," "The Climb" is consistent with most teen pop as far as delivering a lyrical message of perseverance and self-determination. More specifically, the message is that what matters is the *process* or "the climb" towards success and, more importantly, executing "the climb" in the right way. Again, Miley Stewart signifies "the climb" and the arduous effort needed to potentially achieve the American Dream while Hannah Montana signifies the American Dream as "rock star" fully realized in all of its glitz and glory.

The initial rupture in *HMTM* occurs precisely at the moment Hannah Montana quits performing "Rock Star," a song exemplary of the Hannah Montana brand of teen pop music, and Hannah Montana ceases to exist when Miley Stewart removes the wig that makes her Hannah Montana, the teen pop star and cultural commodity. Miley elects to become Miley and performs "The Climb" instead as an ode to labor and process, and it is not coincidental that "The Climb" is New Country as much as teen pop. Throughout *HMTM*, country music is used to signify an "authentic" America and its traditional values. The aforementioned initial fundraising concert features performances of pop-country songs by the characters Robby Stewart and Miley Stewart as well as Taylor Swift. The country band Rascal Flatts appears in *HMTM* as neighbors playing an acoustic country song at Ruby's birthday party. "Butterfly Fly Away," a song Miley wrote after she returned to Crowley Corners, is both an ode to parental authority and self-determination; it is performed as an acoustic country duet by Miley and Robby.

The crowd collectively responds to "The Climb" with the classic stadium-rock gesture of approval by raising their arms and swaying back and forth. For the second time in the film, Miley Stewart and *her* music serves as the force that fosters community. The first is the "Hoedown Throwdown," where the local community formed by Miley at the fundraiser quickly evaporates with the presence of big-city capitalist Mr. Bradley, and the town must counter his corporate power with the star power of Hannah Montana. The second time is after the fiction of Hannah Montana is definitively revealed by Miley, followed by the performance of "The Climb," which ostensibly serves as Miley's farewell and even eulogy to Hannah Montana.[19] However, as Miley turns to exit the stage, the camera pans and zooms in on a young girl in the audience pleading, "Please ... Please be Hannah. We'll keep your secret." Not only the traditional American symbol or cliché of innocence, the tween girl also represents the "consumer citizen" that sustains the Hannah Montana franchise. With the contradictions of Hannah Montana ruptured, the tween girl becomes the initial point of "damage control" and the inhibition of the contradiction. Travis, Vita, and Lilly implore Miley to continue being Hannah Montana until the crowd erupts in a chant of "Hannah! Hannah!..." *demanding* Miley that remain Hannah Montana; it is, after all, the *imaginary* that forges and sustains community, as evidenced by the fact that Crowley Corners can and will survive with the capital generated by a Hannah Montana benefit concert and not any "feeling" of community Miley Stewart briefly produces (twice) in the film through her musical performances.

Another rupture immediately follows when Oswald snaps a cell-phone photo just as Miley puts the wig back on to resume the role of Hannah Montana; he can now reveal the truth behind Hannah Montana to the world. Suddenly, Oswald's two teenage daughters, both devout Hannah Montana fans, arrive at the concert courtesy of special invitations provided by Vita, who in turn confronts Oswald: "You not going to destroy *their* dreams, are you? Because that's what Hannah is all about!" Seeing his ecstatic daughters meeting Hannah Montana in the flesh — or, more correctly, Hannah Montana as the dream made flesh — Oswald realizes what Hannah Montana is indeed "all about." Hannah Montana is the American Dream of individual self-determination leading to personal happiness and success, but not a local or even national dream. Hannah Montana is a global dream in the era of multinational capitalism. Both personally emboldened and ethically redeemed, Oswald calls the tabloid owner, tells her off, and quits his job. While his Englishness serves as the Other to America throughout *HMTM*, here "Oswald" can also be read as a reference to Lee Harvey Oswald, the accused assassin of John F. Kennedy, and the national trauma of JFK's murder in 1963 as the symbolic demise of the American Dream. Oswald "shoots" Hannah Montana with his cell phone camera and can potentially destroy the American Dream represented by Hannah Montana. What prevents Oswald from "pulling the trigger" and hitting the send button is the realization that his teenage daughters, as consumer citizens, have already bought into the dream and, as part of a global "Hannah Montana nation," they will be among the casualties in the potential symbolic assassination. Instead, Oswald decides to conceal the truth as well and sustain the imaginary of ideology. In doing so, the payoff is not financial but ethical. Oswald becomes a "better person" in the process.

The scene cuts to the benefit concert for a final musical number, with Hannah Montana performing "You'll Always Find Your Way Back Home"—another song well within the almost patented Hannah Montana brand of teen pop merging of bubblegum, New Wave, and stadium rock.[20] The lyrical message of "You'll Always Find Your Way Back Home" is that the real person always comes through no matter how circumstances, moods, settings, or trends may change. The contradiction is that "You'll Always Find Your Way Back Home" concludes *HMTM* and is performed by the "inauthentic" Hannah Montana in her formulaic brand of teen pop rather than Miley Stewart and the "authentic" of country music established throughout *HMTM*.[21] Ostensibly, *HMTM* is about Miley's journey back "home" and rediscovering her real self, and what Miley discovers is that she "can't do this"—be Hannah Montana—"at least not here. This is home." Yet *HMTM* ends with Miley accepting the role of Hannah Montana in the one place she learns she *cannot* be Hannah Montana. One might say that "home is where the Hannah Montana is" and for Miley Stewart "home" becomes the spectacle society where, as Guy Debord previously suggested, "Each individual is necessarily unable to recognize [his/her] own reality. Here ideology is at home."

This becomes part of a highly problematic conclusion that necessitates brief discussion of *HMTM*'s opening sequence. The film begins with cross-cuts of pre-concert scenes (a stadium, excited teenage crowds) and a shot of a visibly frustrated Robby Stewart, who is *not* in his Robby Ray Montana disguise. More correctly, Robby sits next to a mannequin head with a blonde Hannah Montana wig shown as a *reflection in the dressing room mirror*. In terms of Jacques Lacan, this not only suggests the mirror-stage, but Robby Stewart represents the "father-image" under whom and through the symbolic order operates. He sits alongside his pop-star creation, whose identity has yet to assumed by his daughter—who is apparently running late.[22] The scene cuts to a jerky pan of the crowd outside the stadium until the hand-held camera locates Miley and Lilly as recognizable faces in the crowd. When Miley and Lilly approach the ticket counter, Miley tells the clerk her name and Lilly quickly adds, "We're on the list." The clerk dismissively answers, "*In your dreams.*" In the symbolic order of language and the name of the subject acting as the initial point of entry, the names "Miley Stewart" and "Lilly Truscott" do not exist in the realm of Hannah Montana; indeed, Miley Stewart and Lilly Truscott do not exist per se in relation to Hannah Montana unless and until they assume the identities of "Hannah Montana" and "Lola Luftnagle." In this sense, Miley and Lilly *only exist* in the Hannah Montana order "in their dreams" and once they occupy their respective roles amid the spectacle of Hannah Montana.

Commandeering a security-team golf cart with security guards in pursuit,

Miley and Lilly reach their destination where the dressing room door bears a large inscription "Hannah Montana," with the name written in its recognizable marketing logo. After insisting that Robby leave, Miley sits in front of the dressing room mirror to complete the transformation from Miley Stewart to Hannah Montana. Returning to Lacan and the mirror-stage, it is not the moment of misrecognition and the paradox of seeing oneself as the self (narcissism) while also seeing oneself as someone else and the world around them (alienation); as Lacan defined it, "The specular *I* turns into the social *I*." [23] In this case, it is "We" instead of "I." Miley Stewart as "the specular *I*" turns into Hannah Montana as "the social *I*" invented by her father for public consumption as a pop-music commodity. If Hannah Montana ostensibly symbolizes stardom's narcissism, Hannah Montana also signifies Miley Stewart's social alienation. During the performance of "You'll Always Find Your Way Back Home," Hannah Montana reaches down to sign the autograph book of the tween girl who first asked her to remain Hannah Montana. Through the very act of writing the name "Hannah Montana," Miley Stewart officially enters the symbolic order *as* Hannah Montana; moreover, she officially "signs on" and agrees to continue playing the role of Hannah Montana as the embodiment of the dream where any difference between the imaginary and real are obliterated in the spectacle society. In the end, Miley Stewart is finally consumed by Hannah Montana: not Hannah Montana as the façade of stardom, but Hannah Montana as the force of ideology.

*HMTM* is far less the tween version of a Frank Capra film that it appears to be on the surface. It better compares to the ideological problematics of John Ford, specifically *The Man Who Shot Liberty Valance* (1962) where there is situation (the outlaw Valance terrorizing the community) → action (Valance's murder and the establishment of a myth of how he was killed by the heroic actions of a common citizen in a shootout) → situation (the revelation that Valance was shot by another cowboy in the back during the famed shootout and the reporter's decision to "print the legend, not the facts"). Social order is built on the community living a lie, and the fiction must become "truth" to maintain order. As Gilles Deleuze noted:

> What counts for Ford is that *the community can develop certain illusions about itself*. This would be the great difference between healthy and pathogenic milieus.... A community is healthy insofar as a kind of consensus reigns ... which allows it to develop illusions about itself, about its motives, its desires and its cupidity, about its values and ideals: "vital" illusions, realist illusions which are more true than pure truth.[24]

In *HMTM*, two large-form scenarios parallel each other and ultimately converge. One is situation (Hannah Montana is taking over Miley Stewart) → action (Miley quits being Hannah Montana) → situation (Miley agrees to continue being Hannah Montana by the decree of the community). The other is situation (Crowley Corners is threatened by corporate capitalism) → action (Hannah Montana performs a benefit concert) → situation (Hannah Montana raises the money to save the community). The seemingly irresolvable rupture that occurs in the conclusion of *HMTM* is that the community becomes fully aware of the imaginary of Hannah Montana, and the community demands and determines that Miley Stewart *remain* the imaginary figure of Hannah Montana as its "vital illusion." The imaginary of ideology must undergo a process of "keeping it real" and the real conditions of existence must undergo a process of "keeping it imaginary" or else the community falls apart and dies. Adorno suggested, "Music is not ideology pure and simple; it is ideological insofar as it is false consciousness."[25] *Hannah Montana: The Movie* demonstrates is that if music is both product and producer of the social order in capitalist society, the community it produces is not only through Hannah Montana as false consciousness made real but by the amount of money the imaginary of Hannah Montana can generate. Print the concert tickets, not the facts.

# 12

# The Boy Brands Are Back in Town (or, Triumph of the Hip): Big Time Rush

> The majority of television shows aim at producing, or at least repro-
> ducing, the very smugness, intellectual passivity, and gullibility that
> seems to fit with totalitarian creeds, even if the explicit message of
> the show is anti-totalitarian.[1]—*Theodor W. Adorno*

## *Meet* Big Time Rush: *The Postmodern Pre-Fab Four*

In 2009, *Big Time Rush* debuted on Nickelodeon, a pop-music sitcom
about a boy band named, of course, Big Time Rush (henceforth *BTR* refers to
the sitcom and BTR the band).[2] *BTR* was created by Scott Fellows, who also
created *Ned's Declassified School Survival Guide*, and both shows are indicative
of Fellow's contemporary sitcom style that borders on live action cartoons.[3]
*BTR* mixes hectic slapstick comedy, over-the-top acting, roving single camera,
exaggerated shot angles, extreme pans and zooms, varying speed images (with
a decided emphasis on fast-motion), non-continuity editing, jump-cuts, subjective inserts, comical audio cues (up to incessant brass or woodwind "wah-
wahs" filling in for the laugh track), and heavy-handed pop-culture
referencing.[4] More specifically, *BTR* is shamelessly derived from *The Monkees*,
both formally and in terms of marketing strategy; as with most Nickelodeon
TV-pop music crossovers, BTR records for Columbia Records. There is usually
a performance of a BTR song within a given episode, which also functions as
the music video and promotional clip for a BTR song that can be used (often
repeatedly) in truncated form during commercial breaks throughout a given
day of Nickelodeon teen programming.[5] As far as ideology marketing, this
chapter examines the *interrelated* treatment of gender, mass culture, and Hipness as the means to "authenticate" the BTR project as oppositional culture
while at the same time manifesting what borders on fascist mentality.

In the pilot episode, "Big Time Audition" (2009), Gustavo Rocque is the

Kendall Knight (Kendall Schmidt, second from left) very much in charge, as usual, in the *Big Time Rush* episode "Big Time Bad Boy" (2010). Also from left to right: Carlos Garcia (Carlos Pena; note the hockey helmet), Kelly Wainwright (Tanya Chisholm), Gustavo Rocque (Stephen Kramer Glickman), Logan Mitchell (Logan Henderson), and James Diamond (James Maslow) (Nickelodeon/Photofest).

arrogant and temperamental chief songwriter and executive producer at Rocque Records, a boy band/girl group label that has fallen on hard times with the decline of First Wave Teen Pop. Trying to salvage his career, Rocque embarks on a cross-country talent search with his final stop in Minnesota. James Diamond desperately wants to become a pop star and goes to the auditions with three friends. Logan Mitchell is planning on becoming a doctor but decides to audition after Rocque's assistant, Kelly Wainwright, tells him that he "has a cute smile, and Justin Timberlake made 44 million dollars last year." Interest piqued by the potential money, Carlos Garcia opts to audition as well. However, Kendall Knight remains thoroughly uninterested. His career goals are expressly either pro basketball or pro hockey (the masculine of sports) and not singing and dancing in a boy band (the feminine of teen pop).

Logan, Carlos and James all fare dismally in their auditions. When Rocque begins to mercilessly berate James, Kendall confronts Rocque by doing an unflattering imitation of the boy band singers Rocque produces and then gets into a slapstick melee with security. In fact, Kendall is exactly what Rocque is looking for in terms of a performer with surplus "bad boy" attitude if not surplus "boy band" talent, and wants to make him the next Rocque Records pop star. Kendall initially refuses but finally agrees on the condition that Rocque takes all four of them and makes them stars as a singing group. With Kendall's mom, Mrs. Knight, and younger sister Katie accompanying them, they move to L.A. and the Palmwoods Apartments to launch their careers. Along with BTR's ongoing struggles against conforming to the demands and standards of the pop music industry, BTR finds a nemesis in Palmwoods manager Reginald Bitters, an uptight Square intent on crushing any and all expressions of male-adolescent fun.[6]

As discussed in Chapter 8, the Beatles' public images were generally defined as the cute one (Paul McCartney), the defiant one (John Lennon), the quiet one (George Harrison), and the funny one (Ringo Starr). The Monkees largely adopted the same arrangement as the cute one (Davy Jones), the defiant one (Mike Nesmith), the quiet one (Peter Tork), and the funny one (Micky Dolenz). *BTR* also uses this arraignment within the group, but clearly establishes a hierarchy with Kendall the acme of white masculine Hipness—even a "Zeus Energy"—that all the other BTR members lack to varying degrees. Indeed, the distinctions were clearly laid out by Rocque in "Big Time Guru" (2011) when he pointed out his problem with each band member: Carlos is dumb, Logan is dull, James is a diva, and Kendall doesn't follow orders.

Carlos is "the funny one" and much of his comic relief is borne out of stupidity and incompetence, especially when it comes to dealing with the opposite sex. The running "joke" on *BTR* is that Carlos frequently wears a hockey helmet as he ineptly goes about his daily activities. In "Big Time Break-Up" (2011), Logan offered two theories as to Carlos's fixation on the hockey helmet. One is that the helmet is a fetish object, and the other is that Carlos is simply "an idiot"; confirming the second hypothesis, in the same episode Carlos pointed out that he has a metal plate in his skull. The hockey helmet also plays on the practice of such protective headgear being used by severely mentally challenged individuals who are at greater risk for personal injury. To put it crudely, the hockey helmet does not signify Carlos as an "idiot" or "brain damaged," but as a "retard." Moreover, Carlos is Latino and the only ethnic (non-white) member of BTR and the *least* Hip in comparison to the three white males.[7] As "the quiet one," Logan is the smartest and most sensible member of BTR, but also something of a dud who actually enjoys intellectual and scholastic endeavors. BTR's resident Square, Logan is the one most likely to accept a normal, routine daily life over the excitement and glamour of pop star life. Conversely, James is "the cute one" which, in terms of *BTR*, is translated into "pretty boy" and the one most willing to sell out to become a pop star. In "Big Time Concert" (2010), BTR is abruptly dropped from their label by Arthur Griffin, who owns Rocque Records as a subsidiary in his multinational corporate empire.[8] BTR disbands, but at Rocque's urging they decide to reform, only to learn James is set to sign with Rocque Records' arch-rival Hawk Records and become "Jamez"—a teenybopper solo artist to be marketed entirely on his good looks. However, Kendall is actually the person Hawk Records would ideally sign because he is the "total package" but is ultimately "too headstrong" to be manipulated by the record industry. Hence, *BTR*'s alpha-male honors belong to Kendall, "the defiant one." Indeed, Kendall doesn't just get what he wants; he gets what he wants by telling people off and doing things his way, and that especially applies to romance and all matters of the opposite sex. In short, while James has the face and Logan has the brains, Kendall has the balls.

## Battle of the Sexes

> KENDALL: Why can't there be a nice, sweet, nice girl at the Palmwoods?
> JAMES: Somebody not crazy or stuck-up — but still really hot! — *"Big Time Love Song"* (2010)

In "Big Time Love Song" teen actress Jo Taylor moves into the Palmwoods and becomes the immediate object of BTR competitive romantic conquest, bordering on sexual harassment. Despite Jo's adamant refusal to date any of them because she has a boyfriend, Jo reveals her secret to Camille, another aspiring actress and Palmwoods resident whose obsessive crush on Logan is part of an overall behavior pattern that amounts to Camille being mentally ill. Jo does *not* have a boyfriend and wants to avoid relationships as her career comes first, even though she enjoys being the center of male attention (read: a cock tease). Guys engage in spontaneous, friendly competition over girls as part of the male-bonding experience; girls are devious, manipulative, and ruthless when it comes to boys.[9] The subsequent "Big Time Break" (2010) focuses on Kendall renewing his efforts to woo Jo and learning about her single status. Kendall pointedly tells her, "I don't like dating girls who lie!" to which Jo indignantly responds, "I don't like dating boys who catch me in my lies!" and then promptly agrees to go out on date with him. The power structure between the new couple is established with the boy acting to correct and *conquer* the "natural" female tendency towards deceit.

The status of the relationship was reinforced with "Welcome Back Big Time" (2010) when Kendall returns from a BTR concert tour and he believes Jo has a new boyfriend. In fact, Jo has gotten a part on a teen drama "New Town High" and is frequently rehearsing with a handsome co-star. Kendall's jealousy worsens, even though Jo points out that he performs concerts with hordes of girls holding up "I ❤ Kendall" signs which doesn't bother her. After Kendall's behavior sabotages a day of shooting on Jo's show, she breaks up with him. Kendall calls her to apologize and asks her to come to the next BTR concert, and if she doesn't, he'll know the relationship is finished. When BTR goes onstage, Kendall sees Jo in the audience happily holding up an "I ❤ Kendall" sign. Male jealousy becomes devotion rather than domination, and it is cleansed of the pathology it assumes with females on *BTR* (i.e., Camille's obsessive relationship to Logan). In turn, Jo learns her place in the BTR order as both groupie and teenybopper. On *BTR*, apparently the only thing a girl wants more than bossing around handsome boys is to be bossed around by a handsome boy.[10]

While representations of girls and women as being "crazy or stuck up" become the modus operandi of *BTR*, this is not uniform; nonetheless, the exceptions sustain the masculine order rather than counter it. Jo Taylor acts as the acceptable norm of the teenage girl as non-threatening and obedient girl-next-door fantasy. Kelly Wainwright is an African-American woman, but her Hipness is not constructed around her racial and gender "Otherness" (e.g., *True Jackson, VP*). Rather, Kelly's Hipness is manifest through her *performance* of gender and relationships with BTR and Rocque by acting like "one of the guys," and thereby making her the part of the masculine norm and not a female "Other." Mrs. Knight is the stereotype of the dedicated and sometimes overprotective mother. Unlike *iCarly*, *True Jackson VP*, or various adult sitcoms (*Everybody Loves Raymond*, *George Lopez*, and *Two and a Half Men* being the most blatant examples), *BTR* does not represent the mother as an Oedipal ogre or domestic dictator. However, as BTR's "stage mom," the representation of Mrs. Knight is highly conservative in valorizing the traditional role of the mother as the unconditionally devoted babysitter of men-children (e.g., Marge Simpson).[11]

Perhaps most important, Katie Knight is the stereotype of the precocious, prepubescent tomboy; she is independent, opinionated, rebellious, smart, and highly sarcastic. While this can be read as *BTR*'s compliance to the Nickelodeon "girl power" agenda, the message is quite different. In fact, Katie's role on *BTR* is antithetical to Megan Parker's ongoing assaults against the male-dominated order on *Drake and Josh*. Katie is often enlisted by BTR as an integral part of their continual pursuit of fun, struggles against Square repression, battles with the record industry, and quest to become pop stars. She acts as BTR's unofficial career-guidance counselor and manager, with Katie's considerable intelligence matched by a predisposition for business and manipulation (the two practices far from mutually exclusive) that rivals *Saved by the Bell*'s Zack Morris. Ultimately, Katie Knight is unlike the parade of "crazy or stuck-up" adolescent girls on *BTR* because she possesses adolescent, rebellious, masculine Hipness. In "Big Time Pranks" (2010) the disordered situation is literally instigated by Kendall. As the reigning "Sir Lord High King of Pranks," he decrees that the annual competition for his crown begins that day. The complication is that Katie is not allowed to enter the prank competition because, as James puts it, she is "too young and too girly." The snub escalates to a collective "boys vs. girls" civil war of pranks at the Palmwoods. "The Jennifers," a clique of three unbearably obnoxious and self-centered Palmwoods girls, are eliminated when they are pranked with superglue in lipstick containers, with the added advantage for the boys being the Jennifers' mouths are sealed shut for the rest the episode. Not understanding the manly code of what has become a battle for gender supremacy, Carlos and James turn on each other to win Kendall's crown and end up in a prank stalemate locked in the Palmwood's supply closet. Indeed, they are "in the closet" with each other as the gender battle flares, leaving Kendall to single-handedly and successfully out-prank all the girls. Eventually, Kendall and Katie are the last pranksters standing, culminating in a squirt-gun-versus-seltzer-bottle stand-off in the Palmwoods lobby. Mr. Bitters angrily declares the prank war over due to the ancillary damage it is causing to building; Kendall and Katie call it a draw and douse Mr. Bitters. Their coronation as co–*Kings* of Pranks is done as obligatory pop culture reference, a gratuitous parody of the end of *Star Wars*. Camille exclaims, "A tie! Nice!" Yet it is anything but an endorsement of girl power or gender equality. Having defeated the female inferiors, Kendall and Katie are both crowned as *male* masters of their milieu.

## Having Your Culture Industry and Fighting It Too

While *BTR* is ostensibly Nickelodeon's rival "teen idol" brand to Disney's Jonas Brothers, ideologically *BTR* serves as a response to *Hannah Montana*. More correctly, *BTR* is the antithesis of *Hannah Montana* except for the surface messages affirming traditional American values. In "Big Time Fever" (2010), Mr. Bitters closes the Palmwoods pool to everyone but himself, and posts a sign banning children specifically. With aid of a Magic Marker, Kendall alters the sign so its reads that kids are welcome; a stampede of toddlers jump into the pool, much to the ire of Mr. Bitters. Camille gushes, "You guys are *great!* A few months in Hollywood usually changes people, but you're still the same down-to-earth guys you were when you got here." However, James succumbs to "Hollywood Fever" and becomes addicted to "Mangerine" tanning spray (in other words, a male fruit). Carlos soon follows and joins the Jennifers, while Logan becomes a bongo-playing hippie. Kendall remains immune and realizes, "I never got Hollywood Fever because I never lost touch with my roots"—as a visual signifier, Kendall is wearing a University of Minnesota hockey jersey with "home team" colors (and, in this sense, Kendall's "roots" are jock as much as Midwestern). Assisted by a wood chipper and ice cubes, Kendall converts the lawn of the Palmwoods into a winter wonderland, and Hollywood Fever is eradicated with an old-fashioned snowball fight.

As discussed in the previous last chapter, Hannah Montana represents ideology as the contradiction between "the expression of the relation between [people] and their 'world'.... The imaginary relation between them and their conditions of existence ... a relation that expresses a will ... a hope or nostalgia, rather than describing a reality."[12] While most pronounced in *Hannah Montana: The Movie*, this contradiction is frequently expressed in Hannah Montana songs as well (e.g., "Supergirl"). Exemplified by Kendall, *BTR* affirms dominant ideology as middle-class, Midwestern, All-American "down-to-earth guys" representing a composite of rugged individualism, teenage rebellion, and the masculine authentic of rock ideology that leads to the achievement of the American Dream, but always doing it on their terms. As Kendall succinctly laid down the BTR law in "Big Time Demos" (2010), "You don't *wait* for your dreams to happen, you *make* them happen." Lyrically, BTR songs celebrate driving ambition, attaining fame, and the joys of social supremacy that come with stardom ("Big Time," "Halfway There," "Famous," "City is Ours," or the none-too-subtle "If I Ruled the World").[13] Musically, the BTR brand of Second Wave Teen Pop is largely a merger of the boy band genre and stadium rock.[14] As a boy band, BTR utilizes the genre staples of Hip posturing, stylized choreography, dance beats, and bubblegum-rap-white soul group vocals which, in the case of BTR, are saturated with studio effects (vocoder, pitch modulations, phase shifting, etc).[15] As a conscious effort to manufacture rock "authenticity," the musical arraignments and especially the chorus sections owe considerably to 1980s stadium rock anthems. "This Is Our Someday," "Famous," "Halfway There," "City Is Ours," or "'Til I Forget About You" are as musically reminiscent of the arena rock of Journey or Bon Jovi as they are New Kids on the Block or Backstreet Boys.[16]

In this respect, while *The Monkees* is the obvious model for *BTR*, another point of comparison is the film version of *Josie and the Pussycats* (2001). *Josie and the Pussycats* was originally a comic book published by Archie Comics (1962–82) about a racially mixed, all-female pop-music trio. As discussed in Chapter 8, in 1968 CBS launched *The Archie Show* as Saturday morning cartoon series; the Archies as a cross-marketed pop band had a smash hit with "Sugar Sugar." Capitalizing on the success, Hanna-Barbera developed a pop-music cartoon series for CBS Saturday mornings, *Josie and the Pussycats* (1970–1). Unlike the Archies' bubblegum pop-rock, Josie and the Pussycats' cross-marketed musical product was a mix of soul, pop, and bubblegum particularly informed by the Jackson Five.[17] In 2001, two major competing discourses in popular music were Alternative versus First Wave Teen Pop. For the film version of *Josie and the Pussycats*, the trip was converted into a struggling pop-punk power trio playing at the local bowling alleys. Conversely, the most popular band in America is Du Jour, a boy band whose lyrics have none-too-subtle homoerotic subtext; their popularity stems from their label, Mega Records, using subliminal messages that brainwash listeners into unthinking consumers. Villainous record company executive Wyatt Frame discovers Josie and the Pussycats and proposes to make them the next Mega Records superstars; instead, Josie and the Pussycats discover the nefarious activities, bring down the company, and, in the process, become rock stars on their own.[18] Fighting corporate capitalism and mass culture, and attaining stardom as the American Dream at the same time, is possible through rock music.

Like *Josie and the Pussycats*, BTR overtly attempts to satirize mass culture and the Culture Industry while valorizing rock ideology. In *Josie and the Pussy-*

*cats*, the binary was constructed between authentic rock and its ideology represented by the trio (masculine rock in the form of women) versus mass culture and its complicity represented by Du Jour (effeminate teen pop in the form of men).[19] With *BTR*, the boy band and masculine of rock ideology attain synthesis and the dialectic entails the inherent enemy becomes "female mass culture" in its myriad manifestations. In turn, the *BTR* brand of teen culture Hipness is thoroughly "boy power" as masculine bravado combining comical rambunctiousness and confident swagger. Terry Eagleton suggested,

> Modern society, as the post-structuralists would say, is "phallocentric"; it is also ... "logocentric," believing that its discourses can yield us immediate access to the full truth and presence of things. Jacques Derrida has conflated these two terms to the compound "phallogocentric," which we might roughly translate as "cocksure." It is this cocksureness by which those who wield social and sexual power maintain their grip.[20]

BTR is not charming *despite* being "cocky" but charming *because* they are "cocksure" and this phallogocentricism permeates the BTR line of cultural product (sitcom, music, videos, live performance, advertising, etc.). In "Big Time Bloggers" (2010), Deke is a powerful on-line music critic; in keeping with stereotype, he is also a diminutive Asian-American teenager who is a tech geek and, the viewer can safely assume, does not have a girlfriend. Deke is set to pan BTR in his blog as "overdressed corporate puppets ... just another band full of rehearsed sound bytes, choreographed body language, and no real substance." In effect, he states the standard critical attack on boy bands in order for *BTR* to refute it, but not in the expected manner. After spending a day caught up in the usual BTR shenanigans, Deke uses his blog to proclaim that "Big Time Rush are four dedicated, smart, and fun-loving guys who share a passion for music and life. My day with Big Time Rush is one I'll never forget. And I'm looking forward to hearing their album." It is not the quality of their "rehearsed sound bytes" and "choreographed body language" that wins Deke over, but the "real substance" of the BTR experience as rebellious male adolescence rather than their generic boy-band sounds.

This inflated masculinity is manifest precisely to counter the commercial liabilities of boy bands being critically tagged as not only corporate and manufactured but, even worse, the critical disparagement that boy bands are lame, wimps, femmes, or flat-out "gay." As Gayle Wald observed, "Such apprehensions about the sexuality of contemporary boy bands are not 'merely' homophobic, but conflate homophobia (expressed particularly as the fear of male homosexuality) *with a misogynist contempt for girls and girls' pleasures.*"[21] In this respect, "Big Time Photo Shoot" (2010) centers on BTR having a publicity still taken for "Pop Tiger" teenybopper magazine (a parody of *Popstar!* and *Tiger Beat*). The photographer, a flaming homosexual stereotype, is intent on shooting BTR dressed as kitschy matadors. BTR balks at the plan, and the usual chaos ensues until BTR gets the photograph they want as four buddies arm in arm, dressed normally, and looking thoroughly cool. However, the episode is told in flashback by the severely injured BTR members, with the final revelation being that they were trampled in a stampede of tween girls seeking the autograph of current teen idol Dak Zevon (another obvious parody, in this case *High School Musical*'s star Zac Efron). To add insult to injury, the BTR photo is printed on the page opposite the newest pin-up photo of Dak Zevon. BTR will be on the walls of thousands of teenage girls' bedrooms, but facing the wall while girls adoringly gaze at Dak Zevon as "teen idol" and not BTR as "the real thing." While the joke is ostensibly on BTR, underneath it all *BTR* ridicules feminine mass culture while simultaneously pandering to the "teenyboppers" in the hopes that they buy a product that holds them in contempt.

Another gendered conflict around mass culture was constructed with "Big Time Girl Band" (2011), an episode in which where the decidedly "mixed messages" bear close examination. Rocque becomes smitten with a girl group, "Kat's Crew," giving them a song originally intended for BTR to record and putting a Kat's Crew poster in the lobby of Rocque Records ahead of BTR. Of course, the girls in Kat's Crew are obnoxious opportunists. They are also literally "catty" and punctuate their stream of derisive remarks with meowing sounds, clawing gestures, and taunting BTR by reminding them, "You can't hit us!" (This also implies that they know they "deserve" to get hit for mouthing off). BTR's fear that they could be dropped by Rocque Records is strengthened when they learn Rocque's first boy-band success, a group called "Boyz in the Attic" (BIA), was dumped by Rocque to make room for the girl group "Angel Angel." To make matters worse, BTR meets the members of BIA; they are now are a quartet of pathetic, middle-aged, mirror images of BTR desperately trying to relive their youth and make a comeback in the music business. As the feud between BTR and Kat's Crew escalates, BTR resorts to a series of pranks that inevitably backfire when Rocque becomes the unintended casualty of a waxed floor that sends him careening through a wall, or a stink bomb planted in the Rocque Records restroom. BIA advises BTR to up the ante with egging, late-night crank calls, and flaming bags of poop. When Logan inquires as to why BIA spent all their time harassing Angel Angel rather than refining their music, the BIA equivalent of Kendall emphatically points out, "This isn't about music: it's about getting rid of a girl group!" This ostensibly suggests an element of self-criticism. BTR gets a glimpse of their potential future in the form of BIA, and a rather sickened Kendall points out that if they continue to act like BIA they will share the same fate as BIA.

However, the hidden message undercuts this overt message. Rocque summarily ends the feud by announcing that he is only keeping one of the groups due to the intense animosity between the two bands, and *already* decided to retain BTR and not sign Kat's Crew. While Kat's Crew is more talented and probably has the greater commercial potential, BTR has continually proven their "loyalty" to Rocque Records, as Rocque simply puts it, "No matter how stupid they are!" The immature, adolescent behavior is proof positive of their dedication to becoming pop stars, regardless of musical ability or professionalism. It also demonstrates their trustworthiness, whereas Kat's Crew could and would sign with any record company that offers them the most lucrative deal (read: whores). Their supremacy retained in the gender politics of pop music, BTR then does the magnanimous thing by insisting Rocque sign Kat's Crew and they apologize for their behavior. It is only through BTR's benevolence that Kat's Crew gets their much-coveted record deal. Having learned and accepted their secondary position to BTR, Kat's Crew agrees to sign with Rocque Records on the condition that BTR records the song that Rocque first intended for them. In turn, BTR agrees on condition that they and Kat's Crew collaborate on the song and the video—a cheesy science-fiction-themed saga of BTR and Kat's Crew as space warriors battling an evil galactic overlord, played by Rocque.

Yet the message of the video that BTR and Kat's Crew are now united in rebellion against the despotism of Rocque (i.e., the record industry and corporate mass culture) is also subverted. After the music-video segment, Rocque reveals an addition to the Rocque Records lobby Kelly describes as "long overdue." A much larger BTR poster has replaced the Kat's Crew poster, which is now consigned to the end of the hall; moreover, the punch line is that the members of BIA sneaked into Rocque Records and vandalized the Kat's Crew poster—much to everyone's amusement. While BIA might be doomed to remain sorry losers, the hidden message is that there is always room for some adolescent misogyny at Rocque Records. As far as narrative, the trajectory is situation (feud between BTR and Kat's Crew) → action (Rocque ends the feud by siding with BTR out of loyalty) → situation (BTR gets Kat's Crew signed to the label and peace is achieved at Rocque Records through BTR). Ideologically, it is situation (male domination challenged) → action (male domination justified) → situation (male domination sustained).

In this respect, another and very much related aspect of *BTR*'s ethical form, as it repeats itself from episode to episode, is situation (BTR is involved in some aspect of pop-music production) → action (BTR does things their way and not the industry way) → situation (BTR achieves immense success by doing things their way). While episodes like "Big Time Bloggers," "Big Time Photo Shoot," "Big Time Concert," and "Big Time Girl Group" typify the *BTR* formula, "Big Time Live" (2010) reached the point of unintentional self-parody.[22] BTR is scheduled to perform on a live morning show, but they are bumped at the last minute by the show's humorless, dictatorial producer "Jane Kennedy" (a parodic conflation of iconic liberals Jane Fonda and John F. Kennedy). She refuses to cut a long cooking segment with "Chef Hollandaise" or a lengthy spot with Ed Begley, Jr. (playing himself), promoting his new and useless line of green products.[23] As natural-born rebels, BTR insist on performing, sabotaging the telecast at every possible moment until they get their way. Meanwhile, Mr.

Griffin has suddenly decided Rocque Records lacks financial viability and the fate of the entire label hinges on the success of BTR's now-canceled performance, a development unknown to BTR at the TV studio. As the telecast descends into Loony Tunes-derived chaos, the producer adamantly refuses to let BTR perform "as long as I'm standing" and is then immediately (albeit accidentally) run over by Katie with Begley's eco-friendly golf cart. Problem solved, BTR performs one of their boy band-stadium rock anthems— the aptly selected "'Til I Forget About You"— and are their usual astounding selves. BTR simultaneously defeats the tyranny of female-controlled mass culture in the form of TV and, as fate would have it, save their male-run record company though their "natural" predilection for adolescent-male rock rebellion.

While *BTR* continually presents BTR as subverting the Culture Industry from within, *BTR* amounts to a half-hour advertisement for BTR as a bona-fide boy band and their musical product, and manufactures their legitimacy around teenage rebel attitude, cocksure masculinity, and Middle-American values. In "Big Time Demos," BTR learns that Mercedes Griffin, the insufferable daughter of Arthur Griffin, is in charge of picking demos and BTR has to satisfy her every whim. She makes their lives unbearable until Kendall exhibits the testicular fortitude to tell her off. Mercedes threatens to ruin their careers on the spot and storms out, only to immediately and contritely return after the commercial break. Having been put in her place, Mercedes apologizes to BTR and tells them, "Kendall's right... I'm a rich spoiled bully who dresses hot and thinks your songs are great." She also admits she lied the whole time because the guys in BTR are "cute" and that she is not actually in charge of picking demos, but picking *up* the demos to deliver to the record company while a "top secret record executive," a business-suited chimpanzee named Rollo, actually selects the bands. The overt joke is that the record industry is literally run by monkeys in suits; the underlying joke is that primates can be trusted to make better decisions about popular music than teenage girls. After BTR's demo is rejected by Rollo (he gives it "the fart noise"), Mercedes Griffin makes an impassioned and persuasive plea to her father: "These guy's songs have infectious melodies, classic pop hooks, and Big Time Rush will crush the 6–16-year-old demographic!" Impressed, Mr. Griffin makes Mercedes his new head of record company A&R. Thanks to BTR (again, specifically Kendall) and learning her place in the pop-music hierarchy, Mercedes also demonstrates she learned the first rule of the pop-music business: conquering the target audience. The episode concludes with BTR performing one of their anthems to ambition and domination masked as social mobility and stardom, "Halfway There." Ultimately, it is not so much a contradiction as sheer calculation and unbridled conquest. Or, as the announcer on the TV commercial for the *BTR* season1, volume 1 DVD proclaimed: "Big Time Rush is taking the world by storm!"

# Conclusion: The Youth of Today Are the Leaders of Tomorrow

You guys are the future. Take good care of us. —*Johnny Depp, 2011 Kids' Choice Awards*

In *Marxism and Literature* (1977), Raymond Williams formulated the structure of "dominant culture" in terms of two equally important constituent elements, "the residual" and "the emergent." Obviously, Williams did not have American teen sitcoms and teen pop in mind, but his formulation can be applied to analyze the current situation of teen culture and its numerous problematics.

As Williams defined it, "'Residual' ... [is] different than the 'archaic,' although in practice they can be very hard to distinguish.... The residual, by definition, has been formed in the past, but is still active in the cultural process, often not at all as an element of the past, but as an effective element in the present."[1] Discussing modern England, Williams pointed to the continued existence of the monarchy, organized religion, and the idea of rural community as three examples of residual culture that remain facets of dominant culture. The ideal of "community" in American political thought also functions as part of residual culture's presence in dominant culture. *Hannah Montana: The Movie* romanticizes rural community, while at the same time the film collapses when trying to sustain that ideal amid the real of social existence. The *iCarly* episode "iBeat the Heat" offers a satirical critique of the individual-versus-community tension in American life; it is less clear whether individualism or community bears the brunt of the joke, and the extent ideals of traditional American community in the neoliberal era are, in effect, represented as "archaic." While Madonna's song "Music" champions the ideal of popular music as the vehicle for manifesting a progressive community and unitary culture, Britney Spears's song "Circus" assaults the same ideal. Hence, the residual is very much part of the present, subject to internal debate within and across cultural texts, and teen culture is no exception.

173

The other aspect is "emergent culture" which Williams defined as "new meanings and values, new practices, new relationships ... continually being created.... It is exceptionally difficult to distinguish between ... elements of a new phase of dominant culture ... and those which are substantially alternative or oppositional: emergent in the strict sense, rather than merely novel."[2] In post–World War II America, the "emergent culture" was television and rock music. Nonetheless, the extent to which this was truly "emergent culture" by 2011 is debatable, and how this proved to be a "new phase of dominant culture" rather than "substantially alternative or oppositional." In the case of television, certain programs in certain historical moments may have indeed been sites of rupture, with *The Smothers Brothers Comedy Hour* an example of a show shut down by a TV network for political rather than economic motivations. However, the claim that TV is a field of cultural opposition becomes harder to substantiate. Indeed, TV is often the bastion for conservatism in terms of form as well as content. Arguments that TV sitcoms have reached a new level of "maturity," through what amounts to the standardization of the contemporary sitcom over the classical sitcom, can also be interpreted as the triumph of novelty in which postmodernism is now the highest stage of TV comedy.

Rock music offers it own problematics as "a new phase of dominant culture" rather than "emergent." Rock is obsessively committed to defining itself in terms of perpetual opposition to the Establishment, with *School of Rock* one of the more strident examples. This is not to deny that rock music has been the product and producer of political rupture points in specific historical moments, from its raucous birth in the 1950s, as a soundtrack to the widespread unrest of late 1960s, or the unprecedented aggression of the punk movement in the 1970s. The problem is that rock ideology is largely American liberalism, and even then fraught with contradictions around identity politics, especially gender and sexuality. Rock and roll "opposition" exists only within the conflicts generated around the liberal-conservative binary, with most rock musicians being liberal (Ted Nugent and Johnny Ramone being the most vocal exceptions). Above all, rock ideology is "liberal" in the classical sense of the term. It is rooted in the primacy of individual freedom, autonomy from social regulation, and self-determination. It celebrates "doing what one wants when one wants" and the chance to achieve unlimited success in the process. Recalling Tom Petty's observation that being a "'rock and roll star' is probably the purest manifestation of the American Dream," Hannah Montana would not necessarily disagree, except that Hannah Montana as "rock and roll star as the purest manifestation of the American Dream" is also revealed to be the imaginary of ideology.

By the mid–1950s, rock music and TV were already becoming staples of American popular culture. As decades progress, they are not only part of *dominant culture* but are becoming forms of *residual culture*. The drive of TV is establishing a continued relevance as a cultural medium supplying more sophisticated cultural product for a more discerning consumer demographic. In short,

Hipper shows for Hip audiences. Conversely, as rock becomes more and more Establishment, it steadfastly defines itself more and more as anti–Establishment. What *iCarly* addresses, albeit in its own problematic ways, is that the emergent culture is not necessarily to be found in the novelty of style or the embrace of tradition, but in the means of cultural production and the possibilities of personal computers and the internet for DYI youth culture. At the same time, *iCarly* and *Hannah Montana*'s reliance on classical sitcom form and 1980s pop-rock (as far as the cross-marketed music product) does not suggest any sort of radical subversion, or even any kind of postmodern reimagining or reinvention beyond the pop-culture referencing. If *iCarly* and *Hannah Montana* can be posited as a kind of emergent *tween culture* out of teen culture, it is also being expressed through a simple replacement of the old forms with the same old forms housing new and younger practitioners.

Teen culture is a complicated and contradictory set of competing discourses engaged in ideology marketing. In the end, this also reflects the complexities and contradictions of cultural production and consumption, liberal vs. conservative American politics, and a Generation Gap that is not so much closing but *being closed*. In this context, Williams stresses another aspect to the formation and maintenance of dominant culture: "*No mode of production and therefore no dominant social order and therefore no dominant culture ever in reality includes or exhausts all human practice, human energy, and human intention ...* they select from and consequently *exclude* the full range of human practice."[3] In the "pedagogic regime" of popular culture, teens are increasingly taught to *exclude themselves* from their own emergent tween and teen cultures and embrace the residual and emergent culture endorsed by the older generations, to learn cultural literacy and not cultural history, to eventually reject what is not sanctioned as "adult" by adults, to disown their own "inauthentic" generational signifiers of the present in favor of "authentic" generational signifiers of past decades, to understand their teen culture is inherently inferior to adult culture, and that their own "allegiances and identities" manufactured around teen culture are inferior as well.

In short, the message in the twenty-first century is that adults long ago cornered the teen culture market as teens whose culture was vastly superior *then* and as adults whose culture is still vastly superior *now*. Jacques Attali proclaimed, "Janis Joplin, Bob Dylan, and Jimi Hendrix say more about the libratory dreams of the 1960s than any theory of crisis."[4] This is not in dispute. The point is that Britney Spears, *iCarly*, and Hannah Montana might also say more about the myriad contradictions of American society in the twenty-first century as any theory of crisis as well — and whether the older generation considers what is being said as even worth hearing.

One of the iconic cultural discourses of the counterculture era, *Easy Rider* (1969) is probably best remembered for its conclusion and the hippie-biker heroes being murdered by trigger-happy rednecks, constructing counterculture martyrs as the 1960s were drawing to a close. What is less remembered — or ignored — was when Captain America (Peter Fonda) gave his succinct assessment of their road trip across America: "*We blew it.*" This is precisely the message concertedly avoided in the crisis of American popular culture. When Johnny Depp told million of teens that they "are the future" and to "take good care of us," it was not only a direct challenge to teens to make the world a better place, it also carried an implied challenges to adults. The older generation might consider doing the unthinkable and step aside because the younger generation may end up doing a better job of running things. At the risk of cynicism, it is hard to imagine them doing any worse. If teens are the future, the insistence on instilling the residual culture of adult generations as the *only* authentic voice, and expressing themselves only by echoing the past, leads to the inevitable conclusion that they will blow it as well.

# Appendix

## Cast Listings

The following is a brief cast listing of the primary teen sitcoms and films discussed in the course of this project. Only main and selected supporting casts are listed.

### Teen Sitcoms

**Saved by the Bell** (NBC, 1989–93). Mark-Paul Gosselaar (*Zack Morris*), Mario Lopez (*A.C. Slater*), Justin Diamond (*Samuel "Screech" Powers*), Tiffani-Amber Thiessen (*Kelly Kapowski*), Lark Voorhies (*Lisa Turtle*), Elizabeth Berkeley (*Jessie Spano*), Dennis Haskins (*Mr. Belding*). Originally *Good Morning, Miss Bliss* (Disney Channel, 1988–9; Gosselaar, Diamond, Voorhies, and Haskins only) and retooled into *Saved by the Bell* for NBC. *Good Morning, Miss Bliss* episodes, as well as the spin-off *Saved by the Bell: The College Years* (NBC, 1993–4; Gosselaar, Lopez, Diamond, and Thiessen only) were all consolidated into the *Saved by the Bell* syndicated rerun package. Another spin-off, *Saved by the Bell: The New Class* (starring Haskins and Diamond with a shifting cast of teens), ran on "Teen NBC" Saturday mornings from 1994–2000.

**Clarissa Explains It All** (Nickelodeon, 1991–4). Melissa Joan Hart (*Clarissa Darling*), Jason Zimbler (*Ferguson Darling*), Joe O'Connor (*Marshall Darling*), Elizabeth Hess (*Janet Darling*), Sean O'Neal (*Sam Anders*).

**Drake and Josh** (Nickelodeon, 2004–7). Drake Bell (*Drake Parker*), Josh Peck (*Josh Nichols*), Miranda Cosgrove (*Megan Parker*), Jonathan Goldstein (*Walter Nichols*), Nancy Sullivan (*Audrey Parker-Nichols*), Scott Halberstadt (*Eric Blonwitz*), Alec Medlock (*Craig Ramirez*), Yvette Nicole Brown (*Helen Dubois*), Jerry Trainor (*Crazy Steve*).

**Zoey 101** (Nickelodeon, 2005–8). Jamie Lynn Spears (*Zoey Brooks*), Victoria Justice (*Lola Martinez*), Erin Sanders (*Quinn Pensky*), Sean Flynn (*Chase Matthews*), Christopher Massey (*Michael Barrett*), Matthew Underwood (*Logan Reese*) Paul Butcher (*Dustin Brooks*), Christopher Murray (*Dean Rivers*), Abby Wilde (*Stacey Dillsen*), Austin Butler (*James Garrett*). Original cast members

Alexia Nikolas (*Nicole Bristow*) and Kristin Herrera (*Dana Cruz*) were subsequently written out of the show.

**Hannah Montana** (Disney Channel, 2006–11).   Miley Cyrus (*Miley Stewart/"Hannah Montana"*), Billy Ray Cyrus (*Robby Stewart/"Robby Ray Montana"*), Emily Osment (*Lilly Truscott/"Lola Luftnagle"*), Jason Earles (*Jackson Stewart*), Mitchel Musso (*Oliver Oken/"Mike Standley III"*), Moisés Arais (*Rico Suave*). Fourth and final season (2010–11) titled *Hannah Montana Forever*.

**iCarly** (Nickelodeon, 2007- ).   Miranda Cosgrove (*Carly Shay*), Jennette McCurdy (*Samantha "Sam" Puckett*), Nathan Kress (*Fredward "Freddie" Benson*), Jerry Trainor (*Spencer Shay*), Noah Munck (*Gibby Gibson*), Mary Gross (*Mrs. Benson*), Reed Alexander (*Nevel Papperman*), Tim Russ (*Principal Franklin*), Mindy Sterling (*Ms. Briggs*), David St. James (*Mr. Howard*), Andrew Hill Newman (*Mr. Henning*), Jeremy Rowley (*Lewbert*), Deena Dill (*Mrs. Gibson*).

**Wizards of Waverly Place** (Disney Channel, 2007–12).   Selena Gomez (*Alex Russo*), Phil Henrie (*Justin Russo*), Jake T. Austin (*Max Russo*), Maria Canals Barrera (*Theresa Russo*), David DeLuise (*Jerry Russo*), Jennifer Stone (*Harper Finkle*).

**True Jackson, VP** (Nickelodeon, 2008–11).   Keke Palmer (*True Jackson*), Ashley Argota (*Lulu*), Matt Shively (*Ryan Laserbeam*), Robbie Amell (*Jimmy Madigan*), Danielle Bisutti (*Amanda Cantwell*), Greg Proppes (*Max Madigan*), Ron Butler (*Oscar*), Trevor Brown (*Mikey J.*), Jordan Monahgan (*Kelsey*).

**Big Time Rush** (Nickelodeon, 2009- ).   Kendall Schmidt (*Kendall Knight*), James Maslow (*James Diamond*), Carlos Pena (*Carlos Garcia*), Logan Henderson (*Logan Mitchell*), Stephen Kramer Glickman (*Gustavo Rocque*), Ciara Bravo (*Katie Knight*), Tanya Chisholm (*Kelly Wainwright*), Challen Chase (*Mrs. Knight*), Katelyn Tarver (*Jo Taylor*), Erin Sanders (*Camille Roberts*), David Anthony Higgins (*Reginald Bitters*), Matt Riedy (*Arthur Griffin*).

**Victorious** (Nickelodeon, 2010- ).   Victoria Justice (*Tori Vega*), Leon Thomas III (*André Harris*), Matt Bennett (*Robbie Shapiro*), Elizabeth Gillies (*Jade West*), Ariana Grande (*Cat Valentine*), Avan Jogia (*Beck Oliver*), Daniella Monet (*Trina Vega*), Eric Lange (*Mr. Sikowitz*), Michael Eric Reid (*Sinjin Van Cleef*).

# Films

**School of Rock** (Paramount, 2003).   Jack Black (*Dewey Finn*), Joan Cusack (*Rosalie "Roz" Mullins*), Mark White (*Ned Schneebly*), Sarah Silverman (*Patty*

*Di Marco*), Miranda Cosgrove (*Summer Hathaway*), Joey Gaydos, Jr. (*Zack Mooneyham*), Kevin Clark (*Freddie Jones*), Rebecca Julie Brown (*Katie*), Robert Tsai (*Lawrence*), Maryam Hassan (*Tomika*), Brian Falduto (*Billy*). Directed by Richard Linklater. Written by Mark White. Rated PG-13.

**What a Girl Wants** (Warner Bros., 2003). Amanda Bynes (*Daphne Reynolds*), Kelly Preston (*Libby Reynolds*), Colin Firth (*Lord Henry Dashwood*), Oliver James (*Ian*), Eileen Watkins (*Lady Jocelyn Dashwood*), Jonathan Pryce (*Alistair Payne*), Anna Chancellor (*Gynnis Payne*), Christian Cole (*Clarissa Payne*). Directed by Dennie Gordon. Written by Jenny Bicks and Elizabeth Chandler. Adapted from *The Reluctant Debutante* (1958; directed by Vincente Minnelli, written by William Douglas-Home). Rated PG.

**Hannah Montana: The Movie** (Disney, 2009). Miley Cyrus (*Miley Stewart/Hannah Montana*), Billy Ray Cyrus (*Robby Stewart*), Emily Osment (*Lilly Truscott*), Lucas Till (*Travis Brody*), Vanessa Williams (*Vita*), Peter Gunn (*Oswald Granger*), Margo Martindale (*Ruby Stewart*), Melora Hardin (*Lorelai*), Barry Bostwick (*Mr. Bradley*). Jason Earles (*Jackson Stewart*), Mitchel Musso (*Oliver Oken*), and Moisés Arais (*Rico Suave*) have only minor parts in the film. Directed by Peter Chelsom. Written by Daniel Berendsen. Rated G.

# Chapter Notes

## Introduction

1. Neoliberalism is a somewhat nebulous term, and used to describe the political philosophy of the Reagan Revolution as much as the New Democrats. Labor historian Nelson Lichtenstein argued that Jimmy Carter was also part of the neoliberal shift in the late 1970s; see *State of the Union: A Century of American Labor* (Princeton, NJ: Princeton University Press, 2002), 235–6. While neoliberalism represents a kind of post-industrial update of the classical liberal model and serves as the ideological basis for both the Democratic and Republican parties, American politics remains steeped in the "liberal-conservative" binary, with substantial differences around identity politics and social issues (gay marriage, illegal immigration, etc.) and the regulatory role of the government (business, health care, Wall Street regulation, etc.). In this sense, the Democratic Party and Clintonism can be termed a "progressive neoliberalism" and the Republican Party and Reaganism a "conservative neoliberalism."

2. Sarah Banet-Wesier, *Kids Rule!: Nickelodeon and Consumer Citizenship* (Durham: Duke University Press, 2007), 71.

3. Here "nation" has to be differentiated from "the State." "Nations" are populations that share culture, ethnicity, history, language, etc. "The State" is the constructed institutional political framework, namely government, but also the Church, school, etc. In this way, there are nations which do not exist as a State (the Palestinians, for example) as well as States made up of disparate and conflicting nations (as evidenced by the collapse of the Soviet Union as a State and the resulting, often violent, restructuring of Eastern Europe in the 1990s). In some respects, America can be seen as a State of various nations in terms of geographic politics (North versus South, Coastal versus Middle America) and generations, particularly in the 1960s, and a schism between older and younger nations (race and Black Nationalism could be added here as well). Nickelodeon has branded itself around a "nation" of adolescent viewers; the theme song of *iCarly* specifically uses the word "nation" instead of "generation."

4. John Hartley, "Invisible Fictions: Television Audiences, Paedocracy, Pleasure," in *Television: Critical Concepts IV*, ed. Toby Miller (London: Routledge, 2003), 58.

5. Pierre Bourdieu, *The Field of Cultural Production: Essays on Art and Literature*, ed. Randall Johnson (New York: Columbia University Press, 1993), 101. Emphasis added.

6. Lester Bangs, *Mainlines, Bloodfeasts, and Bad Taste: A Lester Bangs Reader*, ed. John Morthland (New York: Anchor Books, 2003), 357.

7. Gilles Deleuze, *Cinema 1: The Movement Image*, trans. Hugh Tomlinson and Barbara Habberjam (Minneapolis: University of Minnesota Press, 1986), Chapter 9, especially 142–7. Admittedly, my utilization of Deleuze is a simplified modification and also takes some liberties with Deleuze's intent, discussed in Chapter 3.

8. "Teen Pop" as a genre certainly existed before the mid–1990s. The early 1970s included teen pop performers like the Jackson Five, the Osmonds, and the Cowsills; the mid–1980s teen pop included Menudo, Debbie Gibson, and New Kids on the Block. In the context of this study, First Wave Teen Pop specifically refers to 1995–2003 and Second Wave Teen Pop 2006–2011.

9. While popular music is discussed and specific songs are analyzed in some detail through-

out this project, the reader will note that there are no lyrics quoted; a general interpretation or summation of the lyrical message is provided. The concern is how music manufactures "message" rather than lyrics, and lyrics are frequently overemphasized in the discussions of popular music at the expense of textual analysis of music itself.

10. By "stadium rock" (sometimes termed "arena rock)," I am referring to rock bands emphasizing a commercial hybrid of hard rock, heavy metal, and pop. Boston, Foreigner, Loverboy, REO Speedwagon, Styx, and especially Journey and Bon Jovi were among the most commercially successful stadium-rock bands of the 1970s and 1980s, but my definition could include Aerosmith, Def Leppard, Van Halen and the 1980s "hair bands," such as Poison or Warrant. In this respect, my usage of the term departs from Edward Macan's definition of "stadium rock" as a North American, commercialized merger of the English heavy metal and progressive rock genres, although stadium-rock bands like Rush, Kansas, and Styx were certainly influenced by both metal and progressive rock. See Edward Macan, *Rocking the Classics: English Progressive Rock and the Counterculture* (New York: Oxford University Press, 1997), 186.

## Chapter 1

1. Theodor W. Adorno, *The Culture Industry: Selected Essays on Mass Culture*, ed. J.M. Bernstein (New York: Routledge, 1991), especially "Culture Industry Reconsidered," 98–106.

2. In this respect, Adorno's position has been reduced to high culture snobbery. What is often omitted from these criticisms is that Adorno applied his rigorous and frequently acerbic standards of critique to high culture as well as mass culture/popular culture.

3. Theodor W. Adorno, *Essays on Music*, ed. Richard Leppert, trans. Susan Gillespie (Berkeley: University of California Press, 2002), 445.

4. Eileen R. Meehan, *Why TV Is Not Our Fault: Television Programming, Viewers, and Who's Really in Charge* (Lanham, MD: Rowman and Littlefield, 2005), 54–5.

5. TimeWarner and News Corporation are involved in a share of the teen culture market. TimeWarner utilizes the CW (originally the WB and later merged with UPN to form the CW) as a niche network for teen dramas ranging from *Dawson's Creek, One Tree Hill, Veronica Mars, Gossip Girl, 90210, Hellcats, The Vampire Diaries*, etc. News Corporation, owner of FOX, developed early FOX teen dramas like *21 Jump Street* (which starred the up-and-coming Johnny Depp), *Beverly Hills 90210, The O.C.* and, most recently, *Glee*.

6. On *Sonny with a Chance*, Sonny Monroe (played by Demi Lovato) is a cast member of "So Random!," which is a parody of Nickelodeon's now-extinct brand of comedy-variety shows (*All That, The Amanda Show*). Moreover, an ongoing subplot is that "So Random!" shares their studio with the cast and crew of "McKenzie Falls," a turgid teen drama.

7. *Big Time Rush* routinely features a music-video segment in each episode, which also serves as the "official" music video for the song. In the case of *Victorious*, Victoria Justice music videos are not a part of given episodes, but are very much connected as far as cross-promotion. The videos are credited to the "*Victorious* cast, featuring Victoria Justice" and Justice's co-stars appear in the videos (except "Best Friend's Brother"). *Victorious* episodes frequently include musical performances by Tori Vega (played by Justice) and the other characters written into plot lines. Miranda Cosgrove's pop-music career has largely been separate from *iCarly*, although the show's theme song, "Leave It All to Me," was sung by Cosgrove and released as her first single, and the *iCarly* episode "iDo" concluded with Carly Shea performing "Shakespeare" at a wedding reception (a song from Cosgrove' debut CD *Sparks Fly*). The *iCarly-Victorious* crossover movie, "iParty with Victorious," ended with a collective cast performance of a mash-up of "Leave It All to Me" and the *Victorious* theme song "Make It Shine."

8. Disney Channel performers generally record for Disney's subsidiary, Hollywood Records; Nickelodeon partners with Sony Music and its subsidiary Columbia Records for many of its pop-music crossover projects. Exceptions are Jennette McCurdy, a "New Country" teen-pop performer on Capitol Nashville, and Keke Palmer, who is on Interscope Records. The Jonas Brothers went the opposite route and had the teen sitcoms *JONAS* and its retooled

version *JONAS L.A.*, built around their pop-music stardom (the shows ran on Disney Channel from 2008–10).

9. *Glee* soundtrack CDs are produced in partnership between 20th Century-Fox and Columbia Records.

10. Dave Marsh has been extremely critical of Bono's political posturing. While this criticism is well deserved, it need also be considered in terms of Marsh's own championing of Bruce Springsteen as the rock ideal of progressive populism.

11. Norma Coates, "Teenyboppers, Groupies, and Other Grotesques: Girls and Women and Rock Culture in the 1960s and Early 1970s," *Journal of Popular Music Studies*, vol. 15, no.1 (2003): 76.

12. As of 2011, the Monkees and Kiss have yet to be inducted into the Rock and Roll Hall of Fame. The exclusion from a historic perspective alone is difficult to justify, and suggests more that they are still being "punished" for their dubious pasts.

13. Simon Frith, *Sound Effects: Youth, Leisure, and the Politics of Rock 'n' Roll* (New York: Pantheon, 1981), 56–7. The underlying issue for Frith (the defense of popular music's potential to act as oppositional culture) necessarily allies him with the "consumption" side, even as aware as Frith is of capitalism's determinate role in cultural production.

14. Antonin Artaud, *Selected Writings*, ed. Susan Sontag, trans. Helen Weaver (Berkeley: University of California Press, 1988), 252.

15. What *Malcolm in the Middle* and *Everybody Hates Chris* also shared was a representation of the mother as a raging control-monger and the underlying cause of family's dysfunction.

16. As quoted in Jonathan Dee, "Tween on the Screen," *New York Times* (April 8, 2007).

17. On *Victorious*, the Hip adult figure is Mr. Sikowitz, the decidedly weird-with-a-beard hippie drama teacher. In "The Bird Scene" (2010), Tori learned she cannot participate in any school play productions until she passes "the Bird Scene" test proctored by Mr. Sikowitz. After failing "the Bird Scene" on her third try, Tori lost her temper and told Mr. Sikowitz that, whether he liked it or not, her version of the Bird Scene was good. As the class burst into applause, Mr. Sikowitz proudly informed Tori she now *passed* the Bird Scene test. It was not any better or worse than the other versions, but Tori finally owned her performance and considered it a success, no matter what anyone else thought of it. As Mr. Sikowitz told her, "It was only wrong when you asked if it was right" and provided the message that individualism as non-conformity and self-determination are mutually related.

18. The word "chiz" is the standard and frequently used euphemism for "shit" on *iCarly* and *Victorious* ("It's the chiz," "It's total chiz," "It's serious chiz," "That sack of chiz," etc.).

19. Banet-Weiser, 71.

## Chapter 2

1. Frith, *Sound Effects*, 24. Emphasis original.

2. Norman Mailer, "The White Negro," in *Advertisements for Myself* (Cambridge: Harvard University Press, 1992), 339. Emphasis added.

3. Dick Hebdige, *Subculture: The Meaning of Style* (London: Routledge, 1987), 46–7.

4. Timothy D. Taylor, *Beyond Exoticism: Western Music and the World* (Durham: Duke University Press, 1997), 169. In this respect, Frith raised a crucial issue in *Sound Effects*, 23–32. During the 1960s, folk music effectively replaced country music as the primary white music component of rock and roll, the former considered politically progressive, and the latter politically conservative. What is less satisfactory in Frith's analysis is situating folk as inherently progressive and country as inherently conservative music, and the 1960s saw what amounted to a more natural synthesis between white and black music, formally and politically.

5. A remake of *Footloose* is set for 2011 release. Zac Efron was originally cast in the lead role, but withdrew from the project; he was eventually replaced by professional dancer-actor Kenny Wormald.

6. See also John Waters, "Ladies and Gentleman ... The Nicest Kids in Town!" in *Crackpot:*

*The Obsessions of John Waters* (New York: Vintage, 1987), 88–100. Written in 1985, *Hairspray* is a tribute to *The Buddy Deane Show*, a highly popular local Baltimore teen dance show that ran from 1957–64, and eventually subsumed by racial politics of the era.

7. Outlaw Country performer Waylon Jennings performed the theme song for *The Dukes of Hazzard* and narrated the episodes (billed as "The Balladeer"). However, the 2005 film version of *The Dukes of Hazzard* replaced Southern Hipness with a post–*School of Rock* "eternal teenager/rock rebel" Hipness. Bo Duke sported a Led Zeppelin T-shirt in the film, as opposed to a Lynard Skynyr or Charlie Daniels Band T-shirt. While Lynard Skynard, Charlie Daniels Band, Molly Hatchet, and Allman Brothers Band appear on the soundtrack, the presence of 1970s Southern Rock was part of the film's overall emphasis on 1970s classic rock, and also included songs by AC/DC, James Gang, Mountain, and ZZ Top. The inclusion of Outlaw Country icon Willie Nelson (as "Uncle Jessie") and *Smokey and the Bandit* star Burt Reynolds (as "Boss Hogg") seemed to be further attempts at referential irony than any engagement of Southern Hipness.

8. *High School Musical* co-star Ashley Tisdale signed to Warner Bros. Records (as opposed to Disney subsidiary Hollywood Records) and moved to the CW as a co-star on *Hellcats*, playing Savannah Monroe. However, in 2011, Tisdale's Disney film *Sharpey's Fabulous Adventure* was released, a "spin-off" film based on her *High School Musical* character Sharpey Evans (the Paris Hilton to Hannah Montana-as-Britney Spears). *Hellcats* star Aly Michalka (who portrayed Marti Perkins) was a cast member of the Disney Channel teen sitcom *Phil of the Future* (2004–6) and her band, 78violet, recorded for Hollywood Records from 2004–10.

9. However, two popular teen sitcoms were set in the South. *The Famous Jett Jackson* (Disney Channel, 1998–2001) was a reversed scenario to the subsequent *Hannah Montana*. Jett Jackson was an African-American teenage male and TV star, weary of life in L.A. He convinces the producers of his hit show to relocate production to his small, rural hometown in North Carolina so he can lead a more "normal" life while still being a TV star. *Just Jordan* (Nickelodeon, 2007–9) was similar in that the title character was an African-American male who moved from L.A. to Little Rock with his mother after his parents' divorce.

10. A pilot for a 1995 primetime CBS sitcom in which Clarissa Darling was now living in NYC and interning at the *New York Post*. CBS declined to pick up the show. Melissa Joan Hart subsequently starred as the title character on *Sabrina, the Teenage Witch* (ABC, 1996–2000; WB 2000–3), a primetime sitcom based on the Archie Comics character, which had been a successful Saturday morning cartoon in the 1970s.

11. Similarly, on *Sonny with a Chance*, Sonny Munroe is a Midwestern (Wisconsin) teenage girl who moves to L.A. after she gets a job on a popular teen comedy-variety show. Sonny is enthusiastic, friendly, and hard-working; her West Coast counterparts tend to be less so.

12. *Kenan and Kel* ran on Nickelodeon from 1996–2000, and created as a sitcom vehicle for *All That* regulars Kenan Thompson and Kel Mitchell playing relatively poor African-American males living in inner-city Chicago. *Kenan and Kel* was not without controversy, and was accused by some critics as being little more than a teen sitcom version of *Amos 'n' Andy*. See Banet-Wesier, 158. To note, Kenan Thompson became a long-time regular cast member of *Saturday Night Live*.

13. While *Wizards of Waverly Place* initially compares to the *Harry Potter* franchise, ideologically *Wizards of Waverly Place* had much in common with the 1960s "magic sitcoms," specifically *Bewitched* and *I Dream of Jeannie*. A recommended discussion of the magic sitcoms is by David Marc, *Comic Visions: Television Comedy and American Culture*, 2d ed. (Malden, MA: Blackwell, 1997), Chapter 4. As Marc observed, "The message is clear: Don't be fooled by the glitz and glamour of the easy way (i.e., magic) of doing things. The discipline and respectability of nine-to-five, Thank-God-Its-Friday existence are valorized as far more satisfying than the freedom to gratuitously manipulate the world to one's individual pleasure" (109). This message is the same on *Hannah Montana* if one substitutes "stardom" for "magic."

14. This is not to say there is an absence of minority representation on teen sitcoms. The title characters of *Kenan and Kel*, *The Famous Jett Jackson*, *That's So Raven*, *Corey in the House*,

and *Just Jordan* were African-Americans; the teen sitcom *Taina* featured a Latina main character.

15. Americanism was also very much the theme of the *iCarly* movie "iGo to Japan" (2008, a 90-minute episode) in that Carly and her friends travel to Japan after 'iCarly" is nominated for a best international comedy webshow award. True to stereotype, the French nominee is a pompous ass; the Japanese contenders are ruthless cheaters in global competition trying to sabotage the success of their American counterparts at every opportunity.

16. Lester Bangs, *Psychotic Reactions and Carburetor Dung*, ed. Greil Marcus (New York: Anchor, 2003), 278. Emphasis added.

17. Ibid., 279.

18. Popular music celebrating the American experience is by no means exclusive to rock; other examples include MOR (Neil Diamond's "America"), folk pop (Simon and Garfunkel's "America"), and funk (James Brown's "Living in America"). Country music has also produced a range of overtly patriotic songs (Merle Haggard's "Fighting Side of Me," Lee Greenwood's "God Bless the U.S.A."). However, rock music has produced its own share of jingoist anthems, ranging from Billy Joel's "We Didn't Start the Fire," Sammy Hagar's "VOA" [Voice of America] and Metallica's "Don't Tread on Me." The last was somewhat surprising considering that previous Metallica songs, "Disposable Heroes" and "One," were vehemently anti-war songs.

19. See Macan, *Rocking the Classics*, Chapter 8, especially 172–8. While this tome is informative, Macan makes highly reductive claims concerning rock critics and their objections to progressive rock (naming names: Lester Bangs, Robert Christgau, Simon Frith, and Dave Marsh), peppering his analysis with the term "Neo-Marxist" as a kind of critical Red-baiting, as if rock critics are engaged in an ideological conspiracy against good taste. Macan also makes the particularly absurd assertion that this so-called Neo-Marxist critical cadre "by the late 1970s ... had become notorious for its rejection of all but the most obscure punk/New Wave bands" (176). Dave Marsh has long been an unabashed champion of Bruce Springsteen, hardly someone who is "obscure punk/New Wave."

20. Punk was an American "invention," although the U.S. and U.K. punk scenes developed distinctly national identities within their specific context. Malcolm McLaren briefly managed the NYC proto-punk the New York Dolls in 1974, and witnessed the emerging punk music and fashion trends in the NYC music scene which he later utilized (some would say stole) in his management of the Sex Pistols. The Ramones' July 4, 1976 concert at the Roadhouse in London was a pivotal moment in sparking the U.K. punk movement.

21. Simon Reynolds, *Rip It Up and Start Again: Postpunk 1978–1984* (New York: Penguin, 2005), 326–7. Emphasis added.

22. Ibid., 347–8.

23. Ibid., 342. Reynolds's defense of New Pop ultimately flounders due to a highly contradictory argument. He champions New Pop as subversive for challenging rock ideology's traditional tenets of "authenticity" while at the same time relying on the most essential tenet of rock ideology as far as asserting the "authenticity" of New Pop: the influence of black music. Indeed, Reynolds trumps the fact that the Art of Noise's 1982 hit "Beat Box" was mistaken in America as the work of black musicians (362–3). The fact that "Beat Box" was actually the product of white studio engineers fiddling with a sampled Yes drum track merely demonstrates the extent to which "authenticity" is, and always has been, a self-fulfilling critical construct.

24. Ibid., 348.

25. Ibid. Second emphasis added.

26. William L. O'Neill *Coming Apart: An Informal History of America in the 1960s* (New York: Times, 1972), 196.

27. As quoted in Legs McNeil and Gillian McGill, *Please Kill Me: An Uncensored Oral History of Punk* (New York: Penguin, 1997), 47.

28. Coates, 67.

29. Ibid., 69.

30. "Bisexual" was a term used by Elton John and David Bowie to define their sexuality in the 1970s. John is now openly gay. Bowie used the term more as part of the "bisexual chic"

of the decade to explicitly associate himself with gay subculture in the decade of glam and disco, and pursue his interest in areas of decadence and transgression. Bowie has since been publically non-committal about his sexual orientation as bisexual or heterosexual (Bowie has also been married to model Iman since 1992). It was not until Freddy Mercury of Queen died of AIDS in 1991 that issues of male rock stars and same-sex relationships were acknowledged, let alone addressed, by the mainstream rock community. In 1998, Rob Halford of Judas Priest was the first heavy metal performer to come out as gay. In retrospect, what was more striking is how little effort Mercury and Halford made to conceal homoerotic subtext in the songs, image, and live performances and how apparent it became after the fact.

31. Al Spicer, "David Bowie," in *Rock: The Rough Guide*, 2nd ed., eds. Buckley, Jonathan, Orla Duane, Mark Ellingham, Al Spicer (London: Rough Guides, 1999), 118.

32. *Sound Effects*, 227. For a counterargument against the "cock rock" critical stance, see Susan Fast, *In the Houses of the Holy: Led Zeppelin and the Power of Rock Music* (New York: Oxford University Press, 2001), Chapter 5. Fast effectively points out that the frequent criticisms of "cock rock" rely on traditional "rock-masculine/pop-feminine" critical binary logic. What is less compelling is Fast's defense of Led Zeppelin around the alleged "irony" and "parody" as well as "androgyny" over phallocentricism. Cock rock can also be read as not so much an acknowledgement of femininity but a conquest of it, meaning that the feminine can be assumed by men in order to further exclude the woman from the "masculine" order.

33. Coates, 68, 71.

34. Ibid., 68. Emphasis added.

35. By way of personal example, as a tween and teen ca. in the early-to-mid 1970s, my tastes in rock music — or band/brand loyalty-was the progressive rock of ELP and Jethro Tull as well as the hard rock/metal of Bachman-Turner Overdrive, Black Sabbath and Kiss. From the perspective of dominant rock criticism, namely *Rolling Stone* and *Creem* (at least as far as prog-rock was concerned), this may have been evidence of developing more "mature taste" but developing "good taste" would have been quite another matter. In 1978, after seeing Devo on *Saturday Night Live*, my brand loyalty shifted to punk, a "correct" consumer choice as far as rock critical discourse, but Devo was far from the "correct brand" as opposed to the Ramones or the Sex Pistols.

36. Teen sitcoms are rated TV-G largely to reflect an assumed "tween audience" versus TV-Y and TV-Y7 "kiddie audiences," as well as TV-PG and TV-14 "teen audiences." However, teen sitcoms tend to feature a certain amount of bathroom humor, boys being hit in the groin, and *double entendres*, provided one is willing to concede that teen sitcoms are actually capable of coming up with *double entendres*.

37. Prior to 1975, very few women were "rock stars" and the short list included Grace Slick, Janis Joplin, Joni Mitchell, and Suzi Quatro. As far as all-women bands, Fanny and the GTOs were the only two that attained any sort of national attention prior to punk; the GTOs were not so much a band as an avant-garde parody of the 1960s "girl groups" composed of ex-groupies, with Frank Zappa acting as producer and musical director. As far as rock (excluding punk) was concerned, Heart, a mixed-gender band fronted by Ann and Nancy Wilson, released their debut album in 1976. Fleetwood Mac released the phenomenally successful *Rumors* in 1977 and by that point was a mixed-gender band featuring Stevie Nicks as co-lead vocalist and front person. Pat Benatar released her debut album in 1979. Girlschool released their first album in 1980, and arguably the first all-woman heavy metal band, depending on how one classifies the Runaways. Historically, women as cultural producers had a much greater presence in black music genres, mainstream pop, and country music. Indeed, given the common criticism of country as inherently conservative, country music was much more open to women performers than rock.

38. Andreas Huyssen, *After the Great Divide: Modernism, Mass Culture, Postmodernism* (Bloomington: Indiana University Press. 1986), 62.

39. In this respect, *George Lopez* offered a blatant double-standard as far as gendered adolescent rebellion. The misbehavior of his son Max was impetuous mischief and his highly active interest in the opposite sex, including a number of romantic advances towards his first

cousin, was evidence he was "a player" (read: not gay). Daughter Carmen's misbehavior was spiteful disobedience, while her interest in the opposite sex effectively made her a potential slut.

## Chapter 3

1. Milton Berle appeared on NBC as *Texaco Star Theater*, 1948–52; *The Buick-Berle Show*, 1952–3; *The Milton Berle Show*, 1953–9. Sid Caesar starred on *Your Show of Shows* (NBC, 1950–4), *Caesar's Hour* (NBC, 1954–57), *Sid Caesar Invites You* (ABC, 1958). *The Red Skelton Show* ran on CBS from 1953–70, bracketed by runs on NBC (1951-3, 1970–1). The original *Jackie Gleason Show* ran on CBS from 1952-5 and from 1956-9, with Gleason's own foray into the sitcom *The Honeymooners* running from 1955–6.

2. Marc, 73.

3. See John Ellis, *Visible Fictions: Cinema, Television, Video*, rev. ed. (London: Routledge, 1992), 129, 137.

4. *The Wonder Years* and *Everybody Hates Chris* both used the motif of the main character narrating events from his childhood depicted on the screen. However, *The Wonder Years* was a classical sitcom with dramatic elements whereas *Everybody Hates Chris* was a contemporary sitcom, and the tone of *The Wonder Years'* narration wistful nostalgia versus *Everybody Hates Chris's* sarcastic commentary.

5. In the 1970s, Norman Lear's sitcoms including *All in the Family, Maude, Good Times*, and *The Jeffersons* were hailed as evidence of the TV sitcom entering a new era of "maturity." Lear's sitcoms were very much within the classical sitcom mode, but placed greater emphasis on complex characters, dramatic moments, a greater sense of "realism," and socially relevant content. Conversely, Ernie Kovacs conducted radical and surreal experiments on TV form that make contemporary sitcoms pale in comparison in the 1950s and early 1960s. While the move towards contemporary sitcom formalism can certainly be demonstrated, it is more difficult to claim this represents a definitive break as far as TV comedy, let alone one that is inherently superior. Again, this can be argued not so much as "innovation" but "novelty" as far as dressing up the sitcom into a "new and improved" brand of TV comedy.

6. Deleuze, *Cinema 1*, 164.

7 Ibid., 147, In *Comic Visions*, David Marc suggested the sitcom is fundamentally a formula of "Episode = Familiar Status Quo → Ritual error made → Ritual lesson learned → Familiar Status Quo" (190). In this sense, I concur with Marc in that the sitcom ethical form of situational disorder → transformative action → situational order is a structure of *restoring* a pre-existing social order (i.e., one that exists as the given "before the episode").

8. Adorno, *The Culture Industry*, 166–7.

9. See also my own *Politics and the American Television Comedy: A Critical Survey from I Love Lucy to South Park* (Jefferson, NC: McFarland, 2008), Chapter 10.

10. Robert Bly, *Iron John* (New York: Vintage, 1991), 22–3. Emphasis added.

11. Carl Gustav Jung, *Aspects of the Masculine/Aspects of the Feminine*, ed. John Beebe, trans. R.F.C. Hull (New York: MJF Books, 1989). A combined two-volume set, each volume has its own pagination. For reasons of clarity as well as convenience, I refer to them as *AM* and *AF* in citations, in this case, Jung, *AM*, 85. Emphasis added.

12. Jung, *AF*, 50

13. See Charmaine McEachern, "Bringing the Wildman Back Home: Television and the Politics of Masculinity," *Continuum: The Australian Journal of Media and Culture*, vol.7; no.2 (1994); see also Charmaine McEachern, "Comic Interventions: Passion and the Men's Movement's in the Situation Comedy *Home Improvement*," *Journal of Gender Studies*, 3:1 (March 1999): 5–18. This reading of *Home Improvement* is strongly informed by McEachern's analysis of the show as a satire of the men's movement targeting the spiritual and "feminine" aspects of the movement while valorizing men's movement ideology through traditional symbols of masculinity.

14. In this respect, one underlying shift in the 1990s sitcoms was gendering mass culture

itself. "Good" mass culture is action films, sports, and rock and roll. "Bad" mass culture is chick flicks, daytime talk-shows, and pop music. High culture is uniformly deemed the realm of the feminine-as-intellectual as far as foreign art films, theater, and classical music. As far as literature, men prefer the sports section and comic strips in the newspaper; women embrace the classics as well as popular romance novels.

    15. Jung, *AF*, 98. Emphasis added.
    16. Ibid., 172.
    17. Jung, *AM*, 50. Emphasis added.
    18. Ibid., 50.
    19. *Iron John*, 225–6.

## Chapter 4

    1. Direct address is hardly an invention of the contemporary sitcom, yet alone *SbtB*. On *The George Burns and Gracie Allen Show* (CBS, 1950–8), George Burns frequently addressed the camera. *The Many Loves of Dobie Gillis* (CBS, 1959–63) also featured direct address introductions by Dobie Gillis, a high-school student struggling with the usual teenage problems of parents, romance, and school. Indeed, one could say that if *Miss Bliss* was a Square update of *Our Miss Brooks*, *SbtB* was a Hip update of *Dobie Gillis*.

    2. In the subsequent spin-off *Saved by the Bell: The College Years*, Zack was majoring in "finance."

    3. *Revenge of the Nerds* (1984) is the most famous exception as far as pop culture representation of nerds and geeks, and goes to great lengths to satirize the popular guys and jocks. Nonetheless, while *Revenge of the Nerds* champions the nerd, it is also saturated with the sophomoric sexism ingrained in the "college comedy" genre. *SbtB* served as the rather virulent "anti-nerd" competing discourse that retained the sexism.

    4. Zack and Kelly married in the series finale of *Saved by the Bell: The College Years*. "Properly balanced" American masculinity and femininity were strengthened and unified through couple logic.

    5. Brian Massumi, *A User's Guide to Capitalism and Schizophrenia: Deviations from Deleuze and Guattari* (Cambridge, MA: The MIT Press, 1992), 122. Emphasis original.

    6. In "Check Your Mate" (1991), Screech, the reigning Bayside chess champion, competed against a Russian exchange student from a rival high school. Screech's opponent was repeatedly and disparagingly referred to as a "Commie," with every utterance of "Commie" matched by cheers and applause on the laugh track. On *SbtB*, the Cold War was alive and well despite the collapse of the Soviet Union. Of course, the only student preaching *détente* was Jessie Spano.

## Chapter 5

    1. Banet-Wesier, 32.

    2. Within an hour timespan watching Nickelodeon on a Saturday afternoon (3/26/2011), among the commercials personally viewed were Lalaloopsy dolls, Zhu Zhu Pets dolls, the Girl Tech "Password Journal" (an e-diary with built-in MP3 player manufactured by Mattel), Hasbro *Star Wars* light saber toys, Trix and Cinnamon Toast Crunch breakfast cereals, CiCi's chain of pizza restaurants, Head and Shoulders shampoo, Downey laundry detergent, and Nationwide car insurance.

    3. Hartley, "Invisible Fictions," 63. Emphasis added.

    4. Here one could consider the multitude of popular music-centered TV networks, the sheer amount of which would require a study in its own right.

    5. Nickelodeon's teen programming generally runs from 1–7 P.M. Mondays–Thursdays; 1–8 P.M. Fridays; 11A.M.–9 P.M. Saturdays; and 11A.M.–7 P.M. Sundays (all times CST), but this schedule can vary. Moreover, the Saturday and Sunday morning programming (roughly 6–11 A.M.) consists of animated programs shown in the afternoon teen blocs (*SpongeBob SquarePants*, etc.) rather than the weekday-morning Nickelodeon educational programs like

*Dora the Explorer* or *Max and Ruby*; in this way, Nickelodeon teen programming effectively runs all day on weekends. In a typical day from summer of 2010 to summer of 2011, episodes of *SpongeBob SquarePants* and *iCarly* were givens, and almost always *Big Time Rush* and *Victorious*. When the teen sitcom *Bucket and Skinner's Epic Adventures* debuted in summer 2011, it immediately went into the heavy rotation schedule as well. Rounding out the schedule were various animated shows (*The Penguins of Madagascar*, *T.U.F.F. Puppy*, *Planet Sheen*, etc.), new shows (the teen mystery-drama *House of Anubis* and action-comedy *Supah Ninjas*), the kids game show *Brain Surge*, specials (such as *Nick News* or documentaries on various Nickelodeon teen stars), and occasional movies ranging from older films, like *Ghostbusters*, *Pretty in Pink*, or *What a Girl Wants* to Nickelodeon-produced movies, like *The Boy Who Cried Werewolf* (starring Victoria Justice), *Best Player* (starring Jerry Trainor and Jennette McCurdy), or *The SpongeBob SquarePants Movie*. Airings of shows routinely alternated as far as daily time slots (i.e., one day a rerun of *Victorious* might be shown at 3 P.M., the next day a rerun of *iCarly* or *Big Time Rush* or *SpongeBob SquarePants*).

6. Officially, "iParty with Victorious" is considered an *iCarly* special episode, but was effectively a made-for-Nickelodeon film (as of this writing, a two-hour "extended version" is scheduled to air as well, but no specific dates have been announced).

7. Hartley, "Invisible Fictions," 61.

8. Ibid., 65.

9. Ibid., 64. Emphasis added.

10. Ibid., 70. Emphasis original.

11. In this context, *According to Jim* (2001–9), *My Wife and Kids*, (2001–5) and *George Lopez* (2002–6) all ran on ABC, which is owned by Disney. However, *George Lopez* has been a fixture of Nickelodeon's "Nick at Night" nightly bloc of primetime sitcom reruns since 2007, and in fall of 2010 Nickelodeon added *My Wife and Kids* to Nick at Night. In April of 2011, a week of *My Wife and Kids* late-night marathons was promoted with the tag line "Michael Kyle Rules!" Michael Kyle (played by Damon Wayans) is the main character/ husband-father on *My Wife and Kids*. In this respect, Nickelodeon can construct a space where "adults rule" as well.

12. Banet-Weiser, 126.

13. Meehan, 87.

14. Justice, along with *Victorious* cast Leon Thomas III and Daniella Monet, served as the spokesperson for Earth Day 2011 in Big Help public-service announcements and participated in ongoing environmental work in coastal Louisiana amid the aftermath of Hurricane Katrina and the British Petroleum oil spill disaster. Likewise, in summer of 2011 Big Time Rush appeared in a new set of Big Help spots promoting physical fitness.

15. Nickelodeon also sponsors the annual "Halo Awards," in which various celebrities meet selected teens and honor them for their community service. However, promotion of teen community service is not exclusive to Nickelodeon. Miley Cyrus is spokesperson for "Get Ur Good On" in partnership with Youth Service America. *Glee* partnered with American Express for a similar youth community action campaign.

16. Banet-Wesier, 68.

17. As quoted in Diane Joy Moca, "'Clarissa' Gives TV Its First High-Tech Sitcom," *Chicago Tribune* (March 23, 1991).

18. These kinds of subjective insets were later popularized by *That 70's Show*; for example, in one episode Red Forman's thoughts on the situation — the realization that his son and friends used marijuana — was done as a parody of the 1930s exploitation film *Reefer Madness*.

19. On *Gidget* a widowed father was raising a teenage daughter, on *Punky Brewster* an orphaned tween girl was adopted by an elderly man, and on *Blossom* a father was raising his teenage daughter after the mother abandoned the family. On *Hannah Montana* Robby Stewart was a widower raising Miley Stewart.

20. *Family Ties* can be read as attempting to valorize the liberal idealism of the Keaton parents by satirizing 1980s Reaganism (Alex) and consumerism (Mallory). The problem was that Michael J. Fox quickly became the star and the central focus of the show and, in the cli-

mate of Reaganism, became the character to *laugh with* against his liberal parents rather than to *laugh at* as the satirical representative of Reaganism — not unlike how Archie Bunker became the unintended popular spokesman for Nixon's "Silent Majority" on *All in the Family* in the early 1970s. As a critique of consumerism, Mallory maintained the stereotype of the consumer as a dumb teenage girl.

21. They Might Be Giants are probably best known for their opening title song "Boss of Me" on *Malcolm in the Middle.*

22. Banet-Weiser, 126.

23. To this extent, if Nickelodeon teen programming is analogous to Top 40 Radio, Nickelodeon production is comparable to the Hollywood studio system. Nickelodeon specializes in developing and promoting a stable of teen stars from within, with "promotion" used in both senses of the word. Victoria Justice is the clearest example. Justice joined the cast of *Zoey 101* in 2005 and was eventually promoted to star on *Victorious.* Between the conclusion of *Zoey 101* in spring of 2008 and the debut of *Victorious* in spring of 2010, Justice was almost ubiquitous on Nickelodeon, appearing as a guest star on episodes of *The Naked Brothers Band, True Jackson, VP* and *The Troop,* as well as playing the title character in a heavily promoted *iCarly* hour-long special episode "I Fight Shelby Marx" (2009). Justice also co-starred in the made-for-Nickelodeon movie *Spectacular!* (2009).

24. In the *iCarly* episode "iGet Pranky" (2010), Carly was upset that she unable to execute a decent practical joke. As she dejectedly watched a rerun of *Drake and Josh* episode, Carly remarked to herself, "How come that little girl is so good at pranks?" Beyond the self-referential joke, it points out the fundamental difference between the shows. On *iCarly,* Carly is the central figure sustaining community order; on *Drake and Josh,* Meagan was a force of both disorder and restoration of order.

25. Walter Nichols was Josh's father, and Drake and Megan's stepfather. Walter worked as the on-air meteorologist at a local TV station. As well as being a science nerd, Walter was a "soft male" who enjoyed baths, cats, reading, and other "feminine" things. In terms of recent sitcom logic, the "problem" was that while Josh correctly identified with his father, his father was misaligned as far as gendered behavior which misaligned Josh.

26. *Victorious* is also primarily set in a high school, and Tori Vega becomes the figurative "center of gravity" through which the other students as "social atoms" and a "great melting pot" of diverse yet stereotypical teenagers combine and sustain a community. On *Victorious,* there is less emphasis on characters being friends per se (some characters clearly dislike other characters, namely Tori and Jade), but understanding the necessity of managing productive, if not entirely amicable, relationships to their mutual advantage: in short, capitalist society and liberal democracy.

27. *Zoey 101* can be read as the precursor to *iCarly* at two levels. One is the overt representation of the educational apparatus as a bumbling and repressive regime. The other is that the absence of effective adult authority not only "liberates" kids as far as managing their own affairs and exercising personal freedom, but necessitates that they take on adult responsibilities within their social circle. A recurring motif on *Zoey 101* was that Zoey's trouble-prone younger brother Dustin also attended PCA, forcing Zoey to assume a parental role in the relationship by providing guidance, discipline, and occasional mediation between her brother and the PCA administration. On *iCarly,* Carly Shay frequently serves as the parent for her juvenile delinquent best friend, Sam, and her extremely immature older brother, Spencer.

28. Rebecca was played by Daniella Monet (Trina Vega on *Victorious*).

29. After the first season, the character Dana Cruz (played by Kristin Herrera) was written out and replaced by the character Lola Martinez (played by Victoria Justice). After the second season, the character Nicole Bristow (played by Alexia Nikolas) was written out of *Zoey 101* as well. Ironically, given *Zoey 101*'s emphasis on community, Bristow was reportedly removed from the show due to ongoing personal and professional friction with Jamie Lynn Spears. Lola was promoted to Zoey's new best friend and Quinn Pensky (played by Erin Sanders) promoted to Zoey and Lola's roommate. This also trimmed the teen cast members from seven (four girls, three boys) to six (three girls, three boys) for the latter half of the show's run.

30. *Victorious* is constructed on a similar if more complex arrangement of teen stereotypes:

Tori (white-Latina)—popular kid; symbol of democratic community
André (African-American male)—cool kid; symbol of Hip
Beck (white male)—bad boy/chick magnet; symbol of rebellion
Cat (white female)—ditzy girl; symbol of conformity
Robbie (white Jewish male)—geek/loser; symbol of Square
Jade (white female)—mean girl; symbol of authoritarianism
Trina (white-Latina)—self-centered consumerist; symbol of narcissism
Sinjin (white male)—geek/weirdo; symbol of the Other

31. The least "progressive" aspect of *Zoey 101* was the construction of the PCA community "Other" through the recurring character Stacey Dillsen. Stacey was uncool, unintelligent, and spoke with a pronounced speech impediment. In the *Zoey 101* series finale, Stacey assumes a degree of normalcy and begins to fit in at PCA when her speech impediment is cured by being hit by a car.

32. Banet-Wesier, 141.

## Chapter 6

1. *Zoey 101's* fourth season consisted of 13 episodes (plus a previously unaired episode from Season Three) and ran from January to May 2008; however, occasional reruns of *Zoey 101* were part of Nickelodeon's teen programming bloc, well into 2009. Sean Flynn had also left the show, with his absence explained by Chase studying in Europe; the character James Garrett (played by Austin Butler) was added as Zoey's romantic interest in the final season. In the series finale "Chasing Zoey," Chase returned to PCA and he and Zoey officially became a couple. Moreover, the nerd Quinn and rich kid Logan, whose secret romance was a major subplot of much of the final season, announced their couple status to the community.

2. While Obama was something of a political unknown, he was a rising star in the Democratic Party, and initially gained attention for his speech at the 2004 Democratic National Convention.

3. Gibby's promotion to regular cast in one sense transformed the gendered trio into a more "balanced" gendered quartet of Carly (feminine girl), Sam (masculine girl), Freddie (feminine boy), and Gibby (masculine boy). However, Gibby is rather dimwitted, rotund, and "weird." However, he is also brash, hot-tempered, and has a highly active libido (his relationship with his "hot" girlfriend Tasha was central to the episode "iEnrage Gibby"). As much as he is designated comic relief, Gibby can be read as a satire of the recent representations of sitcom masculinity (e.g., *The King of Queens, According to Jim*).

4. The skits performed on the "iCarly" webshow tend to vary from straight parodies of popular culture ("teen chick flicks" or the "teen vampire" trend) to more "avant-garde" as a kind of Dada (the "How to Make Chicken Soup in a Toilet" skit) or Theater of the Absurd, such as the nonsensical banter in skits where Carly plays "the Idiot Farm Girl" and Sam "the Cowboy" with scenarios like the Idiot Farm Girl repeatedly mistaking the Cowboy's moustache for a squirrel or his chicken for a new car. To be sure, the representation of the Idiot Farm Girl and the Cowboy as far as gender and geographic politics becomes problematic in its own right.

5. According to Schneider, *he* serves as the "live audience" supplying the laughter in order to control the pacing of the show; prerecorded laugh tracks are added in post-production editing (as discussed in "Tween on the Screen").

6. This refers to the first season of *The Troop* (2009–10). After a lengthy hiatus, *The Troop* returned to Nickelodeon in summer of 2011. Felix Garcia became a recurring character, and was replaced by Kirby (played by *True Jackson, VP* cast member Matt Shively). While Kirby is a tech geek, it is expressed in a bumbling passion for monster-killing weaponry, more comparable to *Home Improvement's* Tim Taylor's passion for power tools rather than Freddie Benson's computer-geek stereotype. Moreover, Candace (played by former *Unfabulous* cast

member Malese Jow) was added to the regular cast as the high school's masculine-Hip "bad girl" stereotype, which is to say *The Troop*'s answer to Sam Puckett. In effect, for the second season *The Troop* eliminated the feminine altogether from its ranks.

7. This analysis of gender representation on *iCarly* owes greatly to Judith Butler, *Gender Trouble: Feminism and the Subversion of Identity* (New York: Routledge, 1999), particularly Chapter 2.

8. Freddie's vetoing of "Happy Birthday" was also a joke directed at TimeWarner. Warner/Chappell claims ownership of the copyright on "Happy Birthday" and TimeWarner insists on licensing fees for any use of the song.

9. In "iMove Out," the subplot was an "iCarly" skit inadvertently spawned a thriving pet makeover business, resulting in vicious competition instigated by the area's best-known pet photography business "the Petographers" (which can be read as a conflation of "pedophiles" and "pornographers"), owned and operated by an obviously gay male couple.

10. Dee, "Tween on the Screen."

11. In "iWanna Stay with Spencer" (2007), after one of Spencer's sculptured nearly injures Carly during an "iCarly" webcast, Carly's grandfather insisted Carly move to Yakama to live with him, despite Carly's strenuous objections. In the end, he realized that the practical knowledge Spencer accumulated about Carly over the years made Spencer a far more effective guardian than he could be, despite his traditional status as the elder patriarch, although he could still exercise a degree of control in Carly's life.

12. In "iParty with Victorious," Sam not only pointed out that Mrs. Benson hadn't had a date in over a decade, but made a comment that clearly indicated her parents were divorced, or at least separated. It produced an extremely awkward silence among Carly, Freddie, and Gibby. Like Sam and Freddie, Gibby's mother is single (she briefly dated Spencer in "iFix a Pop Star"), but his father has been mentioned as well ("iGet Pranky"), and his parents also divorced.

13. On *Wizards of Waverly Place*, the Hip-Square dialectic was similarly manifest in the relationship between the main character Alex Russo and her older brother Justin in what has become a dominant tactic in teen and adult sitcoms: culturally-coded "gendered behavior." Alex was not just NYC "streetwise" Hip but independent and willfully non-conformist; the effort she put into school and work can be charitably described as lethargic. Justin was mild-mannered, a studious nerd, and a dedicated employee at the family restaurant. The problematic tension of *Wizards of Waverly Place* was that Alex as a teenage *girl* representing masculine Hip (individuality, laziness, rebellion), whereas Justin as a teenage *boy* represented feminine Square (conformity, responsibility, obedience). For added measure, Alex's best friend, Harper Finkle, was fairly dimwitted, obsessed with popularity, and a self-proclaimed "fashionista" with horrible taste in clothes: the stereotypical "teenage girl."

14. "iGo Nuclear" was shown as part of Nickelodeon's Earth Day 2010 celebration. The episode was actually a sardonic take on strident environmentalism and, and at a certain level, satirized the Earth Day celebration.

15. The status of Mr. Belding on *Saved by the Bell* was quite different. On *iCarly*, like *Zoey 101*, the students want a school system that runs democratically. On *Saved by the Bell*, Zack usually managed to run things his way, while Mr. Belding was an effective puppet ruler in his "scheme of things."

16. As quoted in Jacques Steinberg, "I, Little Sister, Becomes 'iCarly,'" *New York Times* (September 7, 2007).

17. Simon Frith argued that the eventual failure of punk was its inability to escape from the confines of traditional record industry practices, no matter how radical punk presented itself musically or culturally. See "Post-Punk Blues," *Marxism Today* (March 1983), 18–9.

18. In this respect, the "culture" that is frequently satirized on *iCarly* is canonical high culture and commercial mass culture. What is celebrated is a "postmodern" approach to "oppositional culture" that is avant-garde and lowbrow (kitsch, novelty act, etc.), manifest in the "iCarly" skits and Spencer's sculptures.

19. Of the recurring characters, Ms. Briggs is played by Mindy Sterling, best known as

Frau Farbissna in the Austin Powers film series. Carly's grandfather is played by Greg Mullavey, who co-starred on the highly controversial 1970s sitcom *Mary Hartman, Mary Hartman*. Gibby's grandfather is played by Jack Carter, a veteran stand-up comedian/actor, whose career dates back to the 1950s.

20. Cruikshank's *Fred* skits are shown on YouTube and tend towards rapid-fire, seemingly random editing of Cruikshank's persona "Fred Figglehorn" blurting nonsensical observations in direct address to the camera while often running about. *Fred* is also done in fast-motion, producing a high-pitched screeching effect on the voices as well as a frenetic visual effect. Cruikshank has since become a "property" of Nickelodeon, having done the made-for-Nickelodeon film *Fred: The Movie* (2010) and a *Fred* sequel began production in spring of 2011.

21. Ginger Fox and her comeback song "Number One," which is a parody of the First Wave Teen Pop ode to narcissism, have become a recurring joke on *iCarly* as well as *Victorious* since appearing in "iFix a Pop Star." In the *Victorious* special episode "Freak the Freak Out" (2010), two girls involved in a karaoke feud with Tori Vega and her friends perform a dreadful version of "Number One." Given the frequency of jokes about urination on *iCarly* and *Victorious*, "Number One" can be read as signifying inauthentic teen pop as a form of mass culture that is so much piss.

22. Jennette McCurdy's debut music video "Not That Far Away" premiered on Nickelodeon as part of a "Just Jennette" Saturday evening special primetime bloc in 2010. It aired between two reruns of *iCarly* that featured Sam Puckett ("iMake Same Girlier" and "iWas a Pageant Girl") and repeats of the two *True Jackson, VP* episodes guest starring McCurdy as Pinky Truso.

23. It is here that rivalry rather than competition becomes important as well. While "iFix a Pop Star" was used to position Miranda Cosgrove as the new and improved brand of teen pop to Britney Spears, Cosgrove records for Columbia and Spears for Jive, both of which are owned by Sony.

24. In "iStage an Intervention" (2008), Spencer battled a woman named Sasha Striker for the world-record score on the "twentieth century" (i.e., 1980s) video game "Pak Rat," an event covered live by the "Video Game Channel." The VGC team of reporters and techs were uniformly less-than-masculine nerds (one used the live broadcast to pathetically plead for *any* girl to contact him). In contrast, Sasha Striker — a legendary video game champion — projected a swaggering, masculine Hipness.

25. This dialectic was similarly expressed on *Beavis and Butt-head* with Beavis and Butt-head's aimless individualist-anarchist rebellion versus the clenched anus personification of ultra-Square conformity, Tom Anderson. Tom Anderson was the obvious precursor to Hank Hill, the main character of *King of the Hill* (FOX, 1994–2009). Both shows were created by Mike Judge.

26. If Carly's speech parodies Frank Capra films, Sabrina's destruction of the model can be read as a parody of the B-Movie horror film *Attack of the 50 Foot Woman* (1958).

27. In fact, Carly's dream bedroom/loft is thoroughly "postmodern." It combines high-tech appliances (a closet with a glass door and motorized clothing rack; a make-up table with a video screen instead of a mirror and built-in hair dryer) and Pop Art furniture (an "avant-garde ice cream sandwich loveseat").

28. As noted, on *Victorious* Mr. Sikowitz is the Hip adult authority figure at the high school. In the Hollywood environment of ambition, artifice, and avarice, Mr. Sikowitz provides rather traditional advice and lessons about hard work, individualism, perseverance, responsibility, and self-determination through his hippie sensibility and the veneer of 1960s anti-Establishment Hipness.

29. In general, New Country is both a genre and marketing term for recent country performers with noticeable classic rock as well as contemporary pop-rock influences.

30. This is *not* to say that Cosgrove's songs are "liberal" and McCurdy's songs "conservative." McCurdy's second single, "Generation Love," contains lyrics emphatically endorsing community, tolerance, and working together for the betterment of society. The music video

featured McCurdy performing the song intercut with a cross section of Americans holding signs with slogans such as "Show compassion" and "Be selfless."

## Chapter 7

1. As an actress, Palmer gained notoriety for her starring role in the film *Akeelah and the Bee* (2006) and co-starred with Corbin Bleu in the Disney Channel film *Jump In!* (2007). As a teen pop singer, Palmer recorded for Atlantic Records from 2005–7; in 2009, Palmer signed with Interscope Records as opposed to Columbia, the almost standard operating procedure of recording Nickelodeon teen sitcom stars.

2. *TJVP* relies on the classical sitcom format, using a multi-camera set-up and recurring sound stage locations (the lobby and offices of "Mad Style" where True works, occasional high school settings, and other locales as plot specifics require). Instead of laugh tracks added in post-production, *TJVP* is filmed in front of a studio audience, specifically stated in an announcement by Palmer that begins each episode.

3. Dan Kopelman also appeared regularly on *TJVP* as Kopelman, an office executive who never speaks.

4. Ashley Argota, who played Lulu, is of Filipino descent.

5. *The Jeffersons* (CBS, 1975–85) was one of the first sitcoms to feature a racially mixed marriage. George Jefferson's son, Lionel, married a woman whose father was white and mother was black. While Lionel's father-in-law was as an unbigoted, upper-class liberal, George was a product of poverty and racially intolerant, frequently referring to his in-laws as the "zebra couple." More recently, the primetime sitcom *The New Adventures of Old Christine* and the teen drama *Hellcats* featured interracial romantic relationships between a white woman and African-American male. As far as teen sitcoms, the issue was broached on *Hannah Montana* and the episode "We're all in this Date Together" (2008). Hannah Montana (Miley Stewart's pop star alter-ego) was part of a celebrity date auction and one of the bidders was Johnny Collins, an African-American boy for whom Miley Stewart had an unrequited crush. In an almost perverse moment, when Johnny offered a bid of $15, 000 to date Hannah Montana, she raised her arm in the Black Power salute and yells "Sold!"

6. In summer of 2011, Nickelodeon launched *Bucket and Skinner's Epic Adventure* (*BSEA*), which effectively replaced *TJVP* as the fourth Nickelodeon teen sitcom, along with *iCarly*, *Big Time Rush*, and *Victorious*. Clearly derived from the Bill and Ted films, *BSEA*'s title characters are a duo of dimwitted California "dudes," whose lives revolve around the pursuit of teenage fun. While Ashley Argota is now a co-star on *BSEA*—playing opposite Bucket and Skinner as their popular, sensible friend Kelly—*BSEA* ostensibly suggests the antithesis of *TJVP* and an affinity for *Big Time Rush* in its reframing of Hip around the white, male, West Coast teenage experience. Kelly's younger sister Piper is the show's requisite tween girl-as-ruthless capitalist (i.e., *BTR*'s Katie Knight, although Piper has an obvious "soft side" underneath her cold-blooded exterior that Katie does not). Conversely, *BSEP*'s male characters are uniformly bumbling morons (the title characters, their rivals Aloe and Sven, Bucket's uncle) whose buddy camaraderie contains a none-too-subtle amount of homoeroticism, which becomes problematic in its own right as far as Nickelodeon's overall treatment of homosexuality. The issue is the extent Kelly is situated as the primary girl-power figure of "common sense," whereas the male ineptitude around her is designed to be *laughed at*— rather than the masculine being *laughed with* at the expense of all things female (i.e., *Home Improvement*, *The King of Queens*, or *Big Time Rush*).

7. As noted in Chapter 1, a "Mad Style by True Jackson" line of clothing was cross-marketed between *TJVP* and Wal-Mart.

8. The *TJVP* episode "True Mall" (2011) focused on the opening of Mad Style's first outlet store at "New York Midtown Mall." It centered on Callie (Emma Lockhart), a friendly but extremely insecure teenage girl whom True promoted to store manager after she fired the obnoxious and authoritarian adult manager. The rift between the manager and Callie began after Callie pointed out the window display is "too black and white" and needed color—

taken almost verbatim from the *TJVP* pilot — and then took the initiative to remodel it so it looked like "a rainbow" (i.e., "the Rainbow Coalition" and the rainbow as the symbol of gay rights). After the fired store manager attempted to sabotage the store opening, Callie's collection of teen stereotype friends (a jock, a brain, a geek, and a "weirdo"), all of whom worked at other stores in the mall, rallied around her to work together and make the grand opening of the store a success. "True Mall" seemed very much a thinly disguised pilot for another teen workplace sitcom, substituting a shopping mall (teen space) for a corporate office (adult space).

9. Then governor of Minnesota, Pawlenty was national co-chair of the McCain campaign and the media point man for the GOP at the 2008 Democratic National Convention; he was considered McCain's likely, if not inevitable, running-mate. Palin's surprise selection, beyond propping up McCain's "maverick" image as his campaign lagged, was fairly obvious campaign strategy to appeal to women voters, particularly disgruntled, moderate-to-conservative Hillary Clinton supporters.

10. In 2009, *TJVP* was second behind *iCarly* as far as the focus of Nickelodeon's teen sitcom line-up. With the additions of *Big Time Rush* and *Victorious*, *TJVP* became a secondary (if not marginal) part of Nickelodeon teen programming. New episodes of *TJVP* were given little (if any) of the promotion, and reruns of *TJVP* became all but non-existent by the latter half of 2010. However, *TJVP* star Keke Palmer was featured prominently in "Big Help" public service announcements, encouraging volunteerism for the less fortunate over the 2010 holiday season. In early 2011, Nickelodeon announced that Palmer was producing and starring in *Rags*, a forthcoming made-for-Nickelodeon movie musical. In the end, as much as the debut of *TJVP* coincided with Obama's political apex, the demise of *TJVP* was perhaps inevitably tied to the declining popularity of the Obama administration. (As of this writing, the cancellation of *TJVP* has been widely reported on internet sources but Nickelodeon has yet to officially clarify *TJVP*'s status. While *TJVP* may still be part of the Nickelodeon's future programming plans, it seems highly unlikely).

11. On *Still Standing* (CBS, 2002–6), the main characters were Bill and Judy Miller, both of whom loved beer, classic rock, professional sports, and shirking adult responsibilities. They were Hip in contrast to the Square embodied by their oldest son Brian (an anagram for "Brain"), whose love of school was only matched by his love of science-fiction and musical theater. In effect, the Millers were a male "same-sex" heterosexual couple who frequently fought but had a solid marriage because, as Bill put it in one episode, Judy was "a guy's wife and not a wife's wife." On *Yes, Dear* (CBS, 2000–6), the binary became more pronounced with the fun-loving Jimmy and Christine Hughes being a heterosexual same-sex "male" couple whereas the uptight Greg and Kim Warner were a heterosexual same-sex "female" couple. *Just Shoot Me!* can also be compared to *TJVP*. Jack Gallo was a fun-loving guy who enjoyed the male trinity of booze, cigars, and womanizing; Mia Gallo was a tightly-wound feminist whose world-view was implied to be the result of sexual repression. This was contrasted to the supporting characters. Model Nina Van Horn was an acerbic, lazy, chain-smoking alcoholic for whom the one-night stand was modus operandi; fashion photographer Elliot DiMauro was a confirmed heterosexual but also a sensitive "soft male" who openly expressed his feelings and pined for a long-term relationship despite the numerous models he bedded. In short, Nina acted like "a guy" whereas Elliot acted like "a girl." To be sure, as a teen sitcom *TJVP* necessarily had to avoid coding gender behavior around adult pastimes (drinking, smoking, promiscuity) but similarly perpetuated the binary of masculine-fun versus female-seriousness.

12. See my own *The American Worker on Film: A Critical History, 1909–1999* (Jefferson, NC: McFarland, 2010), especially Chapter 11 and Conclusion.

## Chapter 8

1. See also Paul Hegarty, *Noise/Music: A History* (New York: Continuum, 2007), 63–4 for a similar analysis of Hendrix's version of "The Star-Spangled Banner."

2. Malcolm Russell, "The MC5," in *Rock: The Rough Guide*, 2nd ed., 619.

3. The Ohio Express was composed of various studio musicians working for Super K productions releasing singles under the band/brand name "Ohio Express" through Buddha Records.

4. The critical problem is that any comparison between the Jackson Five and the Osmonds amounts to pop music heresy. Musically, the Jackson Five's hit "ABC" and the Osmonds' hit "One Bad Apple" were quite similar; in fact, George Jackson wrote "One Bad Apple" intending it for the Jackson Five (they subsequently recorded a version of the song after the Osmonds). The critical difference owes as much to the constructs of Hipness. The Jackson Five were urban, African-Americans teens who recorded for Motown Records (Hip/authentic soul music) whereas the Osmonds were lily-white, wholesome Mormons from Utah (Square/ inauthentic pop).

5. Black Flag offers an example of the critical difference between "noise" and "dissonance." Their final album *In My Head* (1985) is jarring by the sheer amount of hardcore punk "noise" generated (instrument distortion, feedback, Henry Rollins barking and screaming as opposed to singing). However, the songs were built around abrupt structural and tempo changes, juxtapositions of odd signatures ("In My Head" awkwardly alternating between 3/8 and 4/4 or "Black Love" between 7/4 and 4/4), dissonant riffs ("Drinking and Driving" is anchored around a grinding, ascending G-C#-D-F#-F/A# one-bar progression), numerous and deliberately placed "wrong notes," and especially the atonal, free-form guitar solos of Greg Ginn. The *dissonance within the music* as much as the *noise of the music* makes Black Flag particularly "difficult listening," with *In My Head* suggesting a nexus of Black Sabbath and Captain Beefheart. Indeed, by the early 1980s, hardcore and "thrash" had become a highly standardized genre of musical production as much as any oppositional "noise" to the point that many hardcore bands were completely indistinguishable from one another.

6. *Essays on Music*, 450. Emphasis added. As discussed in Chapter 7, *True Jackson, VP* provided a similar "representation of fun ... aimed at relieving the strain of adult responsibilities" by depicting the daily grind of the workplace as both enjoyable and productive provided adults understand the value of adolescent fun and adolescents understand the value of adult responsibility.

7. McNeil and McGill, 206.

8. Hegarty, 102.

9. Similarly, heavy metal is a musical genre with an assumed audience of young white males and classical music's assumed audience is older, educated, middle-upper class. This is frequently reduced to respective stereotypes of "Neanderthals" and "snobs."

10. Stephen Stills auditioned for the Monkees but was rejected. Stills subsequently went on to rock fame with Buffalo Springfield and Crosby, Stills, and Nash. Neil Young was also a member of Buffalo Springfield as well as Crosby, Stills, Nash, and Young.

11. Colgems Records was run in partnership between Screen Gems (Columbia Pictures) and RCA Records.

12. Timothy Leary, *The Politics of Ecstasy* (Berkeley: Ronin, 1998), 174.

13. As quoted in Jeff Grossman, "This Archie Comics Includes a Lawsuit," *New York Times* (September 4, 2005).

14. See *Politics and the American Television Comedy*, 120–4 for an overview of the conflicts and controversies surrounding *The Smothers Brothers Comedy Hour*.

15. *The Archie Comedy Hour* (1969–70) was essentially an expanded version of *The Archie Show* with the addition of another Archie Comics character, "Sabrina the Teenage Witch" in two independent cartoon episodes. *Archie's Funhouse* (1970–1) was a blatant copy of the *Laugh-In* format. *Archie's TV Funnies* (1971–3) was dominated by short episodes starring characters from old newspaper comic strips (Dick Tracy, Nancy and Sluggo, Broom Hilda, etc.). *Everything's Archie* ran from 1973–4 and consisted of cannibalized earlier programs recycled into "new" episodes. The format changed to educational show with *The U.S. of Archie* (1974–6) and Archie and the gang reenacting key events in American history, coinciding with the American Bicentennial.

16. In the late 1960s and early 1970s, Saturday morning cartoon shows were built around the Beatles, the Jackson Five, and the Osmonds. *The Beatles* ran on ABC from 1965–9, and also served a political purpose. As Norma Coates noted, *The Beatles* depicted the band in matching grey suit and "mop top" haircut era of the band. While the Beatles became long-haired, bearded hippies and counterculture icons amid the unrest of the late 1960s, the cartoon kept the band safely and perpetually locked in 1964 (see "Teenyboppers, Groupies, and Other Grotesques": 74–5).

17. The Partridge Family was based on the Cowsills, a successful pop-rock band of made up of five brothers, their sister, and their mother.

18. In fact, Cassidy was Shirley Jones's stepson. It was stressed by all sides that Cassidy got the part through the strength of his audition, not nepotism. In all fairness, Cassidy was a working actor and appeared as a guest star on several network TV shows prior to *The Partridge Family*.

19. Jenny was played by Meredith Baxter, who later portrayed Elyse Keaton on *Family Ties*.

20. The episode ended with Reuben excitedly telling Keith he got him tickets to the Bolshoi Ballet. Keith told him that he and the youngsters were going to the circus instead. Shirley and Laurie informed Reuben they would go to the ballet, with the eldest Partridge *women* fans of (effeminate) high culture. When Reuben tried to back out, and accused of cultural ignorance to boot, Reuben quite reluctantly agreed to attend the ballet and remarked, "I'm full of ... culture."

21. Coates, 75.

22. One of *The Midnight Special*'s programming tactics was generally airing the perform-ances by the rock bands in the latter half to final third of the 90-minute show. While the ra-tional offered was putting more mainstream performers on early in the telecast served as a better transition out of *The Tonight Show* and into *The Midnight Special*, the viewer wanting to see the rock bands had to sit through said mainstream acts and the attending commercials. For instance, when Kiss appeared on *The Midnight Special* (11/28/1975), the other musical guest were MOR stalwarts Helen Reddy, Barry Manilow, and Frankie Valli. As much as MTV, another factor in *The Midnight Special* ending its run in 1982 may have owed to the growing proliferation of VCRs, which rendered this programming strategy moot.

23. When MTV was launched in 1981, music videos were the exception and not the rule in rock music, let alone popular music. Much of the work in music video was coming from punk and New Wave bands, with Devo being one of the pioneers of the music video. Simply put, MTV played what was available and did not set out to be a "New Wave" music-TV net-work. Once music video became a standard practice and MTV the main outlet — which is to say once supply caught up with demand — heavy rotation of videos by "stars" replaced the less "commercial" artists.

24. The irony is that MTV and Paramount, the studio that made *School of Rock*, are both owned by Viacom.

25. However, being in a band with one's dad was not out of the question. Spirit, best known for their excellent *The Twelve Dreams of Doctor Sardonicus* (1970), featured Randy California on guitar and his stepfather Ed Cassidy on drums.

26. Darrell Y. Hamamoto, *Nervous Laughter: Television Situation Comedy and Liberal Dem-ocratic Ideology* (New York: Praeger, 1989), 72. Emphasis added.

27. While unintentionally, this problematic was exposed in the *Victorious* episode "The Diddley-Bops" (also discussed in Chapter 2). André's musical creditably and opportunity to sign with a major label are badly damaged when he writes a kiddie-song, "Favorite Foods," and performs as a member of the Diddley-Bops for money. He reestablishes his credibility as a serious musician by impressing record industry executives with "Song 2 You." However, structurally "Song 2 You" is *identical* to "Favorite Foods" with the only changes being a new arrangement from a children's song into a pop-soul ballad and heartfelt lyrics (in fact, the lyrics to "Song 2 You" are about the sincerity of the song being offered to the listener). In this sense, authenticity has little to do with pop music form — be it formula or formalism. It is

strictly lyrical content and how the song is performed that separates the inauthenticity of "Favorite Foods" and the authenticity of "Song 2 You."

28. As quoted in the liner notes to Henry Cow, *Concerts* (ESD 80822/832: 1995). Henry Cow was an avant-garde rock band, with Frank Zappa the most immediate comparison. As opposed to canonical classical music and be-bop jazz that influenced progressive rock, Henry Cow drew extensively from modern classical and free jazz. While progressive rock relied on the literary classics and popular literature (namely science-fiction) for lyrical inspiration, Henry Cow was primarily informed by Bertolt Brecht.

29. Dave Marsh, *Bruce Springsteen: Two Hearts: The Definitive Biography, 1972–2003* (New York: Routledge, 2003), 482–3.

30. Springsteen began performing a cover of the Edwin's Starr's explicitly anti-war Motown classic "War" in concerts soon after the "Born in the USA" controversy, and a live version became a Top 10 hit in 1986. As noted, Springsteen has since officially aligned himself with the Democratic Party, participating in the anti–Bush "Vote for Change" tour in 2004 and publically supporting and campaigning for Barack Obama in 2008.

31. See also Simon Frith, *Performance Rites: On the Value of Popular Music* (Cambridge: Harvard University Press, 1996), 165–6.

## *Chapter 9*

1. Raoul Vaneigem, *The Revolution of Everyday Life*, trans. Donald Nicholson-Smith (London: Rebel Press, 2006), 132, 134. Emphasis original.

2. The prototype for *Like a Virgin* was Blondie vocalist Deborah Harry's debut solo album, *Koo Koo* (1981). Both records were produced by Nile Rodgers, guitarist of the legendary disco band Chic. On *Koo Koo*, Harry attempted to crossover from (white) New Wave stardom into the "black music" market. It bombed. *Like a Virgin* bore a remarkable similarity to *Koo Koo* as a hybrid of disco-funk dance beats and New Wave pop music. In fact, the robotic male voice chant on "Material Girl" was almost identical to one used (with different lyrics) on Harry's "The Jam Was Moving."

3. Camille Paglia, "Madonna — Finally, a Real Feminist," *New York Times* (December 14, 1990).

4. Gay Talese, *Thy Neighbor's Wife* (New York: Doubleday, 1980), 58–9.

5. With a list price of $49.95 (keeping in mind this was 1992), *Sex* had a metalized plastic cover and was bound with metal ringing like a notebook. It was encased in a silver Mylar wrapper and sold behind the counters of major bookstores, provided they did not refuse to carry it. This effectively forced the consumer to purchase *Sex* in the same way they would have to purchase any other adult materials.

6. Madonna's view of sexual politics very much adheres to the "Repressive Hypothesis." In *The History of Sexuality, vol.1: An Introduction*, trans. Robert Hurley (New York: Vintage, 1990), Foucault systematically dismantled the Repressive Hypothesis that sexual liberation is locked in a monolithic battle with forces of social repression (e.g., Wilhelm Reich's *The Mass Psychology of Fascism*). In Foucault's formulation, constructs of sexuality are produced through multiple discourses concerning sex.

7. In 2004, Madonna was bought out of Maverick by TimeWarner to settle an increasingly sour business relationship that included mutual lawsuits (while the amount was not disclosed, it was reportedly in the area of 50 to 60 million dollars). Madonna remained with Warner Bros. as a contract recording artist.

8. Also hired for *The Mickey Mouse Club* with Spears were Christina Aguilera and Justin Timberlake. Jessica Simpson was cut in the final round of auditions.

9. Again, the issue is the extent to which Spears's debut provoked a rupture in the ideological contradictions of sexual exploitation and capitalist culture. The content of the rupture can described as reprehensible.

10. In 2002, Christina Aguilera released *Stripped*, a CD emphasizing gritty dance music and sexually themed lyrics accompanied by Aguilera adopting a provocative, highly sexualized

public image. With 2006's *Back to Basics*, Aguilera's shift to adult pop-dance was matched by adopting iconic Hollywood imagery derived from Veronica Lake and, of course, Marilyn Monroe. In short, Aguilera ditched the Britney Spears approach in favor of the Madonna strategy.

11. On the reality show *The Simple Life* (FOX, 2003–5; E!, 2005–7), particularly the first season, Paris Hilton and Nicole Richie brought their blasé, pampered bourgeois attitude to various circles of working-class, Middle American Hell. The viewer could equally laugh at the elites (Hilton and Richie) as well as the commons (the yahoos surrounding them).

12. In 2004, a Spears compilation *Greatest Hits: My Prerogative* was released. The lead-off track "My Prerogative" was a cover of Bobby Brown's 1988 "new jack swing" hit song ("new jack swing" a musical style combining R&B, hip-hop, and synthpop that can be heard on the template for the boy bands of the First Wave Teen Pop era). Spears's version converted it into a lumbering, mechanistic dirge that prefigured the "industrial teen pop" later explored on *Blackout* and *Circus*.

13. As of 2011, *Blackout* sold over three million copies, a respectable but relatively modest figure by pop superstar standards.

14. Britney Spears is very much a "brand" of popular music, with Spears the voice and public image while a stable of studio producers and songwriters manufacture much of the music product. The point is that this is no different a procedure than many other pop stars, be it the "artistry" of Frank Sinatra or the Monkees' early hits that are now deemed "classic pop" rather than manufactured bubblegum.

15. "Piece of Me" was written by Christian Karlsson, Pontus Winnberg, and Klas Åhlund, and produced by "Bloodshy and Avant" (the production pseudonyms of Karlsson and Winnberg). To note, Spears performed "Piece of Me" inside a cage on the 2009 "The Circus Starring Britney Spears" concert tour.

16. While the beat in pop music is often used to simply propel the song with a dance rhythm, Britney Spears songs also use the sound of the beat as a way to signify "meaning." On "Womanizer" (*Circus*), the metronomic swing beat suggests the mechanistic swagger of a "cocksure" male as he saunters about in the business of seduction. The popping, hollow backbeat of "Kill the Lights" (*Circus*) suggests unremitting flashbulbs, in keeping with the song as a vehement lyrical attack on the paparazzi.

17. Jacques Attali, *Noise: The Political Economy of Music*, trans. Brain Massumi (Minneapolis: University of Minnesota, 1985), 29.

18. From the perspective of Attali, the incessant media "noise" surrounding Spears is itself part of the "noise" of Britney Spears' music, specifically songs like "Piece of Me," "Freakshow" (*Blackout*) or "Kill the Lights," which explicitly addresses Spears's role as a media commodity.

19. Attali, 117. Adorno also posited a kind of "linkup" of Schönberg's music of alienation and Stravinsky's objectivist music in a form he termed "surrealistic music" that assembled classical music and popular music into conflicting montages and moved from objectivist music into a music of alienation, best realized in the operas of Weil/Brecht such as *The Three Penny Opera* and *Mahagonny* (see *Essays on Music*, 396–7). Moreover, surrealistic music revealed the binary of classical music and popular was itself a representation of class structures in capitalist society (high culture/bourgeoisie versus popular music/proletariat). Richard Leppert observed, "Adorno long lamented the division of all art, but music especially, into categories of high (serious, classical) and low (popular, mass culture); at the same time, he recognized that the categories themselves mirror social divisions ... and helped keep the divisions in place" (109). See Richard Leppert, "Music 'Pushed to the Edge of Existence' (Adorno, Listening, and the Question of Hope)," *Cultural Critique* 60 (Spring 2005): 92–132.

20. Hegarty's *Noise/Music: A History* is a recommended survey into the question of "noise" as far as a link-up between mass music (pop music) and theoretical music (experimental music). Attali is far too generous as to what constitutes "noise," especially his romanticism of 1960s rock and utter dismissal of progressive rock in what amounts to replicating the critical ideology of *Rolling Stone*. Indeed, Attali goes so far to suggest that "[John] Cage and the Rolling Stones ... announce a rupture in the process of musical creation.... They are not

the new mode of musical production, but the liquidation of the old" (*Noise*, 137). Cage's radical deconstruction of musical composition, production, and reception versus the Rolling Stones's reliance on traditional popular music forms, genres, and performance are antithetical musical and ideological projects.

21. An informative analysis of Situationist praxis and popular music is Andrew Hussey, "Requiem pour un con: Subversive Pop and the Society of the Spectacle," *Cercles* 3(2001): 49–59. Hussey suggested "subversive pop" performers like Black Box Recorder "imitate the clean funk lines of a track by ... Britney Spears in order to reveal the darker sexual imagination which shapes those rhythms" (59). However, this constructs a distinction between mass-culture pop music (Britney Spears) and a subversive pop music (Black Box Recorder), or that the latter is a *détournement* of the former (in fairness, Hussy was writing in 2001 and the apex of First Wave Teen Pop). As the analysis of "Piece of Me" and "Circus" contends, Britney Spear's musical output ca. 2007–8 can be read as its own *détournement* of "mass music" and "theoretical music."

22. Again, the crucial difference between noise and dissonance bears mention. Drawing from composer Michael Nyman's formulation, Hegarty distinguished avant-garde music as dissonance (Schoenberg) and, more effectively in Hegarty's view, experimental music as noise (Cage). "The persistence of Western tonal schemes (however dissonant) are avant-garde, but only in a limited way. The true avant-garde is engaged with practices that undermine and dispute western art music as a whole, and is therefore seen as experimental. Notions of finished pieces, competence of performers, composition, means of production (of sounds, of pieces) are all to be questioned" (*Noise/Music: A History*, 11). Hegarty fully conceded that the distinction is tenuous, and a *historical* distinction as much as any *musical* distinction and one that need be assessed in retrospect as much as in contemporary settings (see 12).

23. Adorno, *Essays on Music*, 395–6.

24. Ibid., 555.

25. Ibid., 403. Emphasis added.

26. "Music" was co-written and co-produced by Madonna and Miriwais Ahmadzai.

27. Adorno, *Essays on Music*, 403.

28. *Rolling Stone* named "Music" the best single of 2000; one suspects the honor owed as much to message as music.

29. In 2002, Madonna (along with then-husband Guy Ritchie) did a remake of Lina Wert-müller's *Swept Away*. The story of an obnoxious bourgeois socialite and a Communist sailor marooned on a Mediterranean island following a shipwreck, and the sexual relationship that results, the original *Swept Away* was highly problematic its negotiation of Marxist and gender politics, namely the taming of the bourgeois shrew with the proletariat penis. In the remake of *Swept Away*, the dilemmas of class struggle and gender politics are simply "swept away" through good sex, not unlike how "Music" posits pop music and libidinal release on the dance floor as the resolution to class struggle.

30. "Circus was co-written by Lukasz Gottwald, Claude Kelly, and Benjamin Levin; it was co-produced by Benny Blanco and Gottwald under his production pseudonym "Dr. Luke." As well as Britney Spears, Gottwald/ "Dr. Luke" has been involved in the writing and production of hit songs for several Second Wave Teen Pop performers, notably Miley Cyrus' "Party in the U.S.A." and Ke$ha's "Blow," as well as Miranda Cosgrove (Kissin' U") and Victoria Justice ("Make It Shine").

31. By "performed," it is meant that the Circus Tour shows were much more along the lines of musical revue and theater than the rock concert per se; they involved extensive use of choreography, costumes, props, lighting effects, and video backdrops: for lack of better term, "multimedia." It was common knowledge that there was considerable amount of pre-recorded music and lip-synching during the performances.

32. Reynolds, 131.

33. *Noise*, 6.

34. Vanessa Gringanolis, "The Tragedy of Britney Spears," *Rolling Stone* (February 21, 2008).

# Chapter 10

1. As quoted in Al Spicer, "Nirvana," *Rock: The Rough Guide*, 2d ed., 689.

2. See Gayle Wald, "'I Want It That Way': Teenybopper Music and the Girling of Boy Bands," *Genders* 35. Archived at: http://www.genders.org/g35/g35_wald.html. Accessed: 6/26/10.

3. Ibid.

4. The sitcom *That 70's Show* served the same purpose, simultaneously celebrating teen rebellion and the culture of the 1970s as the acme of teen rebellion.

5. *Rock and Roll High School* was made for Roger Corman's New World Pictures. Corman's copious output of low-budget films, which were geared towards drive-in markets and teenage/young adult film consumers, have become synonymous with post–World War II teen culture.

6. A highly recommended discussion of the early punk movement is Robert Christgau, "Avant-Punk: A Cult Explodes ... And a Movement is Born," *The Village Voice* (October 24, 1977). Christgau defined punk politics as "anti-liberal without being reactionary ... in a love-hate relationship with industrial capitalism."

7. J. Hoberman and Jonathan Rosenbaum, *Midnight Movies* (New York: Da Capo, 1991), 278.

8. As quoted in Veronica Kafman, "The Ramones," in *Rock: The Rough Guide*, 2d ed., 800.

9. Greil Marcus, *Lipstick Traces: A Secret History of the Twentieth Century* (Cambridge, MA: Harvard University Press, 1989), 16.

10. Hegarty, 95.

11. McLaren changed the NY Dolls' image from a trashy-glam band to a radical Left political group by, as NY Dolls drummer Jerry Nolan recounted, "Dressing us up in matching red leather suits and playing in front of a giant communist flag. It was so stupid!" (As quoted in *Please Kill Me*, 191).

12. Frith, 266.

13. Hussey, 57.

14. Produced by Brian Eno, the Talking Heads' *Fear of Music* drew on black popular music (funk, disco, Motown) and white music (punk, 1960s bubblegum, 1970s art rock) infused with a postmodern sensibility. Arguably the defining album of the post-punk era, the Gang of Four's *Entertainment!* was a violent collision of punk aggression, 1970s pub-rock and hard rock, black music (funk, disco, reggae, Motown), half-spoken/half-shouted vocals, mordant Marxist lyrics, and Andy Gill's avant-garde, atonal scattershot approach to guitar that sounded like the aural equivalent of barbed wire or flying shrapnel. The Pop Group was a punk band but primarily influenced by the funk of James Brown and free jazz of Ornette Coleman; they also utilized reggae music and especially dub reggae production techniques to radical degrees, where sounds buried in the mix (vocal, musical instruments, noises) one moment might suddenly overwhelm the mix the next. Needless to say, the Pop Group was the least commercially successful of the three. See also Frith, *Sound Effects*, 158–63, for a highly informative analysis of the limitations of punk formalism and the resulting emergence of post-punk.

15. Steve Waksman, *This Ain't the Summer of Love: Conflict and Crossover in Heavy Metal and Punk* (Berkeley: University of California Press, 2009) is the indispensible study in this regard. Waksman's genealogy quite effectively situates Motörhead as the "missing link" between mid–1970s metal and punk, and the arduous process by which hard punk and speed metal had effectively found common musical and subcultural ground in the 1980s. However, there is a bit of overemphasis on the Runways and the Dictators in discussing the advent of punk in the 1970s, at the expense of the Ramones and the Sex Pistols. Moreover, the Runaways, particularly during the tenure of lead singer Cherrie Currie, were marketed around sex at a level that made Britney Spears and Miley Cyrus pale by comparison (see Waksman, 134–42).

16. Since *Saved by the Bell*, the name Zack has become a trope in teen culture to signify Hip males. In *School of Rock*, Dewey's nickname for Zack is "Zack Attack"—the same name

of Zack Morris's rock band on *Saved by the Bell*. On the Disney teen sitcom *The Suite Life of Zack and Cody*, Zack is the Hip character to Cody's Square. While a coincidence, Zac Efron became a teen idol with the *High School Musical* films.

17. In *SoR*, both Dewey and Zack use highly recognizable and "canonical" guitars. Dewey plays a Gibson SG, popularized by Black Sabbath's Tony Iommi and AC/DC's Angus Young. Zack uses a Gibson "Flying V," so named because of its distinctive V-shaped body and a guitar commonly associated with hard rock and heavy metal guitarists. Katie's bass looks like a cheap, generic relic; however, in the final credits she is seen playing a more "state-of-the-art" but nonetheless generic bass rather than a "classic" bass such as the Fender Precision or Rickenbacker 4001.

18. This is very much reiterated in Linklater's remake of *The Bad News Bears* (2005), in which baseball replaces rock and Little League the classroom.

19. For added measure, Ned dumped Patty and got a job at the prep school teaching the elementary school children to play guitar.

20. "Commentary" in Adorno, *Essays on Music*, 555.

21. *What I Like About You* was co-created by Dan Schneider.

# *Chapter 11*

1. Louis Althusser, *For Marx*, trans. Ben Brewster (New York: Verso, 1991), 233–4. Emphasis original. I have taken the liberty of substituting "people" for "men" in the context of discussing Hannah Montana.

2. Two pop music sitcoms, *A Year at the Top* (CBS, 1977) and *Sugar Time* (ABC, 1977–8), failed abysmally in the ratings. *Kids, Incorporated* ran on Disney Channel from 1984–93, structured as a kind of hybrid between pop-music sitcom and comedy-variety show. Stacy Ferguson, now much better known as Fergie, was a cast member of *Kids, Incorporated* from 1984–9.

3. On her CD *Breakout* (2008), Miley Cyrus covered Cyndi Lauper's 1980s girl-power anthem "Girls Just Want to Have Fun" and "Breakout" was co-written by former Go-Go's drummer Gina Shock, who also did back-up vocals on the song (needless to say, "Breakout" sounds a lot like a Go-Go's song). On *Can't be Tamed*, Cyrus covered Poison's 1980s power ballad hit "Every Rose Has Its Thorn," albeit more as a New Wave-techno ballad. On the live concert DVD included in the deluxe edition of the *Can't Be Tamed* CD, Cyrus covered Joan Jett's signature song, "I Love Rock and Roll."

4. "We Got the Party" was written by Greg Wells and Kara DioGuardi. "Supergirl" was written by DioGuardi and Dan James and "Mixed Up" by DioGuardi and Matt Frederickson. DioGuardi also worked extensively on Christina Aguilera's *Back to Basics*, Hilary Duff's *Dignity*, as well as two tracks on Britney Spears's *Blackout*. However, DioGuardi is best known as a judge on *American Idol* from 2009–10.

5. This interpretation of "We Got the Party" owes to Gilles Deleuze and Félix Guattari, *A Thousand Plateaus: Capitalism and Schizophrenia*, trans. Brian Massumi (Minneapolis: University of Minnesota Press, 1987), especially 385–6, 423. To use their terminology, in "We Got the Party" teen power is represented as a "war machine" as a disruptive "nomadic" force becoming a "machine-assemblage" by which a "deterritorialization" of power occurs to destabilize established power structures.

6. Arguably the first Second Wave Teen Pop performer was Avril Lavigne, whose debut album was released in 2002. Unlike Britney Spears and Christian Aguilera, Lavigne was very much in the Alternative mode (punk-metal-grunge).

7. Of course, this has to be an *extremely* qualified assessment. Fefe Dobson is an African-American Second Wave Teen Pop performer whose music is highly informed by 1980s New Wave; Dobson co-wrote Miley Cyrus's hit "Start All Over." (To note, Dobson was also a guest star and performed a song in the *True Jackson, VP* episode "Mad Rocks"). Rather, using Miley Cyrus as the example, the country and New Country influenced songs ("These Four Walls,"

"Goodbye," or "Stay") sound more "convincing" than the attempts at Latin Pop ("Let's Dance"), reggae ("Clear"), or rap ("Liberty Walk").

8. Billy Ray Cyrus achieved fame in 1992 with his country-novelty song hit "Achy Breaky Heart" and popularizing the mullet haircut. As an actor, Cyrus starred on the family drama *Doc* which ran on PAX (now Ion Television) from 2001–4.

9. For an ideology critique of *The Beverly Hillbillies* and *Green Acres*, see *Politics and the American Television Comedy*, Chapter 5.

10. Another comparison, especially in terms of *Hannah Montana: The Movie*, is the teen sitcom *Darcy's Wild Life* (*DWL*, 2004–6), which ran on Discovery Kids network and as part of NBC's "Discovery Kids on NBC" Saturday morning line-up. Darcy Fields was a rich, somewhat spoiled teenage girl living in Malibu, and whose life mostly consisted of satisfying her consumer wants. Her mother, Victoria Fields, was an actress who decided to quit show business and bought a small farm in a rural community or, as Darcy terms it, the "middle of nowhere." Much of *DWL* revolved around Darcy adjusting to her new environment, with a key step getting a part-time job as an assistant for the local veterinarian. As a Discovery Kid's show, many of the overt messages of *DWL* stressed educational messages about nature and animals, ranging from general trivia on botany and zoology, the proper care of pets and livestock, and the do's and don'ts of dealing with wild animals. However, the hidden messages were ideological. The basic scenario of *DWL* was *Green Acres* to *Hannah Montana's* take-off on *The Beverly Hillbillies*, with *DWL* serving as a defense of traditional American life and community values. Darcy's move coincided with her reaching maturity through learning responsibility and the work ethic in rural, small-town, America: a maturity it would have been difficult (if not impossible) for Darcy to attain while leading the life of a free-spending, self-centered Malibu teenager. In short, *DWL* is an affirmation of Square over Hip lifestyle as Darcy grew up, not only as a teenager, but as an American citizen.

11. In *Running with the Devil: Power, Gender, and Madness in Heavy Metal Music* (Hanover, NH: Wesleyan University Press, 1993), Robert Walser analyzed the Van Halen song "Running with the Devil" as a contradictory song about the imaginary versus real of the rock-star life. Walser suggested, "The verses and the choruses are presented from very different perspectives. The verse relates an individual experience; the singer is reflective and confessional as he describes his life-style. Indeed, during the verses, which are presented musically in a different key, the lyrics are inflected with doubt and guilt. The fantasy is even questioned: the singer admits that running with the Devil is not exactly as he thought it would be.... *But the choruses sweep aside the doubts in a collective affirmation of the fantasy*. It is the backing chorus that is so sure of the fantasy's validity, not the singer, who punctuates the chorus lines with pained/ecstatic screams. *This is fundamentally a social fantasy, one believed in much more completely by those who feel constrained than by the lonely individual on the road, who is able to see its contradictions*" (52, emphasis added). While Walser offered a highly nuanced reading, in "Running with the Devil" the contradiction becomes inhibited as much as a point of rupture. Unlike 'Supergirl' in which two different genres are turned on their heads as well as against each other, the Van Halen song is a mid-tempo, metal anthem, marked only by a subtle contrasts between verse and chorus. Moreover, in "Running with the Devil" the chorus functions as the melodic hook; the title of the song becomes the sing-along catchphrase for "collective affirmation of the fantasy" which inhibits the ambivalence of the verses: the same problem of Bruce Springsteen's "Born in the U.S.A." (see Chapter 8). In this respect, the message of "Running with the Devil" also can be read as conservative. Van Halen singer David Lee Roth qualifies the pleasures of rock and roll debauchery the audience wishes they were living by being rock stars; indeed, they seem comforted by Roth's specious message that *he* wishes *he* lived the mundane, normal life the audience goes home to after the concert. "True happiness" is found in the daily grind of Square life rather than the Hip decadence of rock stardom, and the audience can take solace in the fact they are getting the message from one who knows.

12. Madonna committed what might be termed a "reinvention gaff" when, after her marriage to Guy Ritchie and moving to England, she adopted a stilted English accent in her TV

interviews. In effect, Madonna's error was constructing a new public image around a self-conscious bourgeois Continentialism, which tends to be viewed as Square rather than Hip. Following *American Life*, the effect was not so much being a subversive American expatriate but projecting a stylized anti–Americanism.

13. The contradiction, or at least the irony, has been Miley Cyrus's own propensity to generate controversy as a "bad role model" to teenage girls. In 2008, Miley Cyrus posed for an infamous photo shot for *Vanity Fair* with noted celebrity photographer Annie Liebowitz that included "topless" shots of Cyrus wrapped in a sheet (as a trivia note, Liebowitz also did the notorious David Cassidy *Rolling Stone* cover photo). Cyrus later apologized, but has continued to court controversy, such as the 2009 Teen Choice Awards for what could be called a "teen hooker chic" fashion statement and her brief pole dance segment during her performance of "Party in the U.S.A."

14. Similarly, Miley's friend Oliver knew the secret and appeared in public with Hannah Montana in disguise as "Mike Standley III." The exception was Miley's older brother Jackson Stewart, who was crude, dumb, lazy, and slovenly (read: slacker). While largely excluded from the Hannah Montana order, he frequently exploited his personal connections to "Hannah Montana" for his own advantage (usually to impress girls).

15. Guy Debord, *The Society of the Spectacle*, trans. Donald Nicholson-Smith (New York: Zone, 1994), 152. Second emphasis added.

16. For the final season of *Hannah Montana*, a 13-episode run officially titled *Hannah Montana Forever* (2010–11), Miley revealed the truth about her dual-identity on *The Tonight Show*. The final episodes were a kind of "phased retirement" of Hannah Montana and Miley Stewart's transition to a life without her Hannah Montana persona. This coincided with Miley graduating from high school and ultimately deciding to go to college with Lilly, putting her show business career on hold. In effect, Miley Stewart entered the world of normal adult life while forsaking the teenage fantasy.

17. While Swift is billed as "herself" in the credits, in the film she is not a "guest star" but depicted as a local girl performing at the fundraiser.

18. Emerson, Lake and Palmer covered "Hoedown" (*Trilogy*, 1972), taking "Hoedown" further into the domain of objectivist music by merging the original's classical-folk nexus with rock music. Edward Macan argued, "Progressive rock serves as a forum in which a number of cultural opposites are *reconciled*: high and low culture, European and African-American creative ideas. In the best progressive rock, one senses the tension that results from attempting to *balance* these values" (*Rocking the Classics*, 165, emphasis added). In effect, Macan also argued that the best brands of progressive rock achieve synthesis of dialectic conflict into a unified whole, rather than constructing "montage" around cultural-musical collisions.

19. The subtext is Miley Cyrus's own career trajectory and the fundamental problem for any teen pop star escaping the so-called "teenybopper" image and sustaining a "legitimate" career in pop music. Many teen pop idols, such as the Monkees and David Cassidy, reached their career peak as teen idols. Indeed, both the Monkees and Cassidy went to extreme lengths to rebrand themselves as authentic rock musicians rather than teen idol pop stars at the height of their careers, and the efforts backfired (see Chapter 8). Conversely, Justin Timberlake (of *N Sync) and Mark Wahlberg (who began his career as teen rapper "Marky Mark") have made successful transitions into mainstream acting and/or music, as have Christina Aguilera and (after a particularly arduous "climb" with considerable setbacks) Britney Spears. In the case of Miley Cyrus, the process has been much more gradual far as constructing a separation between the Hannah Montana brand and the Miley Cyrus brand of teen culture while at the same time maintaining the inevitable association between the two brands. In the concert DVD included in the deluxe edition of the *Can't Be Tamed* CD, Cyrus performed "Hoedown Throwdown" and, not coincidentally, closed the concert with "The Climb." In this sense, rather than the sudden and often unsuccessful attempt to construct a definitive break between teen idol and adult star, there has been a conscious and gradual set of transitional stages in "the climb" from Hannah Montana to Miley Cyrus.

20. The performance of "You'll Always Find Your Way Back Home" begins with Hannah

Montana and her troupe of dancers dressed in white-collar business attire; they dart behind the stage and quickly reappear in kitsch rural clothing. The additional ideological message is that corporate capitalism, the force that nearly destroyed Crowley Corners, remains "ethical" only if adheres to traditional values of that form an "authentic" American community.

21. The song "Mixed Up" (*Hannah Montana 3*) bears mention in this context. As the title suggests, lyrically the song is about someone who no longer knows who they are, where they are, or what they are, and expresses the alienation between Hannah Montana and Miley Stewart sharing one existence while leading two different lives. "Mixed Up" is 6/8 power ballad with a discernable New Country and 1970s Southern Rock influence (specifically Lynard Skynard) as much as the bubblegum-New Wave-stadium rock that typifies the Hannah Montana brand of teen pop. In this sense, the musical setting of "Mixed Up" suggests the alienation of the self is being expressed by Miley Stewart rather than image persona signified by Hannah Montana and her Second Wave Teen Pop songs as ironic commentaries on being "rock star" or "super girl."

22. "It is in the *name of the father* that we must recognize the basis of the symbolic function which, since the dawn of historical time, has identified his person with the figure of the law." Jacques Lacan, *Écrits: A Selection*, trans. Bruce Fink (New York: W.W. Norton, 2002), 66. Emphasis original.

23. Lacan, 7.

24. Deleuze, 147–8. Emphasis added.

25. As quoted in Fredric Jameson, "Foreword," in Attali, *Noise*, ix.

## Chapter 12

1. Adorno , *The Culture Industry*, 166.

2. *BTR* was not Nickelodeon's foray into pop music sitcoms; it was preceded by *The Naked Brothers Band* (*NBB*, 2007–9), which was a more concerted attempt to construct a market rival to Disney's Jonas Brothers. *NBB* was also a contemporary "mockumentary" sitcom about the misadventures of a teenage pop-rock band, emphasizing similar anti-adult authority and pro-masculine adolescence messages seen in *BTR*. Unlike BTR, NBB musical product (on Columbia Records as well) was much more in the vein of Second Wave Teen Pop highly influenced by 1980s New Wave. "I Don't Want to Go to School" had a certain unintentional humor as it was sung by Nat Wolff as though he was about to reenact Columbine.

3. Fellows also created the animated series *Johnny Test* for Cartoon Network. In keeping with the gender politics of Fellows' work, Johnny Test is a boy genius pitted against the schemes of his diabolical twin sisters. As far his Nickelodeon career, Fellows was a writer on the animated show *The Fairly OddParents* (the title alone begs an investigation into sexual politics), and co-wrote the live action cartoon spin-off *A Fairly Odd Movie: Timmy Turner, Grow Up!* (2011); it starred Drake Bell (*Drake and Josh*) and Daniella Monet (*Victorious*). The scenario is Timmy Turner is now 22 and has refused to grow up, so he remains an eight-year-old boy with fairy godparents who grant his every wish. The disorder occurs when he begins to fall in love with his childhood friend Tootie, who has grown up from a braces-wearing geek to an attractive liberal environmentalist activist. When the town is jeopardized by oil developers buying up the land, Timmy decides to grow up, fall in love, and save the community although he loses his fairy godparents forever. However, the Fairy Council is so impressed they decree that Timmy can keep his fairy godparents on condition he only uses his wishes judiciously and for the benefit of others. The film ends with Timmy, Tootie, and the fairies embarking on a road trip to help the less fortunate and save the environment. What is crucial is their van bears the name of the new endeavor and becomes a hidden message that mocks the overt message: "Wishful Thinking."

4. *BTR* often recycles parodic snippets of well-known music. When someone is plotting something or executing a scheme, a parody of the *Mission: Impossible* theme is the usual accompaniment. Action and chase sequences are often underscored by a parody of Jet's alternative retro-rock hit "Are You Gonna Be My Girl?" A parody of Marvin Gaye's soul classic

"Let's Get It On" is commonly used when someone is being amorous, becoming "aroused," or an attractive girl is shown walking (usually in slow motion). The *Psycho* "shower scene" music is parodied as an all-purpose cue when someone throws a temper tantrum, shocked by something, or simply to designate someone as a "psycho" (again, often but not always, a teenage girl). Of course, the economic attractiveness of "parody" from an industry standpoint is that it avoids the problem of licensing the actual songs.

5. This is also routinely done with the music videos by other Nickelodeon pop music performers (Miranda Cosgrove, Victoria Justice, and, to a lesser extent, Jeanette McCurdy) as well as Big Time Rush.

6. Mr. Bitters is played by David Anthony Higgins, best known for his reoccurring role as the supermarket manager on *Malcolm in the Middle*.

7. "Welcome Back, Big Time" had a subplot in which BTR are behind in school due to their recent tour. Gustavo Rocque intervened by hiring three nerds to do their schoolwork for them: an Asian-American male, an African-American male, and a white female.

8. The name "Griffin" as the symbol of corporate record industry profiteering can be read as a parody of record industry mogul David Geffen.

9. Similarly, the disordered situation of "Big Time Girlfriends" (2010) was James and Camille passionately kissing while he helped with her acting rehearsals. While Logan and James sorted it out and remained buddies in the spirit of male camaraderie, Logan broke up with Camille, or at least put their romance on hiatus because she cheated on him. In the subplot, Rocque was highly dissatisfied with Carlos's singing on the new BTR song, and hired an actress to get romantically involved with Carlos and then break his heart so he could better "feel" the song. In the end, the actress fell for Carlos because the more "horrible" she was to him the "sweeter" he was to her. Carlos dumped her once he learned she didn't like corn dogs. In this episode, Mr. Bitters and Katie appeared in character but functioned as a kind of "Greek Chorus," watching and commenting about the events as if they were watching a TV show or movie. More correctly, Bitters watched in rapt fascination while Katie made satirical comments. At the end, Bitters burst into tears, overcome with emotion. Katie disgustedly handed him a handkerchief and snapped, "Oh, stop your blubbering!" The status of Bitters as the feminine Square and Katie as the masculine Hip was manifest.

10. Jo was written out of *BTR* in "Big Time Break-Up." After getting the starring role in a trilogy of "teen magic" films that requires her to relocate to New Zealand for three years, Jo initially turned down the project under the pretense of not being able to get out of her "New Town High" contract. Katie, who has reviewed the various contracts of everyone at the Palmwoods, informed Kendall that Jo lied and can get out of the contract but is using that as an excuse to stay in L.A. with him. Kendall begins acting like a lower-class hick in order to force Jo to break up with him, but Jo eventually realizes what he is doing. In the end, Kendall convinces Jo that she should take the part, as much as it might mean the end of their relationship. As much as the overt message that career ultimately comes first, like *Saved by the Bell* it is through the male that the female becomes "empowered."

11. "Big Time Moms" (2011) was promoted as a Mother's Day special episode, with the requisite BTR tune "The Mom Song" being a lyrical tribute for mothers in a kind of Beach Boys-meets-80s-metal musical setting. The sitcom episode completely negated the "tribute" song. The situation entailed Mrs. Diamond (guest star Lisa Rinna)—a career woman and control freak to the nth degree—arriving in L.A. and announcing she was taking James back to Minnesota to help run, and eventually take over, her successful cosmetics business. When the other BTR moms are enlisted to dissuade Mrs. Diamond, they realize that Mrs. Diamond just misses being a mom. In the end, the other BTR moms arrange it so that Mrs. Diamond can be more involved in supporting James's music career. James is able to say "no" to his mom for the first time in his life, Mrs. Diamond lets James stay in L.A., and the BTR moms unanimously and happily agree that they love their "crazy boys" just as they are. For added measure, the guest star in this episode was Lita Ford, the most famous woman performer in heavy metal. The recurring joke of James being reduced to a state of catatonic shock by his mom, and Ford being called on to snap him out of his traumatized state with a high-volume

power chord implies that hard rock can serve as the antidote for emasculating maternal tyranny. In the end, and consistent with *BTR* logic, the message was *not* kids standing up to their parents, but boys standing up to their moms, and males standing up to females.

12. Althusser, 233–4.

13. In what can be read as a riposte to *BTR*, in "iStart a Fan War," Sam Puckett wears a black T-shirt with a large red lipstick imprint and the words "The City Is Mine."

14. There has been something of a stylistic shift with BTR as the franchise has developed, and musically more of an emphasis on the traditional First Wave Teen Pop boy band sound and Justin Bieber's brand of "white soul" teen pop.

15. This is not an accusation that BTR "can't sing." Indeed, the use of vocal augmentation, particularly vocoder and pitch modification, is almost ubiquitous in pop music. Rather, the sheer amount of effects used on the vocals invites criticisms that BTR "can't sing"—especially given the frequent criticisms of female pop stars (Britney Spears or Ke$ha) using the same studio technologies.

16. Selena Gomez and the Scene's song "More" and Ke$ha's song "Blow" offers comparison to BTR songs, and one could add Madonna's "Music" and Britney Spears's "Circus" (discussed in Chapter 9); "Blow" and "Circus" were both co-written and co-produced by Lukasz Gottwald ("Dr. Luke"). Lyrically, both "More" and "Blow" contain lyrical images of conquering the clubs and the city, and in the Ke$ha song domination ends in demolition ("blowing up" the club). The differences are in the *musical* setting of "More" and "Blow." The verses of "More" are propelled by a clomping backbeat doubled by staccato rhythm guitar, a growling fuzz bass line, and a heavily phased- shifted guitar. In the chorus, the drums provide a steadier backbeat while the guitars do not provide riffs but produce atonal stuttering and disruptive washes of distorted phased guitar noise. "More" contains considerable internal violence in which the instruments manifest a kind of apocalyptic "falling apart" as opposed to any "coming together" within the song. As discussed with Hannah Montana's "We Got the Party," in "More" the forces of teen power are represented musically as a *deterritorialized* and *deterritorializing* "war machine" of insurrection. Conversely, "Blow" is highly mechanistic technosynthpop, with the beat acting as a *march rhythm* as much as a *dance rhythm* though which the synthetic parts (samples, monotone synthesizer pulses, heavily processed vocals) are "regimented" into a robotic whole around the march/dance beat. This became particularly pronounced in Ke$ha's rendition of "Blow" in the *Victorious* episode "Ice Cream for Ke$ha" (2011). Ke$ha wore an American flag tunic, hot pants, a beauty pageant sash converted to a bandolier, and combat boots. The backing dancers—who appeared to be four *men* in blonde wigs dressed similarly to Ke$ha—moved in choreographed patterns resembling a military drill as much as dancing. On one level, it becomes difficult to "Blow" as read as anything except fascist, a *reterritorialization* of the teen pop/teen power "war machine" into strict organization and uniform domination; however, an argument could be made that Ke$ha's use of glam and androgyny along with the exaggerated kitsch militarist and nationalist imagery are a form of postmodern "irony," or even overdetermined to the point of (unintended) satire and subversion. In contrast, BTR's cohesive merger of boy band swagger and stadium rock anthem, epitomized by "Famous" or "City is Ours," manifests a seamless organization where the BTR "war machine" is eminently one of *white male* teen pop/teen power reterritorialized into the BTR boy band/stadium rock brand of "domination-lite."

17. In fact, the cartoon series reconfigured the roles of the band members. Patrice Holloway was hired to do the singing parts of "Valarie" on the Josie and the Pussycats recordings; considered the strongest vocalist by the record producers, she was assigned most of the lead vocals. This necessitated Valarie becoming lead vocalist in the cartoons, which provoked controversy as Hanna-Barbera planned to modify Josie and the Pussycats into an all-white band. The impasse was settled, as bizarre as it sounds now, when Hanna-Barbera decided Valarie could remain an African-American.

18. For added measure, *Josie and the Pussycats* concluded with the revelation that Wyatt Frame and the loathsome CEO of Mega Records Fiona went to the same high school and were the standout geeks. When they remove their disguises, Fiona revealed she has buck teeth

and speaks with a pronounced lisp; Wyatt was a balding albino known as "White-Ass Wally" in school (which is to say "whiter than white"). The villainy of mass culture was ultimately represented around whiteness, the female, and the aberration of being a geek in normative teen society.

19. Roger Ebert's introductory remarks in his reviews for *Josie and the Pussycats* and *School of Rock* bear mention. Ebert dismissed *Josie and the Pussycats* by stating the film "is not dumber than the Spice Girls, but as dumb as the Spice Girls, which is dumb enough" (*Chicago Sun Times*, 4/11/01). In contrast, Ebert hailed *School of Rock* and Jack Black as "a living, breathing, sweaty advertisement for the transformative power of rock and roll" (*Chicago Sun Times*, 10/3/03). In fact, *Josie and the Pussycats* and *School of Rock* are both permeated with rock ideology and sustain the contradictory message that someone can be both an anti–Establishment rebel and an Establishment success. Ebert's comments betray the standard sexism and castigation of feminine mass culture by assessing *Josie and the Pussycats* and the Spice Girls as equally "dumb," whereas *School of Rock* in all its perspiration-drenched masculine glory expresses the mythic "transformative power of rock and roll."

20. Terry Eagleton, *Literary Theory: An Introduction* (Minneapolis: University of Minnesota Press, 1983), 189.

21. "I Want It That Way: Teenybopper Music and the Girling of Boy Bands." Emphasis added.

22. "Big Time Video" (2010) and "Big Time Songwriters" (2011) could be included as well, and respectively centered on BTR's efforts to make a video and record an original song as they wanted it, not industry dictates.

23. Ed Begley, Jr. also plays himself in "Big Time Concert." Mr. Griffin initially drops BTR in order to fund a new product line of children's books on tape with "green politics" messages read by Begley.

## *Conclusion*

1. Raymond Williams, *Marxism and Literature* (New York: Oxford University Press, 1977), 122.

2. Ibid., 123.

3. Ibid., 125. Second emphasis added.

4. Attali, 6.

# Bibliography

Adorno, Theodor W. *The Culture Industry: Selected Essays on Mass Culture.* Edited by J.M. Bernstein. New York: Routledge, 1991.

_____. *Essays on Music.* Edited by Richard Leppert. Translated by Susan Gillespie. Berkeley: University of California Press, 2002.

Althusser, Louis. *For Marx.* Translated by Ben Brewster. New York: Verso, 1991.

Artaud, Antonin. *Selected Writings.* Edited by Susan Sontag. Translated by Helen Weaver. Berkeley: University of California Press, 1988.

Attali, Jacques. *Noise: The Political Economy of Music.* Translated by Brain Massumi. Minneapolis: University of Minnesota Press, 1985.

Banet-Wesier, Sarah. *Kids Rule! Nickelodeon and Consumer Citizenship.* Durham: Duke University Press, 2007.

Bangs, Lester. *Mainlines, Bloodfeasts, and Bad Taste: A Lester Bangs Reader.* Edited by John Morthland. New York: Anchor, 2003.

_____. *Psychotic Reactions and Carburetor Dung.* Edited by Greil Marcus. New York: Anchor, 2003.

Barthes, Roland. *Mythologies.* Translated by Annette Lavers. New York: Hill and Wang, 1995.

Bly, Robert. *Iron John.* New York: Vintage, 1991.

Bourdieu, Pierre. *The Field of Cultural Production: Essays on Art and Literature.* Edited by Randall Johnson. New York: Columbia University Press, 1993.

Buckley, Jonathan, Orla Duane, Mark Ellingham, and Al Spicer, eds. *Rock: The Rough Guide,* 2d ed. London: Rough Guides, 1999.

Butler, Judith. *Gender Trouble: Feminism and the Subversion of Identity.* New York: Routledge, 1999.

Christgau, Robert. "Avant-Punk: A Cult Explodes...And a Movement is Born." *The Village Voice* (October 24, 1977).

Coates, Norma. "Teenyboppers, Groupies, and Other Grotesques: Girls and Women and Rock Culture in the 1960s and Early 1970s." *Journal of Popular Music Studies,* vol. 15, no.1 (2003): 76–91.

Debord, Guy. *The Society of the Spectacle.* Translated by Donald Nicholson-Smith. New York: Zone Books, 1994.

Dee, Jonathan. "Tween on the Screen." *The New York Times* (April 8, 2007).

Deleuze, Gilles. *Cinema 1: The Movement Image.* Translated by Hugh Tomlinson and Barbara Habberjam. Minneapolis: University of Minnesota Press, 1986.

_____, and Félix Guattari. *A Thousand Plateaus: Capitalism and Schizophrenia.* Translated by Brian Massumi. Minneapolis: University of Minnesota Press, 1987.

Eagleton, Terry. *Literary Theory: An Introduction.* Minneapolis: University of Minnesota Press, 1983.

Ellis, John. *Visible Fictions: Cinema, Television, Video,* rev. ed. London: Routledge, 1992.

Evans, Sara. *Personal Politics: The Roots of the Women's Liberation in the Civil Rights Movement and the New Left.* New York: Vintage, 1979.

Fast, Susan. *In the Houses of the Holy: Led Zeppelin and the Power of Rock Music.* New York: Oxford University Press, 2001.

Foucault, Michel. *The History of Sexuality, Vol.1: An Introduction.* Translated by Robert Hurley. New York: Vintage, 1990.

Frith, Simon. *Performance Rites: On the Value of Popular Music.* Cambridge: Harvard University Press, 1996.

_____. "Post-Punk Blues." *Marxism Today* (March 1983).

_____. *Sound Effects: Youth, Leisure, and the Politics of Rock 'n' Roll.* New York: Pantheon, 1981.

Gramsci, Antonio. *Selections from the Prison Notebooks.* Edited and Translated by Quintin Hoare and Geoffrey Nowell-Smith. New York: International Publishers, 1999.

Greene, Doyle. *The American Worker on Film: A Critical History, 1909–1999.* Jefferson, NC: McFarland, 2010.

_____. *Politics and the American Television Comedy: A Critical Survey from I Love Lucy to South Park.* Jefferson, NC: McFarland, 2008.

Gringanolis, Vanessa. "The Tragedy of Britney Spears." *Rolling Stone* (February 21, 2008).

Grossman, Jeff. "This Archie Comics Includes a Lawsuit." *New York Times* (September 4, 2005).

Hamamoto, Darrell Y. *Nervous Laughter: Television Situation Comedy and Liberal Democratic Ideology.* New York: Praeger, 1989.

Hartley, John. "Democratainment and DYI Citizenship," in *The Television Studies Reader,* 524–33, edited by Robert C. Allen and Annette Hill. London: Routledge, 2004.

_____. "Invisible Fictions: Television Audiences, Paedocracy, Pleasure," in *Television: Critical Concepts IV,* 54–71, edited by Toby Miller. London: Routledge, 2003.

Hebdige, Dick. *Subculture: The Meaning of Style.* London: Routledge, 1987.

Hegarty, Paul. *Noise/Music: A History.* New York: Continuum, 2007.

Henry Cow. *Concerts* (ESD 80822/832: 1995). Liner notes.

Hoberman, J., and Jonathan Rosenbaum. *Midnight Movies.* New York: Da Capo, 1991.

Hussey, Andrew. "Requiem pour un con: Subversive Pop and the Society of the Spectacle." *Cercles* 3(2001): 49–59.

Huyssen, Andreas. *After the Great Divide: Modernism, Mass Culture, Postmodernism.* Bloomington: Indiana University Press. 1986.

Jameson, Fredric. *Postmodernism, Or, the Cultural Logic of Late Capitalism.* Durham: Duke University Press, 1991.

Jung, Carl Gustav. *Aspects of the Masculine/Aspects of the Feminine.* Edited by John Beebe. Translated by R.F.C. Hull. New York: MJF Books, 1989

Lacan, Jacques. *Écrits: A Selection.* Translated by Bruce Fink. New York: W.W. Norton, 2002.

Leary, Timothy. *The Politics of Ecstasy.* Berkeley: Ronin Publishing, 1998.

Leppert, Richard. "Music 'Pushed to the Edge of Existence' (Adorno, Listening, and the Question of Hope)." *Cultural Critique* 60 (Spring 2005): 92–132.

Lichtenstein, Nelson. *State of the Union: A Century of American Labor.* Princeton, NJ: Princeton University Press, 2002.

Macan, Edward. *Rocking the Classics: English Progressive Rock and the Counterculture.* New York: Oxford University Press, 1997.

Mailer, Norman. *Advertisements for Myself.* Cambridge: Harvard University Press, 1992.

Marc, David. *Comic Visions: Television Comedy and American Culture,* 2d ed. Malden, MA: Blackwell, 1997.

Marcus, Greil. *Lipstick Traces: A Secret History of the Twentieth Century.* Cambridge, MA: Harvard University Press, 1989.

Marsh, Dave. *Bruce Springsteen: Two Hearts: The Definitive Biography, 1972–2003.* New York: Routledge, 2003.

Massumi, Brian. *A User's Guide to Capitalism and Schizophrenia: Deviations from Deleuze and Guattari.* Cambridge, MA: The MIT Press, 1992.

McEachern, Charmaine. "Bringing the Wildman Back Home: Television and the Politics of Masculinity." *Continuum: The Australian Journal of Media and Culture,* vol. 7, no.2 (1994).

_____. "Comic Interventions: Passion and the Men's Movement in the Situation Comedy *Home Improvement.*" *Journal of Gender Studies*, 3:1 (March 1999): 5–18.

McNeil, Legs, and Gillian McGill. *Please Kill Me: An Uncensored Oral History of Punk.* New York: Penguin, 1997.

Meehan, Eileen R. *Why TV Is Not Our Fault: Television Programming, Viewers, and Who's Really in Charge.* Lanham, MD: Rowman and Littlefield, 2005.

Moca, Diane Joy. "'Clarissa' Gives TV its First High-Tech Sitcom." *Chicago Tribune* (March 23, 1991).

O'Neill, William L. *Coming Apart: An Informal History of America in the 1960s.* New York: Times Books, 1972.

Paglia, Camille. "Madonna — Finally, a Real Feminist." *New York Times* (December 14, 1990).

Peck, Abe. *Uncovering the Sixties: The Life and Times of the Underground Press.* New York: Pantheon, 1985.

Ray, Robert B. *A Certain Tendency in American Cinema, 1930–1980.* Princeton, NJ: Princeton University Press, 1985.

Reynolds, Simon. *Rip It Up and Start Again: Postpunk 1978–1984.* New York: Penguin Books, 2005.

Steinberg, Jacques. "I, Little Sister, Becomes 'iCarly.'" *The New York Times* (September 7, 2007).

Talese, Gay. *Thy Neighbor's Wife.* New York: Doubleday, 1980.

Taylor, Timothy D. *Beyond Exoticism: Western Music and the World.* Durham: Duke University Press, 1997.

Vaneigem, Raoul. *The Revolution of Everyday Life.* Translated by Donald Nicholson-Smith. London: Rebel Press, 2006.

Waksman, Steve. *This Ain't the Summer of Love: Conflict and Crossover in Heavy Metal and Punk.* Berkeley: University of California Press, 2009.

Wald, Gayle. "'I Want It That Way': Teenybopper Music and the Girling of Boy Bands." *Genders* 35. Archived at http://www.genders.org/g35/g35_wald.html. Accessed 6/26/10.

Walser, Robert. *Running with the Devil: Power, Gender, and Madness in Heavy Metal Music.* Hanover, NH: Wesleyan University Press, 1993.

Waters, John. *Crackpot: The Obsessions of John Waters.* New York: Vintage, 1987.

Williams, Raymond. *Marxism and Literature.* New York: Oxford University Press, 1977.

# Index

Numbers in **bold italics** indicate pages with illustrations.

ABBA 33
ABC (band) 116
ABC (TV network) 3, 9, 16, 45, 101, 109, 115
ABC Family 6, 16
*According to Jim* 2, 19, 40, 46, 57, 71, 92, 96
AC/DC 103, 136, 141–2
Adorno, Theodor W. 5, 15–6, 18, 43, 56–7, 99, 102, 126–8, 142, 161–2, 199*ch9n*19
adult authority 7–8, 15, 19, 21–2, 55, 57, 68–9, 76–7, 79, 81–2, 87, 89, 91, 95–8, 107, 112–3, 115, 135–6, 140, 142, 147–50, 157
*The Adventures of Ozzie and Harriet* 39
advertising 2, 4, 17, 34–5, 55, 188*ch5n*2
agency 8, 21, 59–61, 65–6, 68, 71, 85, 128, 147
Aguilera, Christina 2, 9, 15, 34, 123–4, ***125***, 135–6, 198*ch9n*8, 198–9*ch9n*10
*All That* 63, 65, 143
*Almost Famous* 133
Altamont 149
Alternative rock 9–10, 34, 56, 134–5, 146–8, 168
Althusser, Louis 59, 146, 167
*The Amanda Show* 63, 143
*American Bandstand* 115
American Dream 10, 28, 117, 123, 132–3, 153, 157–8, 168, 174
Americanism 4, 185*ch2n*15; versus Continentalism 28–30, 51, 116, 143–4, 158
animus/anima (Jung) 45–6, 51, 140
Anthrax 138
anti–Establishment 9–10, 21–2, 30, 53, 59, 101, 107, 133, 136, 138, 141, 175
*Archie* (comic book)108–9
Archie Comics 108
*The Archie Show* 101, 108–9, 168, 196*ch8n*15
Archies 9, 101–2, 109–10, 168
Argota, Ashley 59
*Arrested Development* 40–1
art rock 1, 32, 138
Artaud, Antonin 18
assumed audience 4–5, 30, 49, 89, 91, 104, 148–9, 153

atonality 101–2, 127
Attali, Jacques 99, 110, 126, 129, 138, 175
au pairs 34
audience 4–6, 18, 41, 55, 57, 84, 114; *see also* assumed audience; imagined audience; target audience
authenticity 9–10, 22, 30, 32, 71, 83, 104, 106, 113–6, 118, 133–8, 142, 148, 150–1, 157, 159, 162, 168–70, 175–6
Ayler, Albert 28

B-52s 34
Backstreet Boys 9, 123, 168
Bad Brains 138
Bad Company 32
Bananarama 147
Banet-Weiser, Sarah 4, 55, 59, 70
Bangs, Lester 6, 28–9
Bataille, Georges 121
Bay City Rollers 134
Beach Boys 106
Beastie Boys 134
Beatles 17, 21, 103–5, 107, 164
*Beavis and Butt-head* 58, 134, 193*ch6n*25
Beckett, Samuel 16
Begley, Ed, Jr. 171–2
Bell, Drake 17, 63, 72
Benjamin, Walter 18
Bergson, Henri 151
Berry, Chuck 21, 29, 103–4, 117, 137
BET 4
*The Beverly Hillbillies* 122, 150
Bieber, Justin 6, 104
*The Big Bang Theory* 50
Big Five (TV industry) 16, 21
Big Help 4, 55, 59
Big Time Rush (BTR, band) 10, 55, 59, 162, ***163***, 164–72, 207*ch9n*16
*Big Time Rush* (BTR, sitcom) 10, 16–7, 21, 26, 40–1, 56, 81, 85, 162, ***163***, 164–72
Black, Jack ***20***, 81, 135, ***140***
Black Flag 19, 134, 138, 196*ch8n*5
*Black Knight* 28

black music 9–10, 29–30, 134–5, 138, 144, 155
Black Sabbath 118, 134, 142
Blondie (band) 34, 136, 142
*Blossom* 61
blues 124, 136
Bly, Robert 44–6
Bon Jovi 168
Bonaduce, Danny *111*
Bono 17
*Boston Legal* 42
Bourdieu, Pierre 5
Bowie, David 31–2
boy bands 2, 6, 9–10, 123, 134, 162–3, 168, 172
Boyce, Tommy 105
*The Brady Bunch* 19
brands/branding 4, 6, 8, 55–9, 84–5, 102,
    121–2, 147, 149, 151, 159, 168
Brecht, Bertolt 40
Brown, James 28, 144
bubblegum 8–10, 29, 101–4, 106, 109, 116,
    120, 122, 126, 134, 147–8, 151, 159, 168
*Bucket and Skinner's Epic Adventures*
    194*ch7n6*
Bush, George H.W. 58
Bush, George W. 17, 71–3, 121, 123, 137, 149
Bynes, Amanda 143
Byrds 106

Cage, John 28
Can 126
capitalism 3, 6–9, 15, 17, 49, 51–4, 58, 60,
    62–3, 70, 75, 82, 84, 87–8, 98, 102, 116–7,
    121, 124, 126–9, 155, 158, 161, 168
Capra, Frank 62, 86, 160
Captain and Tennille 115
Captain Beefheart 126
Carlson, Tucker 123
Cassidy, David 15, 109, *111*, 113–4
CBS 3, 9, 16, 46, 101, 108, 115, 168
Charlie Daniels Band 25
Chic 30
Chisholm, Tanya *163*
Circle Jerks 19
"Circus" 9, 128–30, 173
citizenship 4, 59–60, 80, 84, 89, 121, 141, 149,
    153, 158
*Clarissa Explains It All* 8, 25–6, 41, 49, 58,
    60–3, 75
*Clarissa Now* 184*ch2n10*
Clark, Wesley 121
Clash 103, 137
class/class politics 9, 24–8, 36, 49, 54–5, 66,
    70, 73, 78, 85, 89, 96, 122–4, 128, 143–4,
    150–1
classic rock 1, 9, 18, 56, 103, 133, 135–6, 136,
    142, 144, 148
classical Hollywood cinema 39, 41, 60
classical music 1, 24, 29, 56, 81, 113, 155
classical sitcoms 7, 19, 39–42, 48, 60, 63, 65,
    74, 90, 107, 109, 111, 146, 174–5

Clinton, Bill 3, 58, 61, 63, 73, 85
Clinton, Hillary 72–3
Clintonism 3, 8, 58–60, 85
Coates, Norma 17, 31–3, 114
Cobain, Kurt 134, 137
cock rock 32, 138
Colgems Records 106
Columbia Records 162
Comedy Central 16
comedy-variety shows 16, 39, 63, 108, 114–5
commercials *see* advertising
community 8, 21, 42–5, 50, 53–4, 59–60, 66,
    68–71, 73, 75, 78, 80–2, 84–7, 128–30, 139,
    141, 153, 155, 157–8, 160–1, 173
conformity 5, 7, 21, 44, 59–60, 71, 76, 135,
    144–5, 147, 164
conservatism 3–4, 6, 8–9, 23–5, 41, 45, 53,
    58, 62, 71, 73, 79–80, 86, 88–9, 91, 94–5,
    108, 111, 119, 121, 123, 132, 137, 148–9, 155,
    166, 174–5
consumerism 4–5, 7, 35, 58–9, 63, 80, 84,
    87, 89, 126, 138, 158, 168, 174
contemporary sitcoms 7, 40, 41, 42, 60, 65,
    106, 116, 162, 174
Contortions 28
Coolidge, Calvin 3
Cooper, Alice 29, 103
Copland, Aaron 155
*The Cosby Show* 19, 40, 45, 48, 57, 96
Cosgrove, Miranda 15, 17, 59, 64, 73, *74*, *83–
    4*, 89, 104
cosmopolitanism 89, 121, 123
counterculture (1960s) 9, 21–2, 30–1, 44, 53,
    58, 73, 80, 106–9, 112, 114–6, 133, 138, 142,
    174–6
Country Joe and the Fish 106
country music 23, 56, 106, 148, 155, 157, 159
Cream 140
cross-marketing 16–8, 72, 89, 101–2, 104,
    146, 149, 168, 175, 182–3*ch1n8*
Crough, Suzanne *111*
Cruikshank, Lucas 82
*CSI* 42
cultural consumption 6–7, 15–6, 18, 21–2,
    33–4, 36, 41, 43, 80–1, 83, 102, 104, 151,
    175
cultural literacy 41, 61–2
cultural production 6–7, 15–6, 18, 21–2, 33–
    4, 36, 39, 43, 75, 80–1, 83, 102, 104, 149,
    151, 175
Culture Club 29, 116
Culture Industry 5, 10, 15–8, 21, 32, 43, 82–
    3, 107, 122–3, 151, 168, 172
Cyrus, Billy Ray 148, 154
Cyrus, Miley 2, 10, 15, 17, 19, 29, 34, 104, 130,
    148–9, *152*, 154–5, *156*, 202*ch11n3*,
    204*ch11n13*, 204*ch11n19*

*Darcy's Wild Life* 203*ch11n10*
*Dazed and Confused* 135

Dead Kennedys 5, 137
Dean, Howard 80
Debord, Guy 154, 159
Deleuze, Gilles 41–3, 81, 160, 202*ch*11*n*5, 207*ch*9*n*16
democracy/democratic society 19, 37, 51, 57, 68–71, 79–80, 89, 99, 102, 127–9, 132, 140
Democratic Party 3, 44, 71–2, 85, 95, 117, 121, 123
Denver, John 111
Depp, Johnny 173, 176
Derrida, Jacques 169
*détournement* 138
Devo 147
Dey, Susan *111*
Die Kreuzen 138
DioGuardi, Kara 202*ch*11*n*4
direct address 40, 48–9, 63, 74, 106–7, 188*ch*4*n*1
disco 10, 29, 104, 116, 120, 136, 138, 146, 148
Disney 4, 6, 16–7, 72, 82, 146, 149, 155, 167
Disney Channel 4–5, 16–7, 26, 48, 56–7, 72, 82, 84, 122, 151
dissonance *see* atonality
DIY (Do It Yourself) culture 8, 75, 80–1, 83, 85, 149, 151, 175
Dolenz, Micky 105, 107, 164
dominant culture 10, 22, 173–5
*Don Kirshner's Rock Concert* 115
Doors 21, 115
*Dragnet* 42
*Drake and Josh* 1, 8, 16–7, 26–7, 40, 50, 63–5, 71–4, 78, 84–5, 92, 166
Duff, Hilary 17
Duran Duran 29, 116
Dylan, Bob 175

Eagleton, Terry 169
*Easy Rider* 175–6
Ebert, Roger 208*ch*12*n*19
Echo and the Bunnymen 62
educational system 5, 7–8, 68–9, 75, 79, 88, 90, 92, 135, 141–2, 147
Efron, Zac 170
Ellis, John 39
emergent culture 10–1, 173–5
Emerson, Lake and Palmer (ELP) 29, 204*ch*11*n*5
*Employee of the Month* 98
environmentalism 44, 52–3, 59, 79, 110–1, 171
Establishment 9, 22, 31, 80, 94, 101, 107, 136, 140, 142–3, 148, 174–5
eternal teenager 9, 46–7, 57, 77, 103, 107, 135, 141
ethical form 7, 41–3, 45, 68, 93, 98, 110, 149, 171, 187*ch*3*n*7
ethnicity 7, 36, 51, 55, 95, 97, 139, 164, 169
*Everybody Hates Chris* 7, 19, 40–1
*Everybody Loves Raymond* 7, 40, 90, 166

*The Fairly OddParents* 205*ch*12*n*3
*A Fairly OddParents Movie: Grow Up, Timmy Turner!* 205*ch*12*n*3
family 7–8, 18–9, 41, 55, 75–9, 87, 90, 112–3, 147, 153
*Family Ties* 8, 40, 53–4, 62, 189–90*ch*5*n*20
*The Famous Jett Jackson* 184*ch*2*n*9
Fast, Susan 186*ch*2*n*32
*Father Knows Best* 39, 48, 96
Fellows, Scott 41, 90, 162, 205*ch*12*n*3
feminism 8, 35, 44, 46, 51, 53, 63, 66–70, 76, 78, 120
Filmation Studios 109
First Wave Teen Pop 9–10, 34, 83, 120, 122–4, 134, 146–8, 163, 168
Fitzgerald, F. Scott 132
Flynn, Sean *68*
folk music 25, 106, 111, 155
Fonda, Jane 171
Ford, John 42, 160
Ford, Lita 34, 206–7*ch*12*n*11
Forster, Brian *111*
Foucault, Michel 198*ch*9*n*6
FOX 16
Fox, Vivica A. 96
FOX News 4, 56
*Frankie Goes to Hollywood* 29, 91, 116
Franklin, Aretha 136
*Fred* 82
*Fridays* 115
*Friends* 90
Frith, Simon 18, 23, 30, 32, 138
funk 10, 29, 116, 120, 122, 134, 148

Gang of Four 138, 201*ch*10*n*14
geek stereotype 49, 50, 64, 74, 76, 84, 85
gender/gender politics 7–8, 10, 24–36, 40, 41, 43–7, 55–7, 63–71, 75–8, 86, 90, 94–5, 97–8, 136, 139–40, 142–5, 149, 150, 155, 162, 165–7, 169–72, 175
generational politics 5–11, 13, 18–9, 21–2, 28, 32–4, 36, 41, 55, 58–62, 71, 73, 85–6, 90, 95–8, 101, 107, 112–3, 116, 133, 141, 143–5, 155, 174–6
Genesis 29
geographic politics 7, 9, 24–8, 36, 48, 85, 89, 150, 155
*George Lopez* 19, 40, 57, 97, 103, 166, 186–7*ch*2*n*39
*Gidget* 61
girl power 8–9, 41, 63, 65, 75, 78, 84–5, 87, 90–1, 95, 143, 149, 166
Giuliani, Rudy 72
glam 30–2
Glas, Kyle 135
*Glee* 6, 16–7, 33, 78, 130–2
Glickman, Stephen Kramer *163*
globalization 3–4, 58, 81, 158
Go-Gos 34, 147
Godard, Jean-Luc 107

Golightly, Cage 59
Gomez, Selena 17, 34, 207*ch9n*16
*Good Morning, Miss Bliss* 26, 48–9, 53
Gordon, Andy 90
Gosselaar, Mark-Paul *52*
Gottwald, Lukasz (Dr. Luke) 200*ch9n*30, 207*ch9n*16
Gramsci, Antonio 13, 22
Grateful Dead 17
Green, Robin 114
Gringanolis, Vanessa 130
Grohl, David 135
grunge 9–10, 85, 104
Guattari, Félix 202*ch11n*5, 207*ch9n*16
Guevara, Che 121

*H₂O ... Just Add Water* 1
*Hairspray* 23–4
Halvorson, Gary 90
Hamamoto, Darrell Y. 116–7
Hanna-Barbera 168, 207*ch9n*16
Hannah Montana 4–5, 10, 21, 33–4, 72, 104, 146, 148–51, *152*, 153–5, 157–61, 167, 174–5; songs 19, 84, 147, 151, 157, 159, 167
*Hannah Montana* (sitcom) 4, 9–10, 16–7, 21, 26, 40, 57, 61, 72, 81, 83, 85, 113, 124, 146–51, 167, 175
*Hannah Montana: The Movie* (*HMTM*) 10, 21, 28, 148, 151, *152*, 154–5, *156*, 157–61, 167, 173
*A Hard Day's Night* 105
hard rock 1, 9–10, 17–8, 32, 103, 135, 138, 142, 151
hardcore punk 134, 137–8
Harrison, George 105, 164
Harry, Deborah 136, 147, 198*ch9n*2
Hart, Bobby 105
Hart, Melissa Joan 184*ch2n*10
Hartley, John 4, 55–6, 58, 102
Harvey, PJ 34
Hatfield, Juliana 34
*Head* 106–8
*Head of the Class* 48, 63
heavy metal 9, 18, 32, 134–5, 138, 146–7, 153
Hebdige, Dick 23
Hegarty, Paul 103–4, 137–8, 199–200*ch9n*20, 200*ch9n*22
*Hellcats* 25
*Hell's Kitchen* 98
Helmet 147
*Help!* 105
Henderson, Logan *163*
Hendrix, Jimi 101, 117, 136, 142, 175
Henry Cow 117–8, 126, 198*ch8n*28
heterosexuality/heterosexism 30–2, 36, 51, 76, 91, 168
hidden messages 43, 50, 83, 112, 170–2
*High School Musical* films 6, 16, 33
Hilton, Paris 123, 199*ch9n*11
hip/hipness 4, 7–10, 16, 23–8, 30, 32, 34–6,

47–8, 50, 53–4, 57, 58, 62, 64, 65, 71, 73, 76–8, 82, 84–5, 87, 89–91, 94–5, 97, 104, 107, 113, 133, 136, 139, 142–5, 150, 155, 162, 164, 166, 168–9, 175
hip-hop 56, 120, 136, 146, 155
hippies 7, 53, 62, 79, 85–6, 88, 112, 133, 175
Hoberman J. 137
Hodgkinson, Tim 117
Hollywood 1, 16, 34, 105, 115, 167
Hollywood Records 72
*Home Improvement* 19, 40, 45–6, 54, 91, 96
homosexuality/homophobia 31, 46, 51, 64, 76, 78, 84, 91–2, 95, 103, 123, 132, 150, 167, 169, 185–6*ch2n*30
Horatio Alger myth 93, 117
*House* 42
*Howdy Doody* 17
Human League 29, 116
Humphrey, Hubert H. 21
Hussey, Andrew 138, 200*ch9n*21
Huyssen, Andreas 34–5

*I Love Lucy* 39, 63
*iCarly* 1–2, 5, 8, 16–7, 19, 25–8, 34, 40–1, 50, 55–6, 59, 63–5, 71–3, *74*, 75–93, 93, 104, 149, 151, 155, 173, 175
identity politics 7–8, 21, 24, 56, 91–2, 174
ideology marketing 3–6, 21, 36, 55, 58, 60, 80, 101, 104, 162, 175
imagined audience 4–5, 56–7, 84, 104, 109, 133
individuality 10, 21, 24, 44, 53–4, 57, 59–61, 68, 70–1, 78–81, 86–7, 89, 93, 99, 103, 113, 123, 128, 130, 134–5, 140–2, 144–5, 148, 153–5, 158, 168, 173–4
industrial music 2, 104, 126, 129
infantilism 43, 45–7, 56, 102–3, 126
internet 3, 11, 59, 74, 80–2, 92, 175
*Iron John* 44–5

Jackson, Janet 122
Jackson, Michael 15, 30, 102, 122, 134, 146–7
Jackson Five 102, 168, 196*ch8n*4
Jagger, Mick 29, 31
James, Henry 28
James, Kevin 46
Jay and the Americans 29
jazz 1, 56, 101, 124, 136
Jethro Tull 29, 44
Jett, Joan 34, 147
Jonas Brothers 6, 16, 72, 104, 167
Jones, Davy 105, 164
Jones, Shirley 109, *111*, 113
Joplin, Janis 175
Josie and the Pussycats (band) 168, 207*ch12n*17
*Josie and the Pussycats* (comic book/cartoon) 168
*Josie and the Pussycats* (film) 168–9
Journey 168

Jung, Carl 44–6, 139
*Just Jordan* 184*ch2n*9
*Just Shoot Me!* 90, 195*ch7n*11
Justice, Victoria 17, 56, 59, 190*ch5n*23

Kajagoogoo 103
Kant, Immanuel 42
*Kenan and Kel* 184*ch2n*12
Kennedy, John F. 158, 171
Kerouac, Jack 23
Ke\$ha 6, 207*ch9n*16
Kids' Choice Awards 15, 173
King Crimson 29
*The King of Queens* 40, 46, 50, 57, 92, 96–7, 103
Kirshner, Don 105–6, 109
Kiss 17–8, 32
kitsch 62, 77, 169
K-Mart 17
Kopelman, Dan 90
Kraftwerk 126
Kramer, Wayne 31
Kress, Nathan 59, 73, *74*
Die Kreuzen 138
Kriegman, Mitchell 60

Lacan, Jacques 159–60
large form 7, 41–2, 160–1
Lauper, Cyndi 147
Lear, Norman 92, 187*ch3n*5
Leary, Timothy 106–7
*Leave It to Beaver* 18–19, 96
Led Zeppelin 17, 32, 104, 133, 135
Leibniz, G.W. 127
Lennon, John 21, 105–6, 164
Leppert, Richard 142–3
Lester, Richard 105, 107
Lewis, Jerry 64, 105
liberal democracy *see* democracy/democratic society
liberalism 3–4, 6, 8, 17, 21, 23–5, 41, 44–5, 51–3, 56, 58, 61–3, 66, 73, 79, 85–6, 88–9, 91–2, 95, 99, 117, 121, 123, 133, 137, 171, 174–5
lifestyle 4–5, 7, 28, 79
Lifetime 4, 56
Lightfoot, Gordon 62
Linklater, Richard 134–5
*Lizzie McGuire* 17
Loggins, Kenny 24, 115
Logos/Eros (Jung) 45–6
Lovato, Demi 17, 34
Lovin' Spoonful 110
*The Lucy Show* 1
Lynch, Jane 78, 81
Lynyrd Skynyrd 25

Macan, Edward 185*ch2n*19
Madonna 9, 29, 35, 70, 80, 119–24, *125*, 130–2, 134, 146–7, 153, 173

Mailer, Norman 7, 23–4, 28
*Malcolm in the Middle* 19, 40–1, 49, 90
*The Man Who Shot Liberty Valance* 160
Manson, Charles 149
Mapplethorpe, Robert 121
Marc, David 39, 187*ch3n*7
Marcus, Greil 137
*Marcus Welby, M.D.* 42
marketing 21, 29, 55, 101, 105, 115, 122, 160; *see also* cross-marketing
*Married ... with Children* 19
Marsh, Dave 30, 117
Martin, Dean 63
Marx, Karl 60
Marx Brothers 106
masculinity/femininity 7–8, 10, 26, 29–36, 44–7, 49–51, 54, 57, 64, 71, 75–8, 84, 91–2, 96–8, 103, 123, 134, 136, 138–9, 163–72
Maslow, James *163*
mass culture 5–8, 15–6, 18, 57, 79, 81–3, 116, 118, 124, 149–51, 155, 168, 171, 187–8*ch3n*14; as "feminine" 9–10, 34–5, 84, 115, 134, 136, 162, 169–70, 172
mass music 126
Massumi, Brian 51
maturity 2, 46, 57–8, 93; as sign of "good taste" 17, 33–34, 41, 82, 104
MC5 31, 101, 103
McCain, John 59, 73, 94–5, 123
McCartney, Paul 105, 164
McCurdy, Jennette 17, 73, *74*, 89, 93, 104
McEachern, Charmaine 187*ch3n*13
McLaren, Malcolm 138
McNeil, Legs 103
Meehan, Eileen R. 16, 58
Megadeth 138
Mellencamp, John 29
men's movement 8, 44, 54
"The Merchants of Cool" 21
Metallica 138
meter (in music) 101–2, 104, 124, 127–9
Michaels, Bret 13, 22
Michalka, Aly 184*ch2n*8
*The Mickey Mouse Club* (*MMC*) 122, 198*ch9n*8
*The Midnight Special* 115, 197*ch8n*22
mirror-stage 159–60
Monkees (band) 8, 17–8, 101–2, 105–10, 115, 164
*The Monkees* (sitcom) 10, 40–1, 101, 106–9, 111, 115–6, 162, 168
Monroe, Marilyn 119, 121
Moon, Keith 136
MOR music 29, 111, 116
Morley, Paul 30
Morrison, Jim 31, 115
mothers, sitcom representation of 57, 76–9, 96, 103, 166
Mothers of Invention 106
Motown 136

Mott the Hoople 32
MSNBC 56
MTV 2, 4, 9, 16, 29, 48, 115–6, 119–20,
　　197*ch*8*n*23
MTV Video Music Awards (VMAs) 119–20,
　　123–4, **125**, 130
multiculturalism 44, 91, 121, 139
Munck, Noah 73
Murrow, Edward R. 5
"Music" 9, 127–9, 132, 173
music of alienation 127
Musso, Mitchel 17
*My Name Is Earl* 41
*My Wife and Kids* 19, 40, 57

'N Sync 9, 123
*The Naked Brothers Band* 6, 16–7, 205*ch*12*n*2
nationhood 4, 7, 55, 81, 84, 158, 181*intro.n*3
NBC 3, 8, 48, 101, 105, 108, 115
*Ned's Declassified School Survival Guide* 6, 41,
　　72, 75, 162
neoliberalism 3, 7–9, 19, 44, 58, 60–1, 63,
　　71–2, 79, 85, 87, 98, 149, 155, 181*intro.n*1
nerd stereotype *see* geek stereotype
Nesmith, Mike 105–6, 108, 164
*The New Adventures of Old Christine* 19
New Country 89, 104, 148, 157, 193*ch*6*n*29
New Democrats 3, 8, 58, 61, 63, 85, 92, 149
New Kids on the Block 9, 134, 168
New Pop 9, 29–30, 32, 80, 103, 116,
　　185*ch*2*n*23
New Wave (French cinema) 105
New Wave (music) 10, 29, 89, 104, 124, 134,
　　146–8, 151, 159
New York Dolls 32, 138
News Corporation 16
Nicholson, Jack 107
*Nick News* 4, 55
Nickelodeon 1–2, 4–5, 8, 11, 16–7, 19, 27, 35,
　　41, 55–60, 63, 72–3, 75, 78, 80, 82, 85, 89–
　　91, 95, 143, 149, 162, 166–7, 188–9*ch*5*n*5
Nicks, Stevie 136, 140, 147
Nico 29
Night Ranger 29
1910 Fruitgum Company 102
98 Degrees 9, 123
Nirvana 58, 85, 104, 134–5
No Doubt 34, 147
No Wave 28
noise 99, 102, 104, 110–1, 124–7, 129, 137–8,
　　141
Nugent, Ted 174

Obama, Barack 3, 8, 59, 73, 75, 79–80, 89–
　　90, 93–5, 121, 123
Obama, Michelle 59, 81
objectivist music 127–8, 155
Oedipus complex 46, 78, 166
*The Office* 40–1, 65, 98
*Office Space* 98

Ohio Express 102
oligopoly (TV industry)16, 83
*One Day at a Time* 19
O'Neill, William L. 31
oppositional culture 5, 21, 35, 80, 83, 115–6,
　　126, 133, 136, 142–3, 148, 162, 174
Osbourne, Ozzy 142
Osment, Emily 17
Osmond, Donny 15, 102, 115
Osmond, Marie 115
Osmonds 102, 196*ch*8*n*4
Oswald, Lee Harvey 158
others/the Other 23, 31–2, 50–2, 84, 91–2,
　　97, 136, 158, 166
*Our Miss Brooks* 39, 48
Outlaw Country 25
overt message 43, 50, 112, 149, 170–2

paedocracy 56–7, 97, 102–3
Paglia, Camille 120–1, 127
Palin, Sarah 94, 121
Palmer, Keke 17, 59, 90, 194*ch*7*n*1
parents *see* family
Parliament-Funkadelic 30, 127
Partridge Family (band) 9, 101–2, 109–10,
　　***111***, 112–5
*The Partridge Family* (sitcom) 9, 15, 19, 41,
　　101–2, 109–10, ***111***, 112–5, 146, 149
patriarchy 4–5, 44, 57, 77–8, 149
Pawlenty, Tim 94. 195*ch*7*n*9
PBS 3–4, 17, 21–2, 133
Pearl Jam 62
Peck, Josh 63
pedagogic regime 57–8, 97, 175
Pena, Carlos ***163***
*Perry Mason* 42
Petty, Tom 133, 174
Phair, Liz 34, 147
phallogocentricism 169
"Piece of Me" 9, 124–7
Pink Floyd 136, 142
*Pirate Radio* 133
*Playboy* 121
Poison 32
Pop, Iggy 29, 137
Pop Art 62, 77
Pop Group 126, 138, 201*ch*10*n*14
pop music 9, 30, 56, 101, 104, 111, 114, 116,
　　134, 146, 155, 168
pop-music sitcoms 8, 10, 114, 146, 162
*Popstar!* 169
popular music 4, 8, 16, 28, 72, 101–3, 112, 115,
　　118, 126, 129, 133, 136, 146, 173
postfeminism 8, 70, 78, 89
postindustrialism 3, 7–8, 58, 60, 79, 89,
　　155
postmodernism 29–30, 35, 41, 61, 77, 80, 89,
　　119, 121, 124, 128, 134, 143, 174–5
post-punk 1, 29, 34, 138
Presley, Elvis 17, 31

progressive rock 24, 29, 44
progressivism 3, 9, 17, 59, 61, 85, 89, 98, 121, 173
Public Enemy 126, 134
Puer Aeternus 46
Puff Daddy 135–6
punk rock 1, 9–10, 28, 29, 34, 80, 103, 134–8, 140–2, 146–8, 153, 174, 185*ch2n*20
*Punky Brewster* 61

Queen 32

R&B (rhythm and blues music) 23–5, 29, 78, 106
race/racial politics 7–8, 23–31, 35–6, 51–2, 54, 70, 85–6, 90–1, 93–4, 97, 113, 136, 148, 150, 155, 166, 184–5*ch2n*14, 194*ch7n*5
radio 3, 39, 56, 133
Rafelson, Bob 105, 107–8
Raincoats 34
Ramone, Dee Dee 137
Ramone, Joey 29, 137
Ramone, Johnny 137, 174
Ramones 29, 103–4, 133, 135, 137–8, 141–2
rap music 10, 81, 120, 134, 136, 146, 148, 155
Rascal Flatts 157
Reagan, Ronald 3, 117, 137
Reagan Revolution 3, 53, 62
Reaganism 3, 8, 24, 48, 53–4, 61, 80, 121
*Reba* 19
Reed, Lou 29, 32
referencing 40, 60–1, 127, 162, 175
reggae 134
representation 4–5, 8, 25, 27–8, 45, 47, 51, 65, 71, 84, 91, 96–8, 102–3, 119, 123, 128, 130, 132, 149–50, 153, 155, 158, 166–8, 173
Repressive Hypothesis 121, 198*ch9n*6
Republican Party 3, 44, 58, 62, 72, 94–5, 117, 123, 149
Residents 126
residual culture 10–1, 173–6
*Revenge of the Nerds* 188*ch4n*3
Reynolds, Simon 29–30, 129.185*ch2n*23
Rich, Buddy 136
Roberts, Emma 17, 72
*Rock and Roll High School* 135, 141
rock ideology 9–10, 20, 24, 29, 30–2, 36, 115, 134–6, 138, 141, 148, 150, 168–9, 174
rock music 11, 19, 21–23, 30, 34, 71, 101–3, 118, 133–43, 149, 174–5; relationship to TV 9, 114–7
*Rock Star* 133
role models 55, 61, 65, 112–3, 120–1, 143, 153
roles (in society) 119–21, 123, 128, 132, 153, 159–60
*Rolling Stone* 5, *20*, 22, 31, 114, 130, 132–3
Rolling Stones 17, 31
Ronstadt, Linda 105
Roosevelt, Franklin Delano 79
Roosevelt, Theodore 79

Rosenbaum, Jonathan 137
*Rowan and Martin's Laugh-In* 108
Roxy Music 32
Run-D.M.C. 134
Runaways 34
Rush 142
Russell, Malcolm 101

*Sabrina, the Teenage Witch* (comic, cartoon, sitcom) 184*ch2n*10
*Saturday Night Live* 115
*Saved by the Bell* (*SbtB*) 7–8, 10, 25–6, 47–51, *52*, 53–4, 61, 64, 66–70, 88, 92, 166
*Saved by the Bell: The College Years* 42
Schmidt, Kendall *163*
Schneider, Bert 105
Schneider, Dan 19, 63, 71, 73, 78, 90–1
Schoenberg, Arnold 16, 127
school *see* educational system
*School of Rock* (*SoR*) 9–10, *20*, 22, 71, 74, 103, 113, 115, 124, 133–9, *140*, 141–5, 148, 174
Screen Gems 109
*Scrubs* 41
Second Wave Teen Pop 10, 16, 34, 84, 89, 104, 124, 146–8, 150
self-determination 10, 61, 79, 92–3, 96, 104, 113, 120, 141, 147–8, 157–8, 168, 171, 174
*Sex* 121
Sex Pistols 29, 137–8, 142
sexism 9, 30–2, 34, 50–1, 66–8, 71, 115, 170
sexuality 7–8, 36, 113, 120–2, 125, 174
Shakespeare, William 44, 62
*Shindig!* 115
*The Simpsons* 43–5, 50, 61, 75, 166
Siouxsie and the Banshees 34
sitcoms 2, 7, 18–19, 34, 39, 41, 43, 47–8, 50, 57, 71, 77, 91–2, 96, 98, 103, 117, 149; *see also* classical sitcoms; contemporary sitcoms; teen sitcoms
situationists/situationist practice 138, 200*ch9n*21
ska 134, 147
*Slacker* 58, 135
slackers 7, 54, 85, 89, 92, 97, 134, 141
Slade 32
Slayer 138
Slits 34
small form 7, 41–2
Smith, Patti 34
*The Smothers Brothers Comedy Hour* 108, 174
social mobility 8, 10, 92, 113, 121, 123, 141, 145, 172
Sonic Youth 126
Sonny and Cher 115
*Sonny with a Chance* 6, 16–7, 33
Sony Music 122
soul music 29, 104, 116, 124, 168
Soundgarden 138

*South Park* 1, 130
Southern Hipness 25–6, 89
Southern rock 25
Spears, Britney 2, 5, 9–10, 15, 21, 34, 65, 83–4, 104, 118–9, 121–4, *125*, 126–30, *131*, 132, 147, 151, 153, 173, 175
Spears, Jamie Lynn 65, *68*, 72
spectacle society 119, 129, 132, 138, 151, 154, 160
*Spectacular!* 16
Spice Girls 6, 9, 15, 27, 34, 123
Spicer, Al 31
Spike 4, 16, 56
*SpongeBob SquarePants* 6, 55–6
Springsteen, Bruce 5, 24–5, 117–8, 198*ch8n*30
Square 4, 7, 9–10, 16, 23–5, 27–8, 35, 41, 44, 47–8, 57, 62, 64–5, 77–8, 82, 84, 90, 94–5, 97, 112–3, 135–6, 140, 142, 144–5, 150, 155, 164, 166
*Square Pegs* 48
stadium rock 10, 24, 124, 146–8, 151, 157, 159, 168, 172, 182*intro.n*10
*Star Search* 122
*Star Wars* 22, 167
Starr, Ringo 105, 164
Stefani, Gwen 34, 147
Steppenwolf 103
*Still Standing* 50, 96, 103, 195*ch7n*11
Stills, Stephen 105
Sting 62
Stooges 29, 103
Stravinsky, Igor 127, 142–3
*The Suite Life of Zack and Cody* 16, 72
*Supah Ninjas* 6
Sweet 32
Swift, Taylor 6, 154, 157
symbolic order 159–60
synthpop 120, 127, 147, 151

T. Rex 32
*Taking Woodstock* 133
Talese, Gay 121
Talking Heads 34, 138, 201*ch10n*14
target audience 4–5, 35, 56, 98, 135, 172
Taylor, Timothy D. 24
Tears for Fears 116
techno 10, 120, 146
Teen Choice Awards 15, 130, *131*
teen culture 3–7, 10–11, 15, 17–9, 21–2, 35, 59, 80–3, 101, 133, 142, 151, 173–6
Teen NBC 48
teen pop 2, 4, 6, 16, 19, 21, 29, 84, 102, 126, 134–6, 157, 159, 163, 173, 181*intro.n*4; *see also* First Wave Teen Pop; Second Wave Teen Pop
teen sitcoms 1–2, 4, 6–8, 16, 19, 21, 25, 34, 36, 47–8, 50, 55, 72–3, 83, 88, 90–2, 95, 98, 173
teenyboppers 5, 7, 17, 30–34, 62, 84, 103–4, 114, 116, 134, 148, 150, 153, 164, 169–70

television 1, 3–5, 8, 11, 16, 21–2, 34, 39, 55–7, 60, 102, 162, 172, 174–5
Tenacious D. 135
*That '70s Show* 1, 19
theoretical music 126
They Might Be Giants 62
*30 Rock* 33
Thomas, Leon, III 17
Thompson, Kenan 81
Throbbing Gristle 126, 129
*Tiger Beat* 5, 169
Timberlake, Justin 163, 198*ch9n*8
Time Warner 16, 119, 121
Tisdale, Ashley 184*ch2n*8
Tocqueville, Alexis de 37
tonality 99, 102, 104, 128
Tony Orlando and Dawn 115
Tork, Peter 105–6, 108, 164
Townshend, Pete 136
Trainor, Jerry 73, *74*
*The Troop* 6, 59, 75
*True Jackson, VP (TJVP)* 8, 17, 19, 26–7, 40, 59, 63, 79, 81, 85, 87–88, 90–8, 141, 149, 166, 195*ch7n*10
Turtles 110
*TV Nation* 5
Twain, Mark 28
tweens 4–5, 7–8, 15, 18, 32–5, 55, 61, 64, 82–4, 115, 149, 153, 158, 160, 170, 172, 175
Twisted Sister 32
*Two and a Half Men* 2, 40, 45–6, 64, 71, 90, 92, 97, 166

U2 17
Undertones 103
*Unfabulous* 17, 72
Univision 4
upward mobility *see* social mobility

Vaneigem, Raoul 37, 119
Van Halen 32, 203*ch11n*11
Vanilla Ice 121
Velvet Underground 29, 106
VH-1 16
Viacom 16
*Victorious* 6, 16–7, 19, 25–7, 33–4, 40, 50, 56, 59, 63, 65, 85, 88, 90, 183*ch1n*17, 191*ch5n*30, 193*ch6n*28, 197–8*ch8n*27
Vietnam 101, 107, 117, 142
VMAs *see* MTV Video Music Awards

Waksman, Steve 201*ch10n*15
Wald, Gayle 134, 169
Wal-Mart 17
Walser, Robert 203*ch11n*11
*The War at Home* 19, 50
Warrant 32
WE (Woman's Entertainment) 4
Weather Underground 149
Wham! 116

*What a Girl Wants* (*WaGW*) 9–10, 28, 143–5
Whitesnake 32
The Who 22, 103, 136–7
Will, George 117
Williams, Raymond 10, 173–5
Winfrey, Oprah 43, 90
*Wizards of Waverly Place* 6, 17, 26–7, 40, 50, 57, 72, 85, 92, 149, 184*ch2n*13, 192*ch6n*13
women, as cultural producers in rock 34–5, 186*ch2n*37
work 8, 26, 87–8, 90–8, 112–3, 141, 153

Yes 29, 142
*Yes, Dear* 96, 195*ch7n*11
Young, Angus 136
youth culture *see* teen culture

Zappa, Frank 106, 126
Zeus Energy 44–5, 52, 164
*Zoey 101* 1, 8, 19, 26, 57, 63, 65–7, **68**, 69–73, 75, 78, 84, 88, 90, 149